MW01027852

DAS AFRIKA KORPS

Erwin Rommel and the Germans in Africa, 1941–43

Franz Kurowski

STACKPOLE
BOOKS

Published by
STACKPOLE BOOKS
5067 Ritter Road
Mechanicsburg, PA 17055
www.stackpolebooks.com

Printed in the United States of America

10 9 8 7 6 5 4 3 2 1

Library of Congress Cataloging-in-Publication Data

Kurowski, Franz.
Das Afrika Korps: Erwin Rommel and the Germans in Africa, 1941–43/Franz Kurowski
   p. cm.
Includes bibliographical references and index.
ISBN 978-0-8117-0591-2
1. Germany. Heer. Panzerarmeekorps Afrika. 2. World War, 1939–1945—Regimental histories—Germany. 3. World War, 1939–1945—Campaigns—Africa, North. 4. Rommel, Erwin, 1891–1944. I. Title.
D757.55.G4K87 2010
940.54'13430961—dc22
                           2009041826

Contents

CHAPTER 1

The *Afrika Korps*

WHY WERE GERMAN FORCES IN AFRICA?

When Italy entered the war on 10 June 1940, agreements that had been made among the Western Powers as early as March 1939 went into effect. Three of those agreements concerned themselves with the African continent:

1. A disruption of Italy's lines of communications with Libya was planned as a common war goal.
2. A French offensive from out of Tunisia into Tripolitania—the northern part of modern Libya—was considered.
3. The defense of Egypt would be undertaken by British forces, whose objective would be to hold as many Italian forces along the eastern border of Libya as possible.

Mussolini's plans to get a portion of the booty that was being offered by the invasion of France by the Germans did not materialize because the French capitulated too rapidly. Hitler categorically turned down Mussolini's requests to have all of Tunisia and a part of Algeria, let alone some of the claims Mussolini was making on the European continent.

✠

On 30 July 1940, *Generalfeldmarschall* von Brauchitsch, the Chief-of-Staff of the German Army, proposed a five-point plan that concerned itself with the continuation of military operations in the Mediterranean. Part of his proposal contained "armored support for Italy in Africa" and, under point four, did not exclude the possibility of a direct attack against the Suez Canal.

One day later, von Brauchitsch recommended in the course of a general situation briefing the sending of a German expeditionary corps to Africa.

Hitler had been briefed on the same subject the day before by *Generalmajor* Walter Warlimont, the senior operations officer reporting to the Armed Forces Chief of Operations, Jodl. Warlimont recommended placing a *Panzer* corps at the disposal of *Il Duce* for employment in Africa. Hitler had directed that Warlimont determine the exact forces needed and to explore how they and their materiel could be transported to North Africa. Thus, when von Brauchitsch independently broached the subject, Hitler was not unprepared.

1

Italy, which wanted to clear a path to blockaded East Africa, could only do that by means of launching an offensive from Libya through Egypt. Because that move made it imperative to also take the Suez Canal, Italy had assembled a numerically impressive force in North Africa: 2 field armies with a total of 14 infantry divisions that had some 220,000 men under arms. They also had 339 light tanks, 8,000 motorized vehicles, and 1,400 field pieces, most of which were obsolete.

Mussolini had directed the *Comando Supremo* of the Italian forces at the end of June to prepare an offensive against Egypt, with the objective of taking the canal. The Italian high command then pressed hard on the Italian commander-in-chief there, Marshall Rodolfo Graziani, to start an attack. Graziani, in turn, pointed out the low strengths of his divisions and the shortfalls in their equipment.

At the same time this was going on, the commander-in-chief of the Italian forces in East Africa, the Count of Aosta, was given instructions to prepare to attack north through the Sudan and into Egypt in order to link up with Graziani's forces.

✠

The British, for their part, saw through those intentions, especially helped by their long-range communications intercepts. They started to reinforce their forces as rapidly as possible in the Middle East, especially with armored vehicles and aircraft. Through several convoy operations, supplies and weapons were shipped through the Mediterranean, first to Malta and then on to Alexandria. The Mediterranean Fleet was beefed up. The Royal Air Force started to establish a 6,000-kilometer air supply route that started in Takoradi in Ghana, went through Fort Lamy in the French colony of Chad, and ended up in Cairo. In the course of the campaign in North Africa, more than 5,000 aircraft were sent via that route.

✠

On 31 July 1940, Hitler informed his assembled commander-in-chiefs from the army, navy, and air force of his intent to launch a preventative strike against the Soviet Union. At the same time, he stated that sending German forces to Africa as a diversionary maneuver was worthy of consideration. He still had not made any final decisions, however.

Another step in the progression towards the commitment of German forces in North Africa was a memorandum prepared by Warlimont to Jodl and the latter's boss, Keitel. Warlimont cited additional information that reinforced his argument for sending armored forces to North Africa.

One day later, Warlimont sent in yet another proposal, in which he recommended supporting the Italians in their offensive against Egypt.

Hitler vacillated. Starting in September, however, the German Army High Command started making preparations for sending a mixed armored brigade to Africa. It was intended to assemble the force from elements of the *3. Panzer-Division*. On 5 September 1940, Jodl informed the Italian military attaché in Berlin of the *Führer's* intent to offer Mussolini armored forces for Libya. There was no response from the Italians, however. It was apparent to all that Mussolini wanted his own place in the sun by winning the war in Africa against the British.

In fact, the offer seemed to spur Mussolini to action. On 7 September, he ordered Marshall Graziani to attack and "within two days!"

The Italian offensive started on 13 September. Six Italian divisions, supported by eight tank battalions, overran the weak British frontier positions. Within the space of three days, Sidi Barrani was reached—90 kilometers east of Bardia—and taken. Eighty kilometers to the east of Sidi Barrani, the Italian forces then oriented themselves in a shallow arc and set up for the defense. Graziani did not want to continue the offensive before the middle of December. By then, a water line was to have been brought forward from Bardia and the coastal road from the border improved.

Lieutenant General Richard O'Connor, who had moved his armor of the Western Desert Force to Mersa Matruh for rest at the end of July, was not surprised by the blow launched by the Italians. He had withdrawn his weak frontier forces step-by-step.

In the middle of September, the British Commander-in-Chief Middle East, General Archibald Wavell, ordered the commander of the British forces in Egypt, Lieutenant General Wilson, to receive the Italian 10th Army with a decisive blow, should it attempt to advance in the direction of Mersa Matruh.

Wavell prepared a counteroffensive, which had as its objective the pushing back of Graziani's forces to the Libyan border. A second offensive was also planned against Italian East Africa, where the Count of Aosta and his 255,000 men had held British Somaliland since the middle of August.

On the German side, the commander of the *3. Panzer-Division*, *Generalmajor Ritter* von Thoma, was sent to Africa at the beginning of September. He had received orders to determine the options for getting German forces to Africa and the best possible employment for them.

In the meantime, the German military attaché in Rome, *General* Enno von Rintelen, had sent a report to Berlin on 10 September concerning the

Italian forces in Libya. The report demonstrated how the Italian divisions were insufficiently equipped for their employment there and that the Italian armored and motorized forces were still in Italy.

On 14 September, Hitler appeared to have decided to send an armored corps to North Africa. His decision was reinforced by a briefing on 19 September from *Oberst* Liss of the intelligence section of Army Chief-of-Staff Halder, in which the success of the Italians in their thrust on Sidi Barrani was reported.

After the Italian victory, however, Marshall Pietro Badoglio, the Italian military's chief-of-staff, conveyed to his German counterparts that, with the exception of dive bombers to destroy British positions, Italy did not need any assistance, not even any German armor.

Hitler then asked Mussolini for a meeting. The two dictators met at the Brenner Pass on 3 October 1940. During the conversations, Mussolini revealed that he would take up the offensive in North Africa again no later than 15 October. Hitler promised Mussolini he would send 100 tanks and a large number of vehicles.

At that point, everything appeared to be a done deal and, after a few more conferences and meetings, the plans for the movement of the *3. Panzer-Division* to Africa were finished on 14 October 1940. Three days later, Halder received von Thoma's report from Africa. The experienced officer, who had led the German armor contingent in the Spanish Civil War, recommended that every formation sent to Africa be equipped with a motorized reconnaissance battalion that had two armored car companies. In his oral report to Halder, von Thoma also stressed that at least four armored divisions had to be sent to Africa, if the Axis hoped to enjoy success. He stated: "Fewer than that serves no purpose, because smaller contingents will not meet with success. Sending more would also be a mistake, because more than four divisions cannot be supplied on a movement all the way to the delta of the Nile."

Von Thoma stated the same case in front of Hitler a few days later, and *Major* Meyer-Ricks, who had returned from his intelligence-gathering mission in Africa on 25 October, supported the assertions made by von Thoma.

While the discussions were going back and forth, Mussolini revealed yet another surprise by marching into Greece from Albania on 28 October 1940.

The Italians were hoping for a quick success, but they soon learned a hard lesson. The Greek forces threw the Italians back into Albania. Hitler was incensed and threatened to abandon support for Mussolini's "Libyan adventure" entirely. He stated the Italians needed to settle their affairs by themselves, since they had brought it all upon themselves.

During the afternoon of 4 November, Hitler had his senior leadership meet with him. Keitel, Jodl, Halder, von Brauchitsch and Raeder took part in the discussions. Also present were Jodl's adjutant, *Oberstleutnant* Deyhle, and Hitler's military adjutant from the Army, *Major* Gerhard Engel.

Hitler's monologue basically said that he was against sending German forces across the Mediterranean to Africa, across a sea that was dominated by England and which had not yet seen the Italians fighting with full commitment. He thought the Italians wanted to save the blood of their own troops.

Hitler also dismissed the plan to advance through Bulgaria, Turkey, and Syria to advance on the Suez Canal. He only considered it necessary to send air elements to Africa,

It was not until *Führer* Directive No. 18 of 12 November—"Be prepared for all eventualities!"—that Hitler abandoned his obstinacy. The directive stated the following concerning Libya:

> The employment of German forces in North Africa will not be considered until the Italians have reached Mersa Matruh . . . The Army is to earmark one armored division for employment in North Africa. The Kriegsmarine is directed to equip and prepare German ships in Italian harbors as transports for a large number of forces and logistics goods to Libya or Northwest Africa . . . The Luftwaffe is to make preparations for operations against Alexandria and the Suez Canal

Everything was still in the balance, when the British offensive commenced on 6 December. O'Connor had the 7th Armoured Division, the Indian 4th Infantry Division, a battalion of medium Vickers Mark II tanks, and a battle group composed of the garrison from Mersa Matruh.

In terms of reserves, he had the Australian 6th Infantry Division, a brigade from the New Zealand 2nd Infantry Division, and a Polish brigade. Those elements were either still being trained or were conducting security missions along the Nile Delta.

The Western Desert Force's Indian 4th Infantry Division, supported by the battalion of infantry tanks, reached the area southeast of Nibeiwa within 48 hours of the start of the offensive. It was assisted in its movement by fog and clouds of dust.

Near Nibeiwa, an Indian brigade, with the remaining 28 operational tanks, advanced through a gap maintained by a support group from the 7th Armored Division. At the same time, naval elements from the Mediterranean Fleet shelled the Italian coastal installations and aircraft from the Royal Air Force strafed Italian positions. Nibeiwa was taken, with the Italian general, Maletti, being killed in the fighting. Two thousand Italians surrendered. The supply dumps at east and west Tummar were taken the next day. The Italian 2nd Libyan Division was effectively destroyed.

Blow after blow followed. The 7th Armored Division stormed ahead. On 10 December, Sidi Barrani fell to a combined attack by the two divisions. After three days of fighting, the Italians had 38,000 men taken prisoner. There were four generals among them. O'Connor decided to press the pursuit. Wavell and Churchill approved his decision.

On 12 December, the light "Cruiser" tanks rolled into the area south of Sollum. On 13 December, the 11th Hussars advanced across the border west of Fort Capuzzo, supported by both tanks and artillery. They moved on past Sidi Azeiz to the north to the coastal road, which they blocked the following day. That cut off the fortress of Bardia on the border from its rearward lines of communications. There were four Italian divisions in the fortress. There was another division in Tobruk.

Early in the morning of 3 January 1941, the Australian 6th Infantry Division moved out to attack Bardia. The fighting lasted until 5 January. In the end, 40,000 Italians surrendered.

El Adem, just 24 kilometers south of Tobruk, was taken by a brigade of the 7th Armoured Division. On 20 January, Tobruk proper was attacked and brought under British control by 22 January. The Italians lost another 27,000 men captured there. The British tank forces thrust westward in a series of raids. Derna fell on 30 January. Cyrene was up for grabs on 3 February. Graziani radioed to Rome that he was about to evacuate all of Cyrenaica and pull back as far as Sirte. He had already issued orders to that effect on 2 February and had moved his headquarters from Bengasi to Tripoli on 3 February.

When O'Connor received the news that the Italians were retreating from Cyrenaica, he ordered the 7th Armoured Division to advance through Msus and on to Soluch. As part of the advance, O'Connor also moved a mixed battle group through Antelat towards the coastal road to its west. Around 1200 hours on 5 February, the battle group reached the road, blocked it, and stopped the retreat of the Italian 10th Army. More than 20,000 men laid down their arms. The commander-in-chief of the 10th Army, General Tellera, succumbed to his wounds.

The 11th Hussars were already in El Agheila on 8 February. They then started reconnoitering the terrain to the west as far as the *Arco dei Fileni*, the grand marble arch that divided Cyrenaica and Tripolitania in Libya.

The advance of the Western Desert Force, which had been redesignated as the XIII Corps in December, ended there. The corps had covered roughly 1,000 kilometers in eight weeks and eliminated 10 Italian divisions. In the process, it took 130,000 prisoners, knocked out 180 medium and 220 light tanks, and captured 845 artillery pieces.

The situation had turned deadly for Italy.

The sudden turn of events in North Africa was not yet readily apparent to Hitler on 5 December. On that day, he had assembled all those associated with the planning for the assault on Gibraltar and received their reports. Hitler still did not believe he needed to rapidly intervene in North Africa. He thought the situation was too murky in the Balkans and also did not want his planning for operations in the Soviet Union to be negatively influenced.

On that day, Hitler was more of the opinion that an aerial attack on the British Mediterranean Fleet *and* the denial of Gibraltar to the British would help the Italians to master their own problems.

According to Hitler, the *Luftwaffe* would start attacking the English fleet on 15 December. After the attacks, which would be constantly repeated, the *XXXXIX. Armee-Korps*, which had specially selected, would conquer Gibraltar. Starting in March, German forces would then be able to help the Italians in Greece.

Once the operations at Gibraltar had been concluded, Hitler continued, only then could consideration be given to committing an armored division and a motorized division in Africa.

But three days later, the Italian ambassador to Germany, Dino Alfieri, had an audience with Hitler, whom he briefed on the precarious situation in Albania. Hitler dismissed him.

On 9 December, Halder reported to Hitler on the dangerous situation that had developed in Africa. But from then on, all talk was increasingly idle. The British XIII Corps dictated the pace of events.

The 19th of December witnessed a complete turnabout on the part of the Italians regarding Africa. They were now calling for help. The *Comando Supremo* asked von Rintelen to have an armored division dispatched immediately to Tripoli. In addition, war materiel, enough to equip 10 Italian divisions, was requested. Finally, raw materials for war production were requested. Count Cavallero, the Italian chief of staff, had made this call for help on behalf of Mussolini.

General Efusio Marras, the Italian military attaché in Germany, informed Keitel on 28 December that the situation in Africa was doubtful and all of northern Africa would be lost without Germany's help.

The first German air formations were already on their way to southern Italy by then. They included 100 *Ju 88* and *He 111* medium bombers, 60 *Ju 87* dive bombers, 20 *Bf 109* fighters, and a few night fighters. The aircraft established themselves at air bases on Sicily. They were shortly joined by an additional 300 machines. The mission of the *X. Flieger-Korps*: engage the British supply convoys in the Suez Canal and hinder the advance of the British forces in Libya.

Later on, the air corps was given an additional mission: protect the convoys of the *Deutsches Afrika-Korps* bound for Libya.

On 4 January 1941, von Rintelen sent a report to Germany concerning the situation in Libya. It was claimed that General Alfredo Guzzoni, the Italian deputy chief of staff, felt the Italians could hold Bardia. At the same time the report was transmitted, the British were in the process of taking Bardia.

On 8 January, von Rintelen sent another report from Guzzoni. Following that, Hitler had all of the staff officers responsible for planning in Africa to come to the *Reich* Chancellery. At the conference, Hitler stated:

It is important that the Italians do not lose Libya. If that happens, the British forces there will be freed up for employment elsewhere. In addition, the psychological effects of that loss are greater than the actual loss . . .

Italy must be helped. It is important to send a German armored blocking formation to Libya. That blocking formation must stop the British advance and undertake local immediate counterattacks against weak positions of the enemy.

On 11 January, the operations section of the German Army High Command issued directives for the constitution of the German forces for employment in Libya. All of the smaller elements were to be formed from personnel from the *3. Panzer-Division.*

An advance party for the high command went to North Africa on 15 January. *Generalmajor* von Funck, who had been designated to command the blocking formation, arrived in Tripoli that day to personally gain his own impressions of the new theater of war.

The *3. Panzer-Division* designated its *Panzer-Regiment 5* as the iron fist of the blocking formation. In addition, there was the *I./Artillerie-Regiment 75 (mot.)*, *Panzerjäger-Abteilung 39* and *Aufklärungs-Abteilung 3 (mot.)*.[1] Those formed the nucleus of the *5. leichte Division* of *Oberstleutnant Graf* Schwerin.

On 19 January, Hitler and Mussolini met at Berchtesgaden. Keitel and Guzzoni also conferred there. Guzzoni received the offer of the *5. leichte Division* with thanks. The transport of the German forces across the Mediterranean was scheduled to start on 15 February.

On 3 February, Halder wrote the following in his diary: "Rommel (with new chief-of-staff) commander of the German army forces in Libya." Who had submitted Rommel's name for command—the man who had made himself

1. Translator's Note: 5th Armored Regiment; 1st Battalion of the 75th Artillery Regiment (Motorized); 39th Antitank Battalion; and 3rd Reconnaissance Battalion (Motorized).

famous as the commander of the "Ghost Division," the *7. Panzer-Division*, in France—can no longer be ascertained. One thing is certain, however: Hitler approved the decision that took Erwin Rommel, a man whose name would become a household word in both the Allied and Axis countries, to the African theater of war.

On 6 February, Keitel issued final directives for *Operation "Sonnenblume"* (Operation "Sunflower"), as the German operations plan was called. Among the directives was that the blocking formation would be attached to a German corps headquarters.

On the same day, Rommel arrived in Berchtesgaden, having been called back from leave. He reported to the commander of the German Army, and von Brauchitsch gave him the mission of assuming a corps command, which initially was to consist of the aforementioned blocking formation (*5. leichte Afrika-Division*) and an unnamed armored division, which was to be employed in Africa. That afternoon, Rommel reported to Hitler.

The following day saw Rommel meeting with *Oberstleutnant i.G.* von dem Borne,[2] designated chief-of-staff of the new formation, and a few others of his staff officers. Three days later, he flew with his new battle staff to Munich. From there, his staff flew on to Rome. Rommel, *Oberstleutnant* Schmundt (Hitler's chief adjutant), and von dem Borne followed on 11 February. That morning, they had a conference with Mussolini and Guzzoni; that afternoon, they flew on to Catania (Sicily) with General Roatta, the deputy chief-of-staff of the Italian Army. There, Rommel conducted discussions with the Commanding General of the *X. Flieger-Korps, General der Flieger* Geißler. Rommel requested the Commanding General have strong forces attack the port of Bengasi that very same night. He also requested that British troop movements be attacked and eliminated at first light on 12 February.

The next day, Rommel and his party flew on to Tripoli. An hour later, the Commanding General, who had just been promoted to *Generalleutnant* by Hitler, was standing in front of General Gariboldi, who had just taken over command of the Italian forces in Africa. He informed Gariboldi that he intended to defend Tripolitania from the area around the coastal city of Sirte.

An hour later, Hitler flew with Schmundt over the scene of the most recent fighting. When he returned to Tripoli that evening, General Roatta had also just arrived with new orders from Mussolini.

Gariboldi's announced intentions of moving the Italian X Corps to the Sirte–Buerat area in the near future was not enough for Rommel. He was able

---

2. Translator's Note: General Staff Lieutenant Colonel. General staff officers in the German military had the suffix *i.G.* (*im Generalstab*) added to their rank.

to force the issue and have the first Italian division alerted for moving out towards Sirte on 14 February.

Although logistics elements had already arrived for the Germans, the first combat forces did not arrive in Tripoli until 14 February. The German's war in the desert, which the *Luftwaffe* had already opened, would also now start on land.

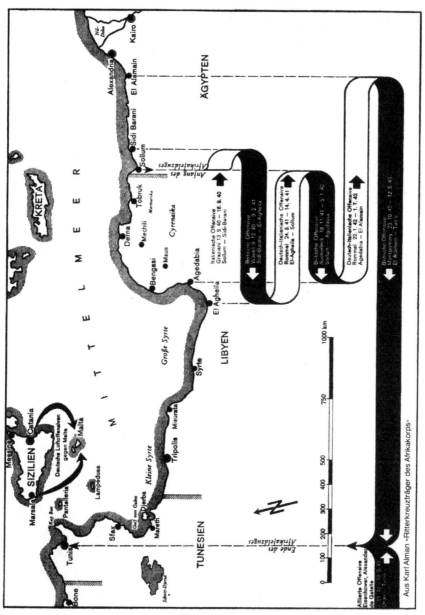

An overall view of the North Afican Campaign, 1940 to 1943. This map clearly indicates the ebb-and-flow nature of the campaign.

An 88mm *Flak* gun being loaded for transport to Africa

General Rommel is an interested observer of the loading process.

The impressive Italian monument, the Fileni Arch.

Panzer IIIs head for the front in the early stages of the campaign. Note the fuel and water (marked with a white cross) containers at the front of the tanks and the extra stowage of essential items.

CHAPTER 2

The Way to Tobruk

THE *X. FLIEGER-KORPS* ABOVE THE DESERT

The first German forces that conducted operations in North Africa were from the *Luftwaffe*. In December, the *X. Flieger-Korps* had been moved to Sicily. The headquarters was billeted in the *Hotel "Domenico"* in Taormina. It was from there that *General der Flieger* Geißler employed the forces under his command.

Attacks against the Suez Canal were considered to be especially important, since the majority of the logistical support for the British forces in North Africa went through the canal as well as those forces intended for employment in Greece. *Major* Harlinghausen, the chief-of-staff for the air corps, recommended that a group from *Kampfgeschwader 26*[1] be moved to Bengasi, from which it could launch attacks against the Suez Canal. Geißler approved the recommendation.

Even before that, there had been collisions between the two powers in the Mediterranean. On 10 January 1941, *Ju 87's* and *Ju 88's* of the corps had attacked the British carrier *Illustrious* some 100 sea miles west of Malta with six 500-kilogram bombs. The carrier was crippled and had to be towed to Malta.

A few days later, 14 machines of the *II./Kampfgeschwader 26* were inbound to Bengasi from the Sicilian airfield at Comiso. The group was led by *Major* Bertram. *Major* Harlinghausen flew along, in order to assist in maintaining contact with the corps headquarters.

Things were in a state of confusion when the German aircraft landed. The Italian air controllers did not provide proper instructions, and three of the aircraft smashed into one another after landing and were lost to further operations.

On 14 January, the first *He 111's* flew to the canal to conduct reconnaissance. They were able to get though without interference and returned to Bengasi in one piece.

This was followed by a second reconnaissance mission on 17 January. When those aircraft returned, they reported that a large convoy was spotted south of the canal and steaming northward. *Major* Harlinghausen saw an opportunity for employing the eight operational aircraft.

---

1. Translator's Note: 26th Bomb Wing.

14

"Gentlemen," he stated to the assembled pilots, "we will approach this in the following way. The first four aircraft will approach the canal from the north and search to the south. The second flight will do the same thing, but starting from the south. That will guarantee we find the convoy."

"It's 1,100 kilometers to the canal, *Herr Major*." One of the pilots tossed out.

"That means," Harlinghausen responded to the unstated question, "that the canal will be outside of our normal range if we aren't stingy with our flying. The best RPM's . . . the best prop settings . . . the properly chosen altitude . . . all those are necessary for us to accomplish the mission. I will assume command." After a pause, Harlinghausen continued: "What do you think, Doc?"

The tall chief-of-staff turned to the group's meteorologist. *Dr.* Hermann looked at the information he had available.

"Getting there is not a problem, of course," he finally said, "on the return flight you'll have an estimated 60 kilometers of head wind. You should be able to overcome that by flying at an altitude of 4,000 meters."

A short while later, the men boarded the first *He 111's*. Piloting the aircraft that Harlinghausen flew in was *Hauptmann* Robert Kowalewski, who had piloted most of the previous flights where the chief-of-staff was on board.

"Everything checking out, Robert?" Harlinghausen asked.

"Everything's fine," Kowalewski responded.

"Off we go!"

✠

They received the signal to start, and they were in the air a short while later. The aircraft formed up and flew east for four hours, before shifting direction a few compass points to the south and reached the city of Suez at the southern end of the canal. Kowalewski turned north and followed the canal.

"There's the Dead Sea!" Harlinghausen pointed out, "go around it and then continue north."

They traced the body of water, but no ships were to be found. The blinking umbilical cord of the canal stretched out below them, devoid of any life.

"We will attack the alternate targets!" Harlinghausen announced to the other aircraft. They flew on to Port Said. Nothing could be found there either, however.

"We need to start thinking about turning back," Kowalewski said, looking at his fuel gauges.

"Go back south for a bit," Harlinghausen said. But they discovered nothing again, except for the ferry at Ismailijja.

Off to the side, the Dead Sea appeared for the second time. Then they discovered the convoy. It had moored along the shore, since it was not allowed to transit the canal at night.

The *Major* issued orders: "Attack the large steamer in the middle!"

They flew directly towards the ship. The bombs were dropped and howled towards the water. But they detonated 30 meters from the vessel.

"Head home!" Harlinghausen ordered, disappointed that they had come so far only not to succeed.

The return flight was a test of nerves for the men of the eight aircraft. They flew back at 4,000 meters but were shaken violently by a storm. That slowed them even more. According to ground control in Bengasi, the storm was gusting at 120 kilometers an hour. The completion of the flight was called into question. *Major* Harlinghausen had calculated a flight time of four and one half hours. But at five hours, the situation turned critical. They still could not see the lights of the airfield. At five and one half hours, they still could see no airfield.

"We have to descend," Kowalewski stated, "otherwise, we'll hit the sand, which won't feel too good!"

Harlinghausen nodded in agreement.

"Belly landing, Robert. We don't know how rough the surface is. Better to keep the legs up!"

Kowalewski, one of the old hands in the *Luftwaffe's* bomber forces, set the aircraft down with self-control and assuredness. The aircraft slid through the sand, ripped down camel thorn bushes, and then came to a halt.

Kowalewski turned everything off. He issued the order to deplane and everyone was off in a flash.

"We need to destroy the aircraft and try to get to the front lines." Harlinghausen told the assembled men. "It can't be too far to Bengasi. Get to work!"

They set the aircraft on fire and then took off on foot. What they did not know was that Bengasi was still 280 kilometers away to the northwest.

They marched the entire night. They were forced to make a detour when they heard the sound of armor off to the east. Back at Bengasi, three machines took off the following morning to find the missing crews. The wreck of the *He 111* was found a few hours later. Additional search missions were started.

All the while, the four aviators from Kowalewski's crew marched through the desert. They rested during the day under outcroppings of limestone over which they would spread a shelter half. The rations were divided equally. When it turned dark, they started out again—chilled by the nighttime coldness of the desert.

During the fourth day, they were spotted by *Oberleutnant* Kaupisch. He set down and picked up the men.

"You took your time, Kaupisch," Harlinghausen said jokingly, when the young officer raced over to the group to report to the corps' chief-of-staff. "Thanks . . . you found the needle in the haystack. What happened to the others?"

"I was able to get back to Bengasi. I ignored the recommendation of the weather prince and flew at 150. There was considerably less wind there."

"And the others? Everyone else an emergency landing?"

"They all landed safely, but apparently three crews were captured by the Tommies!"

They all boarded the aircraft and landed at Bengasi a half hour later. The first attack on the Suez Canal had ended with the loss of seven out of eight machines.

THE ARRIVAL OF *AUFKLÄRUNGS-ABTEILUNG 3 (MOT.)*

The day after various logistics elements arrived in Africa on 11 February, they were visited in their billeting areas outside of Tripoli by Rommel. Rommel then flew to Homs, where he visited an Italian brigade. At noon on 14 February, he returned to Tripoli, where the first combat elements of the *Sperrverband Afrika*[2] were expected that evening.

That evening, the German steamer *Saarfeld* approached the harbor. The steamer had been underway for two days and nights. When the ship docked, *Major* Irnfried *Freiherr*[3] von Wechmar saw a group of German officers at the pier in their new tropical uniforms. Only one of them had on a field-gray tunic. Von Wechmar saw the Knight's Cross and the *Pour le Mérite* at his neck.

"That's Rommel, *Herr Major!*" *Oberleutnant* Thiele, the company commander of the *1./Aufklärungs-Abteilung 3 (mot.)*[4] said to his commander.

"Where did he come from?" the battalion commander responded.

"No idea, *Herr Major*," Thiele answered, "but one thing is certain: The dust will never settle. Wherever Rommel is there is something always going on!"

---

2. Translator's Note Blocking Formation "Africa."

3. Translator's Note: Baron.

4. Translator's Note: 3rd Reconnaissance Battalion (Motorized). This would later be redesignated as an armored reconnaissance battalion, but its basic structure would essentially remained unchanged.

Major Jansa, the commander of *Panzerjäger-Abteilung 39*[5], who was also on board ship, brought the two back to reality.

"Then we should get ready to report, Wechmar," he said in a good-natured fashion. "I think we ought to try to make a good impression on Rommel."

After the gangplank went down, the officers went down to the pier and approached Rommel. Von Wechmar was the first to report. Rommel thanked him and said: "Wechmar, you need to be off the ship and ready to go in five hours. Report that you are ready to march at sunrise."

Rommel said the same thing to the antitank battalion commander.

The murderous work started. The winches, groaning and screeching, lifted the armored cars and radio vehicles, the antitank and other guns, the motorcycles and trucks from the belly of the ship and on to land. Crates of ammunition, barrels of fuel, and rations for the tropics followed. The cargo ferries, which went out to the other ships anchored in the roadstead, came back crammed to the gills with equipment and supplies.

But when the sun came up, they had done it. It had taken six hours, but the first iteration of combat forces were ready to be committed. The soldiers marched out from the quay and formed up in an open square.

Rommel appeared, accompanied by a few high-ranking Italian officers. He greeted the soldiers and bade them farewell in a broad Swabian accent: "Nothing but forward, boys!"

The men then went to their vehicles. An Italian guide on a motorcycle took the lead and took the caravan of steel through the Arab quarters of the city, past groups of palms and wells. They reached the road leading out of the city.

Major von Wechmar took the lead along with his adjutant, *Oberleutnant* von Fallois. The objective: Sirte.

The sun rose in the sky and soon burned down from above. It was noon before the convoy reached the hotel in the desert at Sirte. When von Wechmar jumped out of his vehicle to report to the commander of the Italian's Pavia Division, Rommel came out to meet him from the coolness of the hall.

"Welcome to the desert, Wechmar. I have the following mission for you:

"1. Screen the right flank of the Pavia Division, which is positioned on the hills farther to the east.

"2. Reconnoiter in the direction of En Nofilia–El Agheila.

"3. Coordinate with the Santamaria's reconnaissance battalion, whose commander will be here shortly."

Rommel cleared his throat, then continued: "Your battalion marched well. When will all of you be here?"

"In an hour, *Herr General*," von Wechmar replied.

---

5. Translator's Note: 39th Antitank Battalion.

When the remaining elements of the battalion arrived, Rommel pulled out his Leica and took some photos. His chief-of-staff sent a report to the *Führer* Headquarters: "The first German forces have just arrived at the front in Africa."

"Your code name is 'Tiger' for the time being," Rommel told von Wechmar. "Prove to me you're worthy of it and you will be *that* which you ought to be here in Africa: The masters of the forward area, Wechmar!"

A short while later, when Major Marchese Santamaria arrived, the company commanders and the battalion headquarters had assembled in the large command bus. The Italian major explained to them what was important in the desert.

The first patrol headed out in the morning. It was led by von Fallois. Von Wechmar sent him off with the words: "Don't do anything stupid! Stick to principles: Least loss, greatest reconnaissance gains! Don't risk anything more than necessary to achieve the objective. I only want to see healthy people come back!"

The objective of the patrol was En Nofilia. It was 150 kilometers away. A hot desert sandstorm—a *Ghibli*—blew around and into the 8-wheeled armored cars from the south. When the sandstorm ceased, it was replaced by a *Garbi*, an ice-cold wind form the north. The men moved through the thick veils of sand and felt it enter their ears and noses. They saw "people" who turned out to be camel thorn bushes.

When they reached En Nofilia, they determined it was clear of the enemy. They then returned to Sirte.

The next morning, all of the reconnaissance battalion, the antitank battalion, and Santamaria's battalion moved out for En Nofilia. When the group reached a "crossroads" in the desert—the dirt tracks separated!—an air alert was sounded. Wechmar's driver, Großmann, was just about ready to fire the signal flare indicating it was clear to fire, when the men recognized *Stuka's* making their way to enemy lines. The pilots wagged their wings as they flew past.

Großmann fumbled, however, and the signal pistol went off. The sizzling pyrotechnic buried itself into the upholstery next to von Wechmar, smoldering. Großmann smacked it with his hand, sending it out into the sand, but also slightly burning himself in the process. "If you don't like me, Großmann, just say it!" was the commander's humorous reply.

The advance patrols returned. En Nofilia was still clear of the enemy. The other trek did not encounter any telltale signs of the enemy, either.

En Nofilia, the former Italian desert fort, was taken. The battle group had advanced 150 kilometers without a fight!

The next patrol that von Wechmar dispatched got as far as the *Arco dei*

Fileni, which spanned the *Via Balbia*, the coastal road. Once again, Rommel appeared, seemingly as if by magic. He issued more orders: "Reconnaissance-in-force in the direction of El Agheila!"

Oberleutnant Everth and *Oberleutnant* Behr led the two reconnaissance patrols that were sent forward. They encountered English armored cars. The first rounds fired in anger were exchanged. Three enemy armored cars were knocked out with the 2-centimeter automatic cannon of the German heavy armored cars. The enemy pulled back.

It was 24 February 1941. The Germans took their first light casualties in Africa as well as their first prisoners. They were soldiers from the Australian 6th Infantry Division and a few men from the King's Dragoon Guards. One enemy armored car was captured.

✠

On 21 February, an order was issued that the German forces of the "blocking formation" were henceforth to be referred to as the *Deutsches Afrika-Korps (DAK)*. That applied not only to the forces on the ground, but also to the *15. Panzer-Division*, which was also on its way to Africa. It was intended to send that division and the tank regiment of the *5. leichte Afrika-Division* over as soon as possible.

Generalmajor Johannes Streich, the commander of the light division, had not yet arrived in Africa. During the evening of 18 February, he traveled from Berlin to Rome in a sleeping car. From there, he flew to Tripoli on 24 February. With him were the rest of the divisional staff as well as elements of Rommel's corps staff. When he arrived, Rommel informed him that he would assume command of the forces at the front after the arrival of *MG-Bataillon 8.*[6]

Rommel succeeded in getting Gariboldi's command—Rommel was nominally assigned to support him—to have all of the arriving elements of the light division sent forward to En Nofilia. From there, they were to establish contact with the enemy. The fact that contact had been established two days previously was left unsaid by both parties.

MG-Bataillon 8 had been loaded on ships in Naples on 24 February. *Oberstleutnant* Ponath was the commander. The convoy pulled anchor at 1100 hours on 25 February and consisted of both Italian and German vessels: the freighters *Arcturus, Alicante, Leverkusen,* and *Wachtfels*. It was escorted by four Italian motor-torpedo boats and reached Tripoli exactly 48 hours after it had departed. Outside of the harbor, the soldiers saw a torpedoed hospital ship. In the harbor proper, the hulls of bombed and sunken boats and ships jutted out of the shallow waters. The ships were unloaded with harbor boats.

---

6. Translator's Note: 8th Machine Gun Battalion.

Generalmajor Streich and General Gariboldi greeted the disembarked and assembled soldiers on the morning of 28 February. The companies conducted a pass-in-review along the broad shoreline road. On the morning of 1 March, the battalion headed east, with companies leaving at 10-minute intervals.

The battalion reached the *Arco dei Fileni* after moving through Sirte and En Nofilia. The battalion set up its positions 3 kilometers to the east on both sides of the road. The *6./Panzerjäger-Abteilung 39*, which was an engineer company, established forward positions at El Mugtaa. The vehicles were dug in up to their engines. In the defiles—called *Wadis*—the men were introduced to swarms of flies. They also had their first visits from sand vipers and scorpions. Not to be outdone, a *Ghibli* also made a house call.

The front started to take shape. In addition to the dummy tanks, which Rommel had ordered to move about the desert in a deception campaign, real formations also worked their way forward. On 11 March, *Panzer-Regiment 5* was unloaded from ships at Tripoli.

On 15 March, a reinforced company under the command of *Oberleutnant Graf* Schwerin was sent on a reconnaissance-in-force to the south through Geddahia. It moved into the Fezzan area along an old trek. In addition to reconnoitering, it was sent there by order of Rommel to gather experience with regard to long-range marches in the desert and to test the special tropical equipment the German forces had been equipped with.

The raiding force moved out along the "corrugated sheet metal" trek to Hun, where a small Italian force had an outpost. Sebcha and Murzuk were next, followed by another 300 kilometers further south as far as the area around El Gatrun. None of the men of the force that participated ever forgot that experience.

In the meantime, however, there was movement along the front.

EL AGHEILA IS TAKEN

As early as 7 March, Rommel had informed Streich that he wanted to take El Agheila, as well as Marada.

On 18 March, Rommel flew to Berlin. Prior to doing that, he had consulted with Gariboldi in Tripoli and secured his concurrence for the intended offensive operations.

On 20 and 21 March, Rommel briefed at the *Führer* Headquarters. He stated that the enemy was withdrawing his forces from Cyrenaica and was setting up defensive positions along a line running Agedaiba–Marsa el Brega. Rommel advised that it was time to take up the offensive. He also asked for additional reinforcements, which Hitler turned down. Hitler indicated he did not want any expansive operations in the direction of Libya. That same train of thought was found in one of his directives (21 March 1941), which was released through the German Army High Command. The directive stated that Rommel was to guarantee the defense of Tripolitania and, at the same time, make preparations for taking back Cyrenaica.

It was not until all of the *15. Panzer-Division* had arrived in Africa that he was to take El Agheila as a jumping-off point for further operations.

Let us now take a short look at the status of Rommel's opposing numbers.

✠

After the XIII Corps had been pulled out of the line, the Cyrenaica Command of Lieutenant General Philip Neame was responsible for the "Western Front" of North Africa. His forces included the 2nd Armored Division and the Australian 6th Infantry Division. Since the latter division was earmarked for employment in Greece, it was pulled out of the line at the beginning of March, with only some headquarters elements and a brigade from the Australian 9th Infantry Division taking its place. The remaining two brigades of the inexperienced Australian division were still marching in from Palestine in order to complete unit-level training in the Tobruk–Derna area.

General Morshead, the division commander, knew that his positions at Marsa el Brega could be bypassed at any time by mobile German forces if the latter were to move through the *Wadi el Fargeh* south of the salt marshes.

On 17 March, the British command decided to pull back the exposed Australian brigade and employ it in the area east of Bengasi with another of the division's brigades.

The 2nd Armored Division moved up to the front in the area of Marsa el Brega on 20 March. The two infantry brigades occupied positions between the road and the sea, a sandy sector of 6 kilometers. The tanks went into position south of the road and east of the 8-kilometer-long salt marshes.

The third brigade of the 9th Infantry Division had to remain in Tobruk, since there was no lift capacity available, since all available vehicles were being used to fill the camps of the 2nd Armored Division at Msus and Mechili.

General Wavell eventually sent the Indian 3rd Brigade (Motorized) to beef up the front. It arrived on 29 March in the El Adem area, at a time when Rommel's advance had already started.

✠

It was the afternoon of 23 March when orders arrived at von Wechmar's reconnaissance battalion to take El Agheila.

Von Wechmar, who had been promoted to *Oberstleutnant*, summoned his company commanders: "Behr, take your motorcycles only as far along the *Via Balbia* so that the Tommy outpost in the wooden tower of the fortifications cannot see you. Turn north and spend the night in the dunes next to the sea. At first light, move out so that you can reach El Agheila by 0600 hours. Everyone else will attack from the front."

The motorcycle infantry company took off that night. They dismounted when they thought they were close enough to be heard. They then marched by foot, pushing the motorcycles, through the cold night to the northern outskirts of El Agheila. The main body remained in the dunes, while a patrol went forward to the edge of the town. It reported that the enemy forces appeared to be weak.

Oberleutnant Behr reported the results of the patrol back to headquarters. A short while later, most of the armored cars under *Leutnant* von Seybel reported they had reached the outskirts of the town.

"Behr: Attack! We'll be following behind!" von Wechmar radioed.

The motorcycles raced into the northern part of the town appearing by surprise. A few enemy soldiers appeared. Machine-gun salvoes echoed through the morning stillness. The motorcyclists were soon at the observation tower, where they raised the battalion's flag.

The rest of the reconnaissance battalion stormed into the city, with the four attached tanks in the lead. One of the tanks rolled over a mine and was immobilized. But the battalion had little to do.

A short while later, a column of vehicles approached the desert fort from the west. It was Rommel, who climbed up the observation tower with von Wechmar and the operations officer of the *5. leichte Division*.

Rommel was laconic: "Our next objective is over there . . . Mersa el Brega."

FROM MARSA EL BREGA TO MECHILI

Rommel ordered the attack on Marsa el Brega, 30 kilometers east of El Agheila, for 30 March. The English were expected to put up stiff resistance, since the position—located between the sea and a dried out salt marsh, which could not be negotiated by vehicular traffic—was a bottleneck and offered ideal defensive possibilities.

Streich had *Oberst* Olbrich's *Panzer-Regiment 5* move out at the head of the advancing forces. Streich moved his headquarters close to the English positions. Rommel soon appeared to determine the progress of the attack.

The first attack on the morning of 30 March did not succeed. The Germans encountered massed artillery fire. Streich's command post was hit. The attack stalled.

In the evening, Streich summoned the commander of the machine-gun battalion. He ordered him to move out with his battalion echeloned left at the onset of darkness. It was to move just north of the road and hit the enemy in the flank.

The battalion moved out when darkness fell. He avoided an enemy trench system to the left and then found himself in the enemy's flank. The machine gunners entered the enemy's defenses, with their wiry commander in the lead.

Hand grenades exploded; machine-gun salvoes whipped in the direction of enemy muzzle flashes.

The English proved weak in their flank and were soon fleeing from their positions, leaving behind 50 personnel carriers and 30 trucks.

Streich had his entire division close up that very night in order to prepare for the follow-on attack against Agedabia. Once again, *Maschinengewehr-Bataillon 8* was in the forefront of the action; *Oberstleutnant* Ponath's men were in the advance guard.

During the afternoon of 1 April, the machine-gun battalion attacked along both sides of the coastal road. Initially, the enemy held fast. But then he started to pull back, ever faster. As it turned dark, the companies of the battalion were at Gtafia, some 35 kilometers east of Marsa el Brega. They were stopped there by two batteries of Royal Artillery. In the morning, the British attacked with armored cars and Bren gun carriers, but they were turned back.

The German artillery, which had been brought up in the meantime, started the combat activities on 2 April with a short preparation. The companies moved out, mounted up, but they were soon stopped by a British minefield outside of Agedabia.

At the same time the machine gunners encountered the minefield, a battalion of tanks from *Panzer-Regiment 5* was headed south. Aerial reconnaissance had reported enemy armor located behind the dunes there.

Around 1530 hours, an engagement started with British Mark IV infantry tanks. Seven tanks were knocked out in tank-on-tank engagements. The remaining British armored elements pulled back. They had been from the 2nd Armored Division. Three German tanks sustained battle damage, and the British had been forced out of a potential flanking position.

By the afternoon of 2 April, the machine-gun battalion had approached to within 5 kilometers of Agedabia. A British outflanking maneuver was identified in time and blocked. It was the *5./MG-Bataillon 8*, supported by the

2./Panzerjäger-Abteilung 39, that booked that success. Ponath then sent one of his companies to pursue the withdrawing British. The pursuit forces were able to capture 17 armored cars and 6 trucks, which had gotten stuck in their effort to escape. Thirty British soldiers were taken prisoner.

The attack was pressed home and, after two more hours of fighting, Agedabia was taken by the machine gunners. Following up vigorously, the hills 4 kilometers south of the town were also rapidly taken by the Germans.

Rommel appeared among the men and congratulated Ponath on his success.

At the same time that Agedabia was being cleared, von Wechmar's reconnaissance battalion was advancing rapidly north of the coastal road. It had been directed to bypass Agedabia and feel its way forward in the direction of Bengasi.

Leutnant Wolf and his heavy armored car platoon were in the lead. Just as they passed the forward outposts of *Maschinengewehr-Bataillon 8*, they ran into English two-man tanks, which opened fire with their heavy machine guns. The 2-centimeter rapid-fire cannon on the German armored cars barked in response. Suddenly, however, the Germans started receiving artillery fire. Shells howled overhead and smashed into the forward slope of a hill, where von Wechmar had set up an observation post. He saw an enemy tank that was probably serving as an artillery spotter.

Von Wechmar ordered Pletscher's section forward. As Pletscher stopped by his commander to receive his specific orders, Ponath ran over to him, walking stick in hand.

"Be on your tiptoes, Pletscher!" he warned the noncommissioned officer. ""When you cross the hill in front of us, the road sinks into a *wadi*. There's a bridge there. After that, the *Via Balbia* goes uphill again and Tommy's right behind the next ridgeline."

The three armored cars rolled forward and reached the hill. *Feldwebel* Pletscher saw his first enemy target.

"Fire!" he ordered. The 2-centimeter rounds arched their way over to the enemy. They seemed to harmlessly disappear into the interior of the steel crate, but then flames came roaring out of hatches that had been flung open.

"Enemy armored cars to the right!" Pletscher's gunner reported. He looked over to the right and saw the characteristic antenna frame and eight wheels. Those were no enemy armored cars. It was *Leutnant* Wolf's platoon, which had followed Pletscher.

Wolf then took the enemy artillery observer under fire. It only took three rounds to set the lightly armored English vehicle alight.

Wechmar ordered his men to continue the reconnaissance forward: "We have to hold open the flank of *MG 8* and screen!"

The armored cars and other battalion elements rolled forward and fought it out with enemy elements that were pulling back. Towards evening, elements of the battalion reached the coastal road north of Agedabia. The road was clear of enemy forces, but *Leutnant* Wolf, who had continued to reconnoiter east, reported that there were enemy armored forces some 15 kilometers further on.

When *Oberleutnant* von Fallois brought in the report to the battalion commander, von Wechmar was in the process of shaving. Von Wechmar ordered a telegraph message sent to the *DAK* headquarters and also sent a motorcycle messenger to Agedabia to establish communications with the machine gunners.

Twenty minutes later, the tank regiment commander appeared at von Wechmar's command bus. Together, Olbrich and von Wechmar went forward to take a look at the reported concentration of enemy armor.

Once there and cautiously approaching, the officers determined that it was nothing more than the tank hulks left behind after the English had fought the Italians there the previous winter.

On top of everything else, Rommel then showed up! He had wanted to observe the fighting firsthand. He took it in stride: "The next time, let's see some functioning tanks!"

Although the town of Agedabia had fallen by the time Rommel arrived there on 3 April, the British were still holding out in the fort. Rommel asked Streich what he planned to do.

"I don't think we should afford the enemy the opportunity to reestablish himself!" the division commander responded. "That's why I brought up the entire division, and we'll be finished here in Agedabia shortly."

"Understand . . . I hadn't ordered that, but it's the right decision."

✠

That afternoon, the fort also fell to the Germans. Streich's division continued to move east and established an all-round defensive position in the middle of the desert 20 kilometers to the east that night. The division could go no farther because it was out of fuel.

When Rommel showed up the following morning he ordered all of the trucks of the field trains unloaded. He then had the trucks sent to the rear with two driving teams aboard each of them in order to get ammunition, rations and fuel up front. The contents of the vehicles were placed on tarpaulins in the open desert.

Until the trucks returned, the division was condemned to being immobilized. It was 1,000 kilometers to Tripoli.

The next morning, Rommel again appeared at Streich's location. The division commander had spent the night in his staff car.

"Empty all of the remaining fuel tanks of the vehicles in order to give the tanks fuel. With whatever tanks can then run, advance through Giof el Mater and in the direction of Mechili today. The rest of the division is to follow you after the trucks return."

General Zamboon, who had closed up with his Italian division, vehemently recommended that the risk not be taken: "The trail to Giof el Mater was sewn with thousands of our mines from the retreat last winter. It's a death trap!"

Rommel insisted his orders be carried out. Streich directed the necessary measures. When the tanks had been refueled in the evening, the vehicles moved out in darkness.

In the darkness, the trek could not be identified. Every vehicle had to follow in the tracks of the one ahead of it. Streich moved with the tanks in the middle of the column in his staff car.

The first few mines went up with a thunderous crack. Then there was an ear-deafening detonation ahead of the general.

"That was one of our ammo trucks, *Herr General!*" *Leutnant* Seidel, one of his liaison officers, reported.

"Over there!" The general's driver pointed to the flames welling up mightily over the truck.

"Move around to the right!"

They passed the burning vehicle but were fortunate not to roll over any mines themselves.

"Follow the man ahead of you!" Streich spat out when the driver started to drift off to the left. The driver grimaced in the darkness. The Old Man is hot tonight, he thought.

At that moment, the column came to a standstill. When a staff car further to the rear attempted to pass the stopped vehicles, it had gotten past only three of them when there was another hard blow. The vehicle was blown apart and the crew, all dead, was recovered from the ruins.

"What do you think, now, Schultze?" Streich asked his driver, who would have been in the same spot as the other blown-up staff car. "Follow the lead vehicle!"

"*Jawohl, Herr General!*" the driver responded, unsettled.

✠

The lead vehicles soon got stuck in the fine sand. All of the wheeled vehicles bogged down. Whenever a vehicle attempted to go around a stuck vehicle, it also got stuck.

Streich ordered his prime movers forward. He then ordered his formations to form up around him. He wanted his force assembled, in case the enemy attacked him in this vulnerable position.

The general had the march continue at first light. But only a portion could move out. Once again, the tanks were out of fuel.

Later on, aircraft had to be sent out to find vehicles and crews that had strayed from the general course during the night march. A few had to be resupplied by air—especially with water.

By then Streich was in the lead in his staff car. Towards noon, he reached the dried-out salt lake that was about 20 kilometers south of Mechili. The formation stopped there. By the time they had come that far, the division commander only had six wheeled vehicles and two *Flak* vehicles armed with a single 2-centimeter cannon.

When two *Ju 52's* arrived and landed on the salt lakebed, they were strafed by English fighters as they were unloading and set on fire. The remaining men and vehicles could move no further. For the time being, the advance on Mechili had come to a standstill.

ADVANCE ON DERNA

Since the capture of Derna was of decisive importance for the further success of the *DAK*, Rommel had also initiated a simultaneous advance on it. It was the only place where the serpentines of the Cyrenaican highlands went down to the coastal plain, only to rise again in another series of serpentines to the east. Everything was forced into this bottleneck, which was located between the sea to the north and the *wadi* of Derna to the south. The airfield of Derna was just to the east of the town, which was of decisive importance for the British forces in the Western Desert as well.

On 4 April, *Operation "Ponath"* got underway. *Oberstleutnant* von Ponath's advance guard consisted of a machine-gun company, an antitank gun company, and a combat engineer company. It advanced from Agedabia through the desert; its objective was Derna, after having moved through Giof el Mater–Bir ben Gania–El Mechili. The rest of von Ponath's battalion (under *Hauptmann* Frank) followed along with the rest of the *5. leichte Division*.

Kampfgruppe Ponath had its work cut out for it: 450 kilometers of unknown desert terrain. The more the battle group headed to the south, the hotter it became. In some places, the temperature reached 50 degrees (122 degrees Fahrenheit). Ponath marched by compass. The vehicles constantly bogged down in the soft sand, and the soldiers breathed a sigh of relief whenever they encountered a stretch of rock or pebbles.

What filled the men with confidence, however, were the surprises that Rommel always had in store for them. When they reached the landing strip at Bir ban Gania, for instance, they were not the first Germans there. Two *Ju 52's* were on the strip and Rommel approached the approaching men from out of the shadows of one of the aircraft.

After about 30 kilometers of movement to the northeast, the lead vehicles ran into a minefield. Several soldiers were killed and a few others wounded.

That stopped the advance momentarily, and the battle group rested there while clearing the minefield. On the morning of 6 April, a Fieseler *Storch* circled above and then landed. Rommel deplaned.

"Ponath: Get going immediately and as fast as possible. Objective: Mechili!"

The wild hunt continued, and around 0600 hours, six vehicles, including that of the commander, reached an area 30 kilometers south of Mechili. The rest of the vehicles had gotten stuck and were in the process of trying to catch up. Once outside of Mechili, Ponath was radioed new orders: "Bypass Mechili and head straight for Derna!"

Ponath quickly issued new orders: "Prahl: Stay here and gather the stragglers. Follow as quickly as possible when you have everyone." Prahl saluted and set out to accomplish his difficult mission.

Ponath attempted to inform the elements of his scattered battle group by radio of what was happening. His forces were further dissipated when Rommel ordered him to detach a small group under *Leutnant* Bukow. The two machine-gun crews and an antitank gun went into position on the fork in the road that led to Tmini. Prahl eventually gathered most of the stragglers and took off in pursuit of his battalion commander. Prahl's group ran into Bukow's and was briefed on what had happened.

When Prahl's group ran into a thinly held outpost line around 1630 hours, they moved right through it at high speed and completely surprised the enemy. With the final fuel available, it reached the area around El Ezzeiat. The vehicles were gathered into a *wadi* and camouflaged. The machine guns were unloaded and positioned; the mortars and antitank guns followed.

As the men were preparing their defenses, the sound of engines started to drone in from the east. It became louder and louder. Prahl ordered his men to get ready to engage.

It was a British supply convoy that just happened to show up at that critical moment. When the lead vehicles were only about 15 meters away, the Germans jumped up, weapons at the ready, and completely surprised the bewildered English soldiers.

"Hands up, gentlemen!" Prahl ordered. "No movement or we'll open fire."

The British soldiers surrendered. A search of the vehicles revealed the British had an abundance of fuel, water, and rations, including the 4 officers and 240 enlisted personnel who were then distributed among the 40 captured vehicles.

"Mount up!" Prahl ordered. His men were so few in number that he could only place a single guard on every second vehicle.

During a never-to-be-forgotten night march, with the prospect of the English turning the tables on them at any moment, the Germans finally reached the trail to Derna. Late in the morning, about 9 kilometers outside of the town, another British convoy was spotted. There were about 100 vehicles. The prisoners were left behind with a machine-gun crew guarding them. *Leutnant* Prahl advanced, widely dispersed. Not a round was fired. Did the enemy still believe there was no enemy in front of him?

When they approached the first few trucks, they saw that the Tommies were sleeping. They were fairly upset when they were rudely awakened. Once again, Prahl's small force had taken more than 200 prisoners.

"Damn . . . we need to leave these guys somewhere!" Prahl gave vent to his frustration.

"Why don't we just let them go? They're no threat to us," one of the other officers responded. And so they were released. The look of surprise on the faces of the Tommies was priceless when they were told they could simply disappear.

Prahl continued his quest to find his commander, whom they eventually encountered 3 kilometers outside of Derna. Ponath and his men were busy trying to camouflage themselves and guard their prisoners, two of whom were generals. What had happened while Prahl was trying to find Ponath?

✠

After Ponath had left behind his adjutant, the small advance guard had continued on in the direction of Derna. During the evening of 6 April 1941, General O'Connor, the successor to General Neame, was in Maraua, along with the latter general. They wanted to go on to Martuba, but they missed the turnoff and had continued on to Derna. At the edge of the town there, they were interdicted by outposts of *Maschinengewehr-Bataillon 8*. In addition to the two aforementioned generals, the driver and Brigadier Combe, who had commanded the 11th Hussars against the Italians during the winter campaign, were also taken prisoner. It was *Feldwebel* Borchardt and his men from the *1./ MG-Bataillon 8* who made the important "haul." The next morning, General O'Connor saw Burckhardt again and gave him his camera, telling him he was a "brave soldier!"

Just outside of Derna, Ponath's men captured another group of British soldiers, some 200 in number. The effort to take Derna by surprise attack at first light with the few forces available failed, however. Engaged by tanks and armored cars, Ponath and his men had to pull back.

That was the situation when Prahl and his men linked up with Ponath at 0930 hours. With the new force, Ponath decided to try to take Derna again.

It was 1100 hours when the battle group moved rapidly out of the *wadi* and entered the northern portion of the town, where the airstrip was located. They fired from their vehicles as they advanced and destroyed six British transporters, which were trying to take off.

The advance continued south, through the middle portion of the town, and then on towards the fighter base south of town. When the Germans reached the open area, which was as flat as a washboard, the enemy opened fire. The motorcyclists raced towards the Bren carriers. They tossed grenades in them, either immobilizing or destroying them. But the German attack was stopped, and the British fighters still there took off to the east as quickly as they could get started.

The men of the battle group established their positions along the eastern side of the landing strip. When British elements attempted to break through to the east, they were halted by the concentrated fires of the Germans and driven back. A number of British on the trucks surrendered and were escorted back to the "prisoner defile."

A British field hospital and a mobile maintenance facility were prized booty. Both the Germans and the British worked together to care for the wounded. It was fascinating for the German soldiers to see the stoic resignation with which the enemy accepted captivity. For them, the war was over.

The attack was continued in the afternoon, and the western end of the airfield was reached. The British launched an immediate counterattack with Mark II infantry tanks. Thirty tanks advanced in sections. They would stop to fire and then move out again. *Kampfgruppe Ponrath* was forced back to its initial line of departure on the other side of the airfield. The British tanks then attempted to blast a path through the Germans for their infantry to escape to the east. They moved through the German lines, firing without a pause. But the infantry that followed was separated form the armor and held back by the machine gunners of *MG-Bataillon 8.*

When a rapidly moving staff car approached the German positions around midnight, it was stopped. There were two British generals in it.

At first light on 8 April, *Kampfgruppe Ponath* moved out to attack again. There was still sporadic fighting in Derna until 0900 hours. Then the town was firmly under German control. One of the most dramatic raids of the entire campaign in Africa came to an end. The small advance guard had taken 4 generals, 174 officers and 793 enlisted personnel. The mission had been accomplished with virtually the last rounds remaining.

Reinforcements were requested by air. They arrived in the afternoon via *Ju 52's* in the form of three 2-centimeter *Flak* and 60 men. They were no longer needed for the fighting, however.

Additional *Ju 52's* brought in ammunition, water, and rations in the afternoon. A short while after that, a *Stuka* squadron arrived and took over the airfield. They would support the continued advance of the *DAK* from there.

Rommel arrived from Mechili around 1835 hours. Along with him was the rest of Ponath's machine-gun battalion. Rommel issued orders to the rejoined battalion to continue advancing as the division's advance guard in the direction of Tmimi.

MECHILI IS CONQUERED

On 7 April, when the rest of the division, including the tanks of *Panzer-Regiment 5* of *Oberst* Olbrich, had still not arrived outside of Mechili, Rommel went looking for it in his Fieseler *Storch*. When he found the formations, he landed.

"What's going on, Olbrich? Why aren't you at Mechili?" Rommel said to the regimental commander disapprovingly.

"We got into rocky dessert. Our tanks could not get through, *Herr General!*" Olbrich answered. "We had to regroup, move back, and then go around further to the south."

Portions of the desert simply could not be traversed, tank or no tank.

A few minutes later, *Generalmajor* von Prittwitz, the commander of the *15. Panzer-Division*, arrived with his operations officer. He had come in advance of his division to get an idea of what it was like "on the ground."

Rommel greeted the commander and asked him to bring his division forward as soon as possible.

Later that day, a reinforced *Bersaglieri* battalion also arrived outside of Mechili. It took up positions in the southeastern sector.

Ju 52's landed on the dried-out salt lake to bring in supplies. British fighters tried to strafe the ongoing supply operations. They were engaged by the handful of 2-centimeter *Flak* present, which succeeded in shooting down one of the attackers.

That same evening, the first eight tanks of the *I./Panzer-Regiment 5* arrived. They were led by *Major* Bolbrinker. That gave Streich the first heavy weapons he needed for his planned attack. Rommel gave him the green light for the attack first thing the next morning.

Fortunately for Streich's division, the senior logistics officer for Africa, *Oberstleutnant Graf* von Klinkowström, had arrived in Agedabia on 5 April with three battalions of logistics forces, which brought 330 tons of fuel and 200 tons of rations for the division.

The demand for surrender issued on 6 April was ignored by the English defenders. All of 7 April lay under the pall of a *Ghibli*, which prevented any type of forward movement. During the sandstorm, two emissaries were again dispatched to General Gambier-Parry to seek his surrender. He once again turned down the request, especially since he had received orders that evening to break out. That led to a confusing situation on the morning of 8 April.

Early on the morning of 8 April, Streich moved forward with the leaders of his formations to scout out a good place to potentially penetrate the British lines. Suddenly, the Germans saw a long column of vehicles leave the desert fort. The elements of the British 2nd Armored Division were conducting their breakout!

Major Bolbrinker, who had come forward with his eight tanks at the right time, had also seen the huge dust cloud that had developed.

Bolbrinker radioed his commanders: "Everyone follow me into El Mechili!" The eight tanks moved out. A short while later, Bolbrinker saw that a group of English vehicles was directly approaching Streich's command post. The Germans there opened fire with machine guns.

The majority of the British vehicles then turned off to the right. Streich ordered his adjutant to take the two 2-centimeter *Flak* that were there for the command post defense and overtake and stop the English convoy.

Leutnant Rickert took off at high speed, and Streich followed Bolbrinker's tanks headed for Mechili in his staff car.

Just outside of Mechili, when the tanks had reached the trench system and the foxholes, the English opened fire with antitank guns. Bolbrinker ordered his tanks to stop to fire.

The *Panzer III's* came to a halt. Fire spewed from their main guns, and the first English antitank gun was knocked out. The first German tank was then hit. When the ammunition started to go off, the crew bailed out. Finally, the four enemy antitank guns were silenced, but not before they had immobilized another two German tanks.

After the enemy's defensive belt had been crossed, a large truck convoy suddenly approached Mechili from the west. It was the trucks that *Leutnant* Rickert had pursued. Once they were about to be overtaken, they turned around to seek the sanctuary of the fort.

"Fire a few rounds at the convoy!" Streich ordered the first tank he could reach. The tank pivoted and the first round was quickly fired from the short main gun. The round slammed into a truck and set it alight. The following rounds also hit. The truck convoy came to a halt. The English soldiers did not know where to turn. They dismounted their vehicles with raised hands. In all, there were some 2,000 men, including two generals, one of whom was Gambier-Parry. The convoy had contained two battalions from the Indian 2nd Brigade and rear-area services of the 2nd Armored Division.

During the last phase of the fighting for El Mechili, a new *Ghibli* blew in, which stopped all movement for four hours. Despite the thick veil of sand, the black clouds of smoke could be seen rising from the fuel depots, which the remaining English had set on fire. They did not want the Germans to get their hands on the precious commodity.

The British senior officers requested that Streich allow them to search the now-occupied depots and camps for uniform articles and materials suitable for burning, so that their men, now prisoners, could get through the night better. Streich granted them their request and also let them have trucks to fetch rations from their former supply depots. Streich also let the generals spend the night in their command cars.

✠

Rommel did not want to waste any time. He saw a great opportunity to immediately advance through Tmimi and on to Tobruk. Tobruk was a large port, which the *DAK* desperately needed. Tobruk could be considered the focal point of the entire North African theater. Rommel immediately sent von Prittwitz in the direction of Tobruk with a *Kampfgruppe*. Among the forces of the battle group were the light division's machine-gun battalion and reconnaissance battalion. The light division established its headquarters in Mechili for the time being.

After several hours of maintenance, Olbrich's tanks advanced in the direction of Tmimi. They arrived there the next morning. Streich informed Olbrich to continue advancing along the *Via Balbia*. Streich, for his part, went to the "White House" in Acroma. He was to meet Rommel there to receive orders for the next phase of operations for the light division, especially the armor. Rommel, however, was not there. Streich discovered that he had already gone ahead to the lead elements of Ponath's battalion, which were already at the outer ring of defensive positions for Tobruk. Rommel wanted to take the fortress in a *coup de main*, but he was already several days too late, as he would later discover.

The fortress of Tobruk was established by the Italians in 1935. The first fortifications built were the 128 strongpoints that were designed to protect the city and the harbor along a distance of some 54 kilometers. The ring was established in a semicircle about 15 kilometers around the city. The strongpoints were set up in two parallel concentric lines, with a separation of about 600 meters between them. The rear line of strongpoints was positioned in such a manner that it could support the forward line with fires. On both flanks of the defensive positions, there were only an outpost line and a solitary defensive line, since the *Wadi es Sahal* in the west and the *Wadi es Zeitun* in the east—both located north of the coastal road and extending to the sea—were natural obstacles that would make any breakthrough attempt difficult.

The terrain within the fortress climbed from the sea in two steep steps and reached a height of some 140 to 160 meters and then descended down into the area in front of the defensive sector towards the south and southeast, becoming ever flatter. In the west, the *Ras el Madauar* was the highest point, reaching an elevation of 209 meters. From there, a long ridgeline extended to the west as far as Acroma and almost as high as the *Ras el Madauar.*

Each of the strongpoints in Tobruk consisted of three dugouts, which were protected from the front by concrete but were open above. Each of the dugouts had an antitank gun or a mortar, a machine-gun, and place for 40 soldiers.

The strongpoints in the first line of defense were surrounded by tank ditches, which were 1.2 to 1.5 meters deeps and 3.5 meters wide. Each tank ditch had two crawl spaces that connected with the strongpoint's communications trench. All of the trenches, including the tank ditch, were covered with boards, which had been covered with sand to camouflage them.

All of the strongpoints were also surrounded by wire obstacles that were 1.5 meters tall and 6 meters wide. An additional wire obstacle surrounded the entire ring of defenses. The tank ditches, the area between the wire obstacles, and the trenches themselves were mined. Each of the strongpoints enjoyed good fields of fire and were able to supply flanking fires in support of other strongpoints.

The airfield at El Adem, 25 kilometers south of Tobruk, was connected with the fortress by a concrete road. In the fortress proper, there was also a small airfield for fighters 4 kilometers south of the harbor.

Not of that would have benefited the British, however, if they had not received reinforcements in the nick of time.

General Wavell, who had spent time in Cyrenaica at the beginning of April to get a firsthand look at the terrain, recognized the danger to his western flank. On 3 April, when he returned to Cairo, he requested his superior officer to leave the Australian division, which had been earmarked for shipment to Greece, in Egypt instead. He also requested that the British 6th Infantry Division, which had been earmarked for an attack against the Italian Dodecanese Islands, also be left in the Nile Delta, where it was currently billeted. In addition, he had the Indian 4th Infantry Division move from the Sudan into Egypt. The latter move was possible after the Italians had been defeated there. The Chiefs in London signed off on Wavell's requests.

On 5 April, the 18th Infantry Brigade of the Australian 7th Infantry Division dispatched its main body by sea to Tobruk, with the remaining elements moving by land. The brigade finished its movement on 7 April. Wavell, an able tactician, had the 22nd Guards Brigade, augmented by additional artillery and antitank gun forces, move from Cairo to the Egyptian-Libyan frontier. On 7 April, Wavell received a telegram from Churchill: "Tobruk, so well fortified by the Italians, is to be held to the last man."[7]

Wavell flew to Tobruk on the morning of 8 April, issuing his orders personally once there.

He telegraphed London that he had no more armored forces capable of taking on the *DAK* after the 2nd Armored had been effectively wiped out.

The commander of the Australian division, Major General Morshead, had the two brigades that had been pulled back from Cyrenaica set up in positions on both sides of the coastal road at Acroma, some 25 kilometers west of Tobruk, on the morning of 8 April. Both of the brigades were augmented by an artillery regiment. When Morshead entered Tobruk, he also found his 18th Brigade, which had been brought forward and was going into position on both sides of the road leading to Bardia.

Morshead met with Wavell, who also had Lavarack, another Australian major general, who had been designated as the acting commander of the Cyrenaica Command. All three generals inspected the fortifications, which Morshead already was acquainted with from the winter campaign. On 9 April, they all agreed that the fortress needed to be defended with three brigades in the exterior front lines, while a fourth brigade, along with armored support, to be positioned as a reserve. Morshead was designated as the local area commander.

At the same time, additional reinforcements arrived in Tobruk. These included a tank battalion with 11 Cruiser tanks, 15 light tanks, and 4 infantry Mark II's. Another artillery regiment, as well as additional antitank and antiaircraft guns, was brought forward.

Luftwaffe aerial reconnaissance indicated the harbor at Tobruk was full.

A "Mobile Force" was also established from elements of the British 7th Armored Division. Brigadier Gott was designated as its commander. Among

---

7. Translator's Note: This quote was reverse-translated without access to the original quote.

the "Mobile Force" was the 11th Hussars, although it only had 50% of its subordinate elements. The remnants of the Indian 3rd Infantry Brigade (motorized) and the 2nd Armored Division also constituted part of the force. Supporting the "Mobile Force" were an artillery regiment and an antitank-gun battalion. Its mission was to fix enemy forces south of the coastal road.

Those were forces that could have stood up to an entire corps when they were positioned in a fortress like Tobruk. The *DAK*, by contrast, was barely half that size with the forces it had in the field at the time.

Rommel miscalculated when he thought he could fix the enemy to the front with the Italian forces that had been brought up in the meantime. It was his intent to conduct a right hook with his *5. leichte Division* to take Tobruk from the south.

ASSAULT ON TOBRUK

The elements of *MG-Bataillon 8* reached Tmimi during the morning of 9 April and set up a screening perimeter oriented east and southeast. Mounted patrols reconnoitered in the direction of Gazala. When they reached its outskirts, they were engaged by heavy machine guns and forced to pull back.

Aufklärungs-Abteilung 3 (mot.) arrived around noon. Practically without a break, it continued reconnoitering eastward, with the machine-gun battalion following two hours later. The machine gunners later overtook the reconnaissance elements and continued on to Tobruk. Some 30 kilometers from the city, the men were engaged by small arms from the hilltops along both sides of the road. Artillery fire commenced, and the battalion was forced to dismount. Cursing, the men dug in. *Oberstleutnant* Ponath spotted three batteries of enemy guns through his field glasses; the enemy artillery was firing from open positions. When the first German vehicle was hit, Ponath sent the remaining ones back to a safer distance.

Based on the kilometer marker on the *Via Balbia*, the men were only 26 kilometers from Tobruk. Some of his advance guard had reached the 19-kilometer marker. By the evening of 9 May, the rest of the German forces had closed up to the 31-kilometers marker, along with the Italians' *Brescia* and *Trento* Divisions. On 10 April, Rommel issued his orders for the attack on the fortress. The two Italian divisions were to attack Tobruk from the west in order to fix enemy forces. At the same time, the *5. leichte Division* was to attempt a flanking maneuver to the south, bypassing the fortress and then attacking form the southeast. Rommel had *Generalmajor* von Prittwitz move ahead in a staff car and look for suitable artillery firing positions for engaging Tobruk's harbor. The Commanding General instructed Wechmar's reconnaissance battalion to advance through Acroma and on to El Adem. He instructed the machine gunners, who had been engaged in heavy fighting since the previous day, to continue to try to advance.

Prittwitz took off immediately. He only had his driver and liaison officer with him. After Prittwitz's staff car had disappeared from sight, the lead elements of the *Brescia* Division arrived. *Generalmajor* Kirchheim, who was serving as an adviser to the division, had brought it forward.

"Kirchheim, you're heaven sent!" Rommel called out. Kirchheim was a fellow recipient of the *Pour le Mérite* from the First World War. "Head out on the road and check on the preparations of the Italians. You can get as far as kilometer marker 13 without any problems. According to the last reports, Italian outposts are already there."

Kirchheim was not assigned to the *DAK*. He was part of the Special Headquarters for Libya. Nevertheless, he obeyed Rommel's directive and raced to the front in his staff car, accompanied by two other staff officers. When Kirchheim's vehicle approached the "White House" at marker 18, he saw British fighters racing along the *Via Balbia* on a strafing run.

"Air attack!" the driver yelled out. But it was too late. The machine-gun rounds started slamming into the vehicle from the three Hurricanes. Kirchheim felt a hard blow to his shoulder and then to his arm. He felt a hot pain in his eyes.

The vehicle stopped crosswise to the road. The Hurricanes had already disappeared over the horizon.

"Explosive rounds!" one of the staff officers yelled out. Even more urgently, he exclaimed: "you're wounded, *Herr General!*"

The men dressed the general's wounds on both arms and his shoulders. There was a small piece of shrapnel under the left eye as well. Far behind them, they could hear the hammering of machine guns from the Hurricanes again. That strafing run hit advancing elements of the *Brescia* Division.

Coming out of the desert, a *Kübelwagen*[8] suddenly turned onto the *Via Balbia*. It was the vehicle of *Generalmajor* von Prittwitz. He had his vehicle stop in order to assist.

"Kirchheim! You're a sure bet for going home with that wound!" Prittwitz said, trying to cheer up his stricken comrade. "If you go through Vienna, you can say hello to my wife! Tell her that I'm doing really well. But I have to go on now to find some firing positions."

"Prittwitz," Kirchheim responded, "it's good that you're doing that. I was supposed to recon the lines of departure for the attack on Tobruk. I'm not going to leave the front because of a few scratches. I'll get going again in 15 minutes. Did Rommel tell you that there were Italian outposts as far as marker 13?"

---

8. Translator's Note: A *Kübelwagen* was the rough equivalent of the U.S. jeep. Literally, it meant "bucket vehicle."

"That he did. I don't have to worry until I get that far."

"That's fine. Stay somewhere where I can find you."

A quarter of an hour later, Kirchheim was true to his word and rolled out again.

When they reached kilometer marker 14, they saw Prittwitz's *Kübelwagen* on the side of the road. A few seconds later, a figure came racing towards them through the roadside ditch, waving frantically towards Kirchheim's vehicle. Kirchheim had his vehicle stop, and Prittwitz's liaison officer reported to him: "English AT in front of us! The general has been killed by a direct hit. His driver as well. Both are still in the vehicle."

Kirchheim had the liaison officer get in. They moved back a bit, then turned around. They radioed for medics to come forward and then went on to reconnoiter the positions.

✠

The men of *MG-Bataillon 8* had continued their advance, but they also came under heavy artillery fire again. Ponath had his men dismount and sent the vehicles to the rear. The soldiers continued running forward, even though machine-gun fire was whipping towards them from a great distance. The road led into a steep cliff. Once they reached the relative cover there, they were also able to see the artillery firing positions on the far side of a ravine. A few seconds later, the bridge flew into the air; the enemy had blown it up! Machine-gun fire and artillery shells started raining down on the attackers. When the left flank of the attack group reached a small patch of woods, it started receiving fire from bunkers that had been carved out of the cliffs on the opposite side of the ravine. Everyone took cover and tried to make himself as small as possible.

"We need artillery on those positions!"

Before the messenger could get to the radio operators and have the request telegraphed through, the men in the forward lines went through a living hell. Finally, German artillery replied in kind. One after the other, the enemy guns on the far side of the ravine were silenced. Then the machine gunners saw the British race two trucks forward, which picked up the wounded and the remaining gun crews and raced off again.

"Let's go!" Ponath roared.

The men of the battalion attacked along a frontage of 2 kilometers. They descended into the steep *wadi*, where they were greeted by new bursts of machine-gun fire. Once again, the men had to find cover wherever and whatever it was. They also encountered a thick wire obstacle.

Ponath had no choice but to call off the attack.

Early in the afternoon, a *Kübelwagen* approached the German positions from the west. The solitary German antitank gun that was on the road attempted to halt the vehicle, but the officer inside told the men to get moving, since the enemy was pulling back.

A few seconds later, the vehicle went up in flames. It had been von Prittwitz's vehicle.

✠

On the evening of 10 April, the machine gunners were informed that they were to be relieved by men of the *Brescia* Division, so that they could carry on the attack south of Tobruk.

When the battalion reached the fork in the road to Acroma early in the morning of 11 April, they discovered that their sister battalion—*MG-Bataillon 2*—had already passed that area during the night and that von Wechmar's recon battalion had already reached Bardia.

During the afternoon of 11 April, Streich discovered that his comrade Prittwitz had been killed. He was on his way to see Rommel at the rest area along the Gulf of Bomba. Streich, who was using a captured British armored car—christened the "Mammoth"—as his command and control vehicle, was almost taken out on Rommel's orders by a German antitank gun. At the last moment, the German command pennant was seen.

"What's the idea of using a British vehicle?" Rommel started to dress down the commander. "We almost took you out!"

"Then perhaps the *Herr General* would have lost both of his armored commanders on a single day," Streich responded. Rommel calmed down and got back to business, giving Streich new orders and placing him in charge of the forces on the ground arrayed around Tobruk. On Streich's way back to the front, he received machine-gun fire and mortar rounds. The general and his escort officers jumped out of the vehicle, while the driver attempted to evade the fire by driving in a zigzag pattern towards the north. The dismounted men had to seek cover constantly, but they were eventually able to escape the enemy fire and link up with their vehicle. Streich assumed command of the forces around Tobruk in the "White House" at Acroma.

✠

Before we turn to the assault on Tobruk proper, let us also take a look at the activities of von Wechmar's reconnaissance soldiers in the buildup to the attack.

Late in the evening of 3 April, von Wechmar's battalion had been sent in the direction of Bengasi. As was usually the case, von Wechmar was right at the front of the column with his men. The battalion advanced rapidly along the *Via Balbia*. According to *Oberleutnant* von Fallois, the battalion would be in Bengasi by midnight if it continued its current rate of advance. After short firefights, enemy patrols would pull back rapidly. Suddenly, a *Kübelwagen* approached the battalion rapidly from the rear. Standing behind the window in the open-topped vehicle was a figure in a leather overcoat and goggles mounted to the front of a visor cap—Rommel! When he reached von Wechmar's vehicle, he had the column stop.

"What are your patrols saying, Wechmar?"

"Light contact. Enemy pulling back, *Herr General.*"

"I know," Rommel replied. "That's what the aviators are saying as well. So, on to Bengasi, but be careful! There could be Tommies in the city. I'm attaching a tank company and a section of artillery to you." Rommel paused and smiled: "That's half of the *DAK!*"

Leutnant Wolf rolled forward a short while later with his patrol. At the rest area, where the tanks were supposed to join them, a motorcycle showed up a short while later from the east. It was the priest of the Italian hospital at Bengasi. He had helped himself to an English motorcycle and headed west. He reported that the English were pulling out and that most of the formations that had been there had already departed during the day.

A short while later, *Oberleutnant* Landrock, the tank company commander, arrived. He stated that his company and the attached artillery section would arrive at 2300 hours.

After the other elements of the battalion had refueled and uploaded ammunition, *Oberleutnant* Behr, the commander of the battalion's motorcycle infantry company, received orders at 2305 hours to head straight for Bengasi and take it.

The motorcyclists took off and reached Bengasi at first light. They moved rapidly through the city, which had already been abandoned by the enemy, and waited for the rest of the battalion on the eastern outskirts.

When Rommel showed up in Bengasi in the morning, he ordered the advance to continue at noon. The airfield at Bengasi was reached, and it was determined that it had also been abandoned by the enemy. The next objectives were the high ground around Benina and Fort Benina itself. The motorcyclists were greeted with heavy fires there.

"Tanks up front!" von Wechmar ordered.

Oberleutnant Behr ordered his dismounted motorcycle infantry to follow the tanks, as the tanks rolled past and headed uphill. The enemy artillery fired wildly against the advancing tanks. Then there were three—then a fourth—detonations. The tanks had run into a minefield. Three tanks were immobilized with track damage.

The motorcycle infantry ran up the hill. The enemy was pushed back in close-in fighting, where carbines, submachine guns, and hand grenades were the order of the day. Under the scorching sun, the assault packs of the infantry seemed to weigh a "ton."

As it started to turn dark, the Australian infantry pulled back. Numerous enemy soldiers had surrendered; six artillery pieces were captured. The men of the reconnaissance battalion set up for the night on the hill. The engineers cleared mines along the road, and the tank crews worked with the maintenance platoon to repair the damage to the tracks and running gear. The field mess came forward, and the soldiers were able to enjoy a warm meal in the middle of the night.

When the officers assembled for their daily conference, *Oberleutnant* Behr reported that *Leutnant* Langemann's motorcycle platoon was missing. He had been seen just before darkness, after he had assaulted up the hill and was advancing forward. Could the Australians have captured him and his platoon?

One of the other platoon leaders reported that he thought Langemann had continued advancing in the direction of Fort Benina. Whenever *Oberleutnant* Behr attempted to send out search patrols, they were all greeted by heavy fire from the Australians.

So . . . what had happened to *Leutnant* Langemann?

After reaching the crest of the hill, *Leutnant* Langemann and his men continued hot on the heels of the enemy forces pulling back.

"Follow me!" he yelled out to his platoon. They ran through the onset of darkness, and suddenly, they were in front of the fort. They were greeted by fire. A few seconds later, they also heard Australian-accented English behind them. They disappeared into a fold in the ground and tried to conceal themselves. The Australians ran past them and into the fort. Langemann followed with his platoon. They not only succeeded in entering but also getting to the middle of the compound, where the Australians were forming up. Realizing he would be no match against the enemy force, Langemann pulled back with his men.

In the morning, however, Langemann had one of his machine guns open fire on the concentrated enemy forces. The Australians quickly mounted their vehicles and took off. Langemann and his men had captured the fort!

✠

Rommel ordered the reconnaissance battalion to continue its advance. *Feldwebel* Junger and his section were in the lead. As they advanced, they stopped to pick up a *Stuka* crew that had been shot down and had parachuted to safety.

The advance continued on what barely could be called a trail. The armored cars were in front, the trucks in the middle, and the motorcycles bringing up the rear. They mass of machinery plowed through a thick cloud of dust to the east. It moved up hills and down over flat terrain, through rocks and stones, and across layers of limestone that crumbled under the wheels of the vehicles.

"Watch out," the *Stuka* crew informed Junger, "there are Tommy tanks ahead!"

During a maintenance halt, *Oberleutnant* von Fallois climbed a hill. Surrounded by a thick cloud of dust, he saw some 40 enemy tanks approaching them. But the tanks suddenly stopped in front of the hill.

That night, a patrol under *Oberleutnant* Behr reached five of the tanks that were positioned somewhat closer to the Germans. Three of the tanks were empty; the crews of the other two were taken prisoner.

When the prisoners were interrogated, it was discovered that the tanks had halted due to a lack of fuel. Most of the enemy tanks had pulled back, as best they could. The reconnaissance battalion continued its advance in the morning. Based on a message dropped from Rommel's *Storch*, von Wechmar knew that Ponath's machine gunners were assaulting Derna. Rommel's orders: "Move faster!"

During the afternoon of the next day, the battalion left the trail in order to shorten its approach march. But the difficult terrain did not win the men much time. *Oberleutnant* Everth was in the front. Just as he was about to light a cigarette, his *Kübelwagen* was struck by a mighty blow to its left front. There was the smell of cordite, and dust wafted skyward.

"Stop . . . mines!" he yelled and radioed to the rest. The battalion came to a halt.

Von Wechmar had his engineer platoon move forward to clear the mines. *Feldwebel* Schubert's men cleared the thermos-shaped mines, which seemed to be scattered and emplaced everywhere. They were placed in a pile.

Schubert kept reminding his men to be careful. It took the entire afternoon to remove the danger and create a gap through the minefield through which the vehicles could pass. *Feldwebel* Waschke operated the mine detector. During the evening, a thunderous detonation echoed through the desert. One of the engineers had accidently dropped a mine in the middle of the pile. Bodies flew through the air; there were screams for help. When von Wechmar rushed out of his command bus, he saw a number of men lying on the ground. *Feldwebel* Schubert had been killed, along with two other men. Six other soldiers were wounded. The burial report of *Oberfeldwebel* Schlitt had three new names entered on it.

The vehicles of the battalion returned to the trail; towards midnight, they reached Derna, which had been taken by Ponath's men in the meantime. The next morning—it was 9 April—the battalion received orders from the Commanding General to continue its reconnaissance-in-force, heading towards Bardia while bypassing Tobruk.

"Always do 60, Wechmar. A recon battalion that doesn't do 60 isn't worth a whole lot," Rommel concluded, with a slight smile.

Oberleutnant Everth led the advance guard of the recon battalion as it went around Tobruk in the middle of the night. Attached to the advance guard were the antitank guns of *Oberleutnant* Plüschow. English artillery from Tobruk hammered the route of advance. The men got through that difficult stretch, reached the coastal road, turned right, and headed east. *Leutnant* Wolf took over the lead in the advance guard. Off to the left, there was an occasional glimmer from the sea, which could be seen from time to time in the bright moon light. Off to the right were the eerie sand dunes. Occasionally, the men saw a hill jutting up out of the distant desert. As they approached Bardia, the foothills of the mountains got closer and closer to the *Via Balbia*. Before the sun rose, there was a sandstorm.

When the battalion reached Bardia around 0700 hours, it was greeted by demolitions that had been placed on the road leading to the bay and the harbor. Thick smoke rose over the fuel depots of the British.

The battalion got to the city, which was on a hill overlooking the harbor. The enemy was nowhere to be seen. Bardia was in German hands.

While von Wechmar had Thiele's company remain behind in Bardia, the main body of the battalion continued east to the highlands east of the town, where it occupied former Italian positions.

Let us now turn our attention back to Ponath's men and the assault on Tobruk.

A BATTALION DIES

The attack on Tobruk was continued shortly after noon on 11 April 1941. After the attempt failed to follow the retreating enemy back into the fortress, it was directed that *MG-Bataillon 8* and *Panzer-Regiment 5* attack. The tank regiment had only 20 tanks at its disposal.

Reports had come in that the enemy was evacuating the fortress, however, and the men were ordered to move aggressively. The men gave it their all, including an effort to create a "lot of dust" so as to deceive the enemy as to the true strength of the relatively meager German force in front of it.

Two companies advanced on line at the front, with two other companies echeloned left and to the rear. On the right were the 20 tanks that had made the advance in one piece. After advancing about 2 kilometers. The attack force was met by heavy artillery fire from the fortress.

Ponath ordered his men to dismount. The vehicles were quickly abandoned, the weapons and ammunition gathered. The men then followed their commander. They had to get ahead of the artillery. The tanks turned off to the right and left, attempting to draw the artillery fire. The lead ground elements then started to received antitank-gun and machine-gun fire.

Ponath ordered his men to take cover.

The men feverishly dug into the barren desert with bayonets, entrenching tools, and anything they could lay their hands on to dig with. Small walls of stones were fashioned to offer head protection.

Wounded cried out and attempted to crawl to the rear. Others were hit as they tried to find better cover.

The tanks engaged the enemy's antitank guns. The German tanks started being knocked out or immobilized in the unequal fighting against the antitank guns and artillery. The last remaining operational tanks had to pull back. The attack was called off.

Few soldiers have ever wanted night to fall as much as those soldiers of *MG-Bataillon 8* outside of Tobruk on Good Friday, 1941.

Whenever a head appeared for a brief moment, there was a burst of machine-gun fire or the crack of rifles.

Feldwebel Urban and *Unteroffizier* Weißgerber, two medics, crawled and took short runs—their lives always in the balance—to get from one wounded man to the next. They field-dressed their comrades and carried them back to the rear. They wore Red Cross armbands. Was that the reason they were not hit? Did the enemy recognize the symbol? Apparently, the answer was yes.

During the night, the adjutant, *Oberleutnant* Prahl, went back through the artillery fire to the vehicles and went to the division headquarters in Acroma. He briefed Streich at 0900 hours. When he returned to his battalion, he brought orders with him to attack again. This time, all of the tanks would support the battalion. When Ponath received the reports from his company commanders, he discovered that his battalion had lost 1 officer and 40 men killed.

It was 1100 hours when the German tanks arrived. They moved through the middle of the machine-gun battalion's positions. When the last tank rolled past, Ponath jumped up and issued orders to the messengers: "Follow the tanks closely!" The messengers headed out to relay the message to the companies. A few of them were hit. All of a sudden, however, the tanks came streaming back.

"What's going on?" Ponath shouted to the regimental commander, who had personally led his tanks into battle. Olbrich replied: "We can't get through. There's a tank ditch 400 meters in front of us, with AT behind it."

Ponath's men would have to go it alone. After the dust that the tanks had churned up had settled, the men could see the broad wire obstacle in front of them. Far to the rear, poles could be seen, which had small baskets at the top. Tommies were in there, directing fires.

Prahl worked his way back through the enemy fire to the division command post. He rendered a report that was short and to the point. The battalion received orders to dig in where it was.

During the night, motorcycles from the mess hall attempted to go forward to provide the men in the makeshift trenches with warm food and some water. Two of the motorcycles were lost in the enemy fire.

That same evening, one of the liaison officers, *Leutnant* Helmut Kaatz, was killed. In addition to the 42 enlisted personnel, who had been wounded, the commanders of the 3rd Company (*Oberleutnant* Goedeckemeyer) and the 4th Company (*Oberleutnant* von Rautenfeld) had also been hit. In all, the battalion had suffered 27 dead and 81 wounded during the advance on Derna from 1 to 12 April. In addition, there were 13 missing and 80 incapacitated due to sickness. That left *Oberstleutnant* Ponath with only 500 men.

When morning dawned on 13 April 1941—Easter Sunday—there was incessant artillery fire raining down on the men of the battalion in no-man's-land. The artillery was joined by mortar and machine-gun fire. The enemy observers in their "baskets" were engaged by machine guns that were quickly placed on top of the provisional cover, but despite that, the initial fires were well placed.

A radio message came in: "*Oberstleutnant* Ponath: Report to the division!" Followed by fires from the enemy, the battalion commander raced across the battlefield. When he arrived there at 1700 hours, the commander of the *I./ Flak-Regiment 18* was also there. Ponath reported that heavy enemy fires made every daylight movement suicidal. For its part, however, the *DAK* needed to get the fork in the road south of Tobruk so as to be able to observe directly into the city and harbor.

The battalion was directed to attack again. This time, the assault was to be preceded by a 10-minute artillery preparation commencing at 1830 hours. The *I./Flak-Regiment 18* was directed to support, as well as the tanks and engineer forces.

The three messengers that Ponath dispatched to the companies to relay the orders for the attack were all killed, one after the other. Two others were wounded. As a result, the 2nd and 3rd Companies, which were the farthest forward, did not receive the attack order. They were supposed to have rolled up the enemy lines to the right and left. Ponath personally briefed the commander of the 5th Company.

Everyone waited for the *Flak*, which had been directed to soften up the enemy positions. At 1750 hours, the light *Flak* rolled forward through the enemy fire to the forward lines and set up. The 8.8-centimeter *Flak* positioned itself behind the 5th Company. The enemy seemingly fired with everything he had against those *Flak* batteries. The light battery replied in kind against any and all muzzle flashes it could make out. The first gun was lost, however, followed by a second. Soon, all of the light *Flak* were silent. Only a *Leutnant* and six men returned from the front lines.

The heavy *Flak* succeeded in eliminating a few enemy antitank guns and artillery pieces, which the enemy had positioned forward. The *Flak* fired for 10 minutes in a deadly and bitter struggle. It was then time for the artillery preparation, but it did not come.

Hauptmann Bartsch looked at his battalion commander.

"Do it without the prep, Bartsch!" Ponath ordered.

"5th . . . get up . . . move out!"

The men jumped up. They ran forward, only for many to collapse to the ground, tripping on the rocky terrain or, worse, being hit. They had to cover 300 meters of open ground. The enemy artillery started a fiery rain of death on the men.

Elements of the 2nd and 3rd Companies joined in, even though they had not received any orders to do so. They got as far as the tank ditch, where they were then engaged from the enemy dugouts. They ran and crawled back to their lines of departure.

The 5th Company got as far as the forwardmost line of outposts, where it was forced to stop and take cover.

Ponath had his companies informed that they would continue the attack at night: "We will penetrate the enemy's line and establish a bridgehead through which the tanks can pass."

During the night, squads infiltrated forward. They crossed the tank ditch, took the adjacent dugouts, and established a bridgehead that was approximately 400 meters wide and 100 meters deep. It appeared the point had been reached where further operations could be launched. Ponath ordered his attached antitank guns forward. He told his patrols to scout to the northeast.

The antitank guns were rolled forward by the crews. When the patrols came back, they reported that there was no enemy in front of them. After the war, it was discovered why the patrols had discovered no enemy forces.

They had infiltrated right in the middle between the Australian strongpoints R33 and R35. Since they oriented to the northeast, they also went right in the middle of the two rearward and offset strongpoints, R32 and R34. As the Germans would soon find out, all of the missed strongpoints were fully manned and capable of defensive operations.

Before the Germans could do anything, however, it was the Australians' turn to launch combat patrols. They snuck up on the exposed German lines; soon there was close-in combat. Screams were heard in the night, followed by sudden silence. Then an Australian combat patrol assaulted on the boundary between the *4./MG-Bataillon 8* and the positions of the antitank guns. The Australians were aiming for the left flank of the bridgehead. In close combat, the gun crews were cut down.

Then it was suddenly quiet again. After a while, the song, "It's a Long Way to Tipperary," could be heard from the area the Australians had penetrated. When the last verse of the song died away, it was replaced after a short, but oppressive few moments by a wild "Hurrah!" accompanied by another attack by the Australians against the left flank. The men of the 2nd Company defending there were thrown back to the tank ditch. *Hauptmann* Frank, the company commander, was badly wounded in the close-in fighting. *Leutnant* Hofer from the 7th Company was killed. The life and death of the battalion hung in the balance.

At that moment, *Hauptmann* Bartsch and *Leutnant* Dreschler rallied a few men and launched an immediate counterattack against the Australians, who pulled back from a portion of the terrain they had just retaken.

That night was expensive for the machine-gun battalion: 40 soldiers were lost. In the course of the immediate counterattack, *Leutnant* Dreschler was also badly wounded. Of the 35 soldiers who had advanced forward with him, only 5 returned to the trenches.

On the Australian side, it was Lieutenant Austin Macknell who had launched the incursion into the advanced German positions. The first soldier of the 9th Infantry Division to be recommended for the Victoria Cross for his actions that night was Jack Edmundson, who later received the highest British award for valor.

Panzer-Regiment 5, which had been able to increase its operational strength to 38 tanks, when a few more vehicles were brought forward, was directed to move to the bridgehead at 0200 hours, where it was to initiate the decisive thrust through the perceived gap. It was 0430 hours before the tanks arrived, however. Following the tanks were the last three self-propelled antitank guns from *Panzerjäger-Abteilung 39*. It was imperative that the armored vehicles move quickly, so as to take advantage of the protective darkness, which would not last too much longer.

With the tanks in front and the machine gunners following behind, the force was able to advance 4 kilometers until first light. It rolled right through Strongpoint R32, from which nothing stirred. At the 4-kilometer point, it had another 4 kilometers to traverse before it would get to the fork in the road that Rommel wanted so badly. In a valley depression, the force was greeted by amassed artillery fire. From around 2 kilometers away, all of the guns of the Australian artillery regiment opened up.

The men of the machine-gun battalion jumped into the cover afforded by an enemy trench system, which was half completed. The tanks continued to move and got to a point about 600 meters from the artillery positions. The British antitank guns then took out five *Panzer IV's*, one after the other.

The regimental commander ordered his tanks to try to maneuver out of the way to the east. When they headed in that direction, they encountered a belt of antitank guns arrayed along the Tobruk–El Adem road. Four more German tanks were knocked out in the ensuing engagement, but several Australian guns were also silenced. Some of the crews were able to dismount safely and make their way back to German lines.

The tanks, which had fired all but their emergency rounds, turned away at that point. British tanks and self-propelled antitank guns followed hot on their heels. Eight more German tanks were knocked out; two Mark II infantry tanks were able to account for four of the Germans. It was 0700 hours when the remnants of *Panzer-Regiment 5* were able to leave the battlefield.

A *Stuka* attack had been planned for between 0600 and 0630 hours to support the attack, but it never took place, because the *Stukas* were unable to find their targets in the thick dust of the battlefield. Instead, they attacked the city and harbor of Tobruk.

MG-Bataillon 8, which had been split up into two battle groups, remained behind on the battlefield. The soldiers who had been positioned in the bridgehead that had been taken the previous night were overwhelmed by the enemy, and the antitank guns positioned there were also lost.

Shortly after the German tanks had withdrawn, the Australians attacked Ponath's men from three sides. Using the last rounds of ammunition they had left, the men of the battalion were able to turn back the Australian assault force. The enemy infantry were then replaced by mortar rounds, which slammed into the shallow trenches. Light armored cars also sallied forth, but became more cautious after *Gefreiter* Fichter knocked one out with an antitank rifle.

"We need to pull back, Bartsch," Ponath explained to his company commander during a meeting. "We need to go back at least as far as that hill to our rear, where movement can be seen. Those must be our tanks."

The captain volunteered to provide covering fire for the other men.

"Good . . . we'll pull back and then cover your withdrawal."

✠

After the designated pyrotechnic had been fired, the men of Bartsch's 5th Company threw their weapons up on the parapets and started firing for all they were worth. At the same time, Ponath and the remaining men jumped up and ran to the rear. After about 20 meters, the *Oberstleutnant* collapsed heavily to the ground. Other men around him fell as well.

More and more soldiers were mortally wounded. An enemy tank, which had entered the sector of the 3rd Company, fired from its main gun and machine-gun with everything it had. The 3rd Company was forced to surrender after it had fired its remaining rounds.

Hauptmann Bartsch also decided to throw in the towel. Continued fighting would have only meant certain death for him and his men.

At 1130 hours on that deathly morning, the remaining soldiers of the battalion surrendered. One hundred sixty-eight soldiers went into captivity, a large number of them wounded. One hundred twelve remained behind on the battlefield. *Oberstleutnant* Ponath was killed by a round through his heart. The prisoners were taken to the Arab prison in Tobruk. The dead were evacuated by Australian details and buried.

Thus the initial attempts to take Tobruk—first by surprise and then by force—had failed.

✠

When Rommel heard the news of the loss of the battalion on that bloody Easter Sunday, he became enraged that the tankers had left the machine gunners "in the lurch." But *Oberst* Olbrich had had good reason to call off his attack: In addition to the 17 tanks he left behind on the battlefield, all of his remaining tanks had suffered significant battle damage and many of them were incapable of being operationally employed for the time being.

In the end, though, it was Rommel who bore the ultimate responsibility. He had ordered the attack in an effort to exploit the moment of surprise. His efforts faltered on the stalwart defense of the Australians and the precautions that had been taken by Wavell.

On the evening of 14 April, the remaining soldiers of *MG-Bataillon 8* were informed that Ponath had been put in for a posthumous award of the Knight's Cross.

✠

On 16 April, Rommel attempted to take the *Ras el Madauar* with 18 tanks of the Italians' *Ariete* Division. It had originally been planned for the division to follow *MG-Bataillon 8* and *Panzer-Regiment 5* in their breakthrough on the city and harbor of Tobruk, but the division had moved so slowly to the front that it did not arrive on time. It was not until Rommel personally showed up at the division's staging area that things started to move rapidly. The Italians moved out, but their advance was abruptly stopped by a few salvoes of artillery.

Despite all the setbacks, Rommel was still determined to take the fortress. The enemy position was a thorn in his side. It denied him use of the coastal road for nearly 50 kilometers, if the enemy artillery, which was registered on all of the main roads, was also factored in. The road was of vital importance for operations. Without a route directly through the city, the logistics personnel had to take a detour of nearly 75 kilometers. Moreover, the alternate route was badly chewed up after even just a few vehicles had crossed it, leading to numerous accidents and mechanical failures.

Rommel had the Italians attack again, but the second attack was also a fiasco. They attackers were bloodily repulsed and Bren gun carriers chased behind the fleeing Italians. No less than 1,100 were taken prisoner. The next attack—on 17 April—also failed, even though the 10 tanks from the *Ariete* Division were augmented by the *Trento* Division, which had arrived at the front in the meantime, and *Kradschützen-Bataillon 15* of the *15. Panzer-Division*.

The 10 Italian tanks advanced aggressively. They were able to penetrate far into the area of the fortress, but then were engaged by enemy antitank guns. All but one of the tanks was knocked out. At first light on 18 April, Rommel allowed the Italians to pull back 1.5 kilometers. Rommel was forced to call off the attack on Tobruk until additional elements of the *15. Panzer-Division* arrived.

✠

The calling off of the German attack allowed General Morshead the opportunity to continue improving his fortifications within the depths of the fortress area behind the two lines of strongpoints. The defensive main effort was placed behind the outpost line.

On 22 April, the Australians launched an attack against the *Ariete* Division west of the *Ras el Masauar*. A crisis situation developed, and Rommel personally led a few elements of German forces to push the enemy back. Two groups of "corset stays" were sent behind the Italian lines to bolster their defenses. These consisted of elements from the *15. Panzer-Division*, which was gradually arriving on the battlefield. The acting commander of the division was *Oberst Freiherr* von Esebeck, who assumed command after *Generalmajor* von Prittwitz was killed.

The fact that Rommel was aiming not only for Tobruk, but also the Suez Canal, is reflected in operations that were already being conducted by forces of the *DAK* that were east of the fortress. In addition to von Wechmar's *Aufklärungs-Abteilung 3 (mot.)*, elements of *Kradschützen-Bataillon 15* had also been sent there after its initial support of the *Ariete* Division. It had arrived in Tripoli on 5 April and had covered the 1,800 kilometers to the front in six days under the leadership of its forceful commander, *Oberstleutnant* Knabe. It was still missing two companies, however—the 4th and 5th—which were still stranded in Naples, awaiting ship transport. On 11 April, Knabe received orders from the *DAK* in Ain el Gazala to advance in the direction of Capuzzo. Knabe's advance guard was reinforced with *Panzerjäger-Abteilung 33 (15. Panzer-Division)*, the *1./Flak-Regiment 18* (8.8-centimeter *Flak*), and the *4./Flak-Regiment 18* (2-centimeter *Flak*). The reinforced battalion was directed to advance via Acroma and the crossing of the trails at Point 167 (south of Acroma) and head on through Sidi Azeiz to Capuzzo, where Knabe was to take both the town and the fort.

The remaining two companies of *Kradschützen-Bataillon 15* arrived a few days later and were committed by Rommel against Tobruk under the command of *Major* Schraepler, his adjutant. The two companies failed to achieve the breakthrough needed.

Once Knabe got to the Capuzzo area, he was assigned to *Kampfgruppe von Herff*. Von Herff's mission, which Rommel gave to him on 14 April: "Screen the border to Egypt. Prevent any enemy approach from the east and interference with the encirclement of Tobruk."

The opponent of the Germans in that sector of the desert was the "Mobile Force" of Brigadier Gott. The "Mobile Force" had armored cars and artillery support, as well as help from the air in the form of the Royal Air Force. On the other hand, the Germans were basically bereft of air support, since most of the formations of the *X. Flieger-Korps* had been diverted to support the Campaign in the Balkans, which had just started.

When the 22nd Guards Brigade was sent to Gott from Egypt as reinforcement, the mission of *Kampfgruppe von Herff* had become almost impossible.

Rommel, who left the Tobruk front for one day on 19 April to visit *Kampfgruppe von Herff*, ordered it to safeguard the harbor at Bardia. When the heavy company of von Wechmar's reconnaissance battalion was sent there the next day to carry out the mission, it actually found a British landing party in a *wadi* it was searching. There was a major in command and 59 soldiers, all of whom were taken prisoner.

Oberst von Herff had the fortifications of the two forts of Capuzzo and Upper Sollum improved. In order to prevent the enemy from a flanking maneuver to the south, von Herff recommended to Rommel that Halfaya Pass, which was still under the control of the enemy, be taken. Rommel concurred.

Because the enemy was operating with strong armored formations in screening sector of von Herff, Rommel gave him a typical order: "Conduct an offensive defense along the Egyptian border. Conduct constant combat reconnaissance to the south and southeast, go after the enemy where he is found and defeat him." (From the daily logs of the *DAK* on 24 April 1941)

On 24 April, *Kampfgruppe von Herff* sent elements to the southeast as far as the border fence, where it was forced to turn back in the face of intense enemy artillery fire.

During the afternoon of 26 April, the same effort was mounted again. The motorized riflemen raced through the artillery fire of the enemy. They succeeded in outracing the artillery and also deceiving the enemy, who thought the Germans were advancing with light tanks, even though they were only *Kübelwagen*. By the time it turned dark, the Germans had succeeded in penetrating the defensive lines above Halfaya Pass. At the same time, *Aufklärungs-Abteilung 3 (mot.)* blocked to the west. Because von Herff heard enemy fire well forward, he assumed that an enemy immediate counterattack was in progress, whereupon he had his forces pull back to the frontier fence.

Very early on 27 April, von Herff sent patrols out again. They found the area all the way up to Halfaya Pass clear of the enemy. As later reconnaissance determined, the enemy had pulled all the way back to Buqbuq. Von Herff immediately established a strong outpost line running Sidi Omar–Sidi Suleiman–Halfaya Pass.

On the night of 28 April, the motorcycle battalion and the antitank battalion were pulled from the line and sent back to Tobruk for employment there.

✠

The overall situation in Africa appeared more uncertain than ever in Germany. For that reason, *Generalleutnant* Paulus, who would forever become infamous for the German debacle at Stalingrad, was given a mission on 23 April to assist the German effort in the desert. Paulus at the time was the quartermaster of the German Army. His mission was to provide the five companies of the Engineer Instructional Battalion for the assault on Tobruk, since they were especially trained for the modern equivalent of siege warfare. He was also to send two batteries of coastal artillery and ensure that the remaining elements of the *15. Panzer-Division* be transported from Naples as expeditiously as possible. Replacements for the decimated *5. leichte Division* were earmarked. In addition, more air assets in the form of fighter and bomber formations were promised.

In addition, the German Army High Command sent a request to the Armed Forces High Command for the allocation of two air transport groups to assist in the expeditious transfer of the engineers and motorized riflemen of the *15. Panzer-Division* to Africa.

Since the Campaign in Greece was coming to a close, the *X. Flieger-Korps* was directed on 25 April to oversee the airlift of the elements of the *15. Panzer-Division* in Naples to Derna, using the two transport groups that were provided. The air corps was also directed to safeguard the transports on their sorties to Africa.

"Tell Rommel," Chief–of-Staff Halder informed Paulus, "that he has to hold out until 5 May. By then the main body of the *15. Panzer-Division* will be there." Halder continued: "Tell him that all of the assistance requested is underway. If Sollum should be lost, then you are to explore other options for defense. I am giving you authority to act in my name, Paulus!"

✠

On 25 April, Rommel decided a change in tactics was in order. Previously, he had attacked all along the front with all available forces. He directed that a main effort be formed around the *Ras el Madauar* with the creation of two strong *Kampfgruppen* from both of his German divisions.

He wanted to attack again some time around 1 May. Strong combat patrols were to be sent out on the night of 30 April/1 May to secure bridgeheads in the ring of defenses from which the attack groups could advance the following morning.

When *Generalleutnant* Paulus arrived at the *DAK* command post outside of Tobruk on 27 April, he was briefed on the intended operation. For the first time, it was to be a deliberate attack with *all* available German and Italian forces. Paulus opted not to make any remarks until he could further observe the situation.

Over the course of the next two days, Paulus talked to the two division commanders and discovered that they were also for the attack and thought it had a good chance of succeeding. Once he heard that, he gave his approval in his proxy capacity. Gariboldi had already concurred on 28 April. The attack orders were issued.

THE ASSAULT ON THE RAS EL MADAUAR

Rommel issued orders to the commanders selected for the assault. Rommel was emphatic. Everyone present knew that it was not only imperative to be victorious but to also convince the emissary from the Army High Command.

On the Australian side, the 24th Battalion of the 9th Infantry Division had relieved the 48th Battalion on the small sector on both sides of the mountain on 28 April. The 20th Infantry Brigade, whose sector this was in, believed that the German effort would only be "a half-hearted enemy attack."[9] The brigade headquarters put out that message despite a dive-bombing attack by 20 *Stukas* against the southern slope of the *Ras el Madauar* at 1815 hours, with a second attack by 30 *Stukas* following a short while later against the northern slope.

At 1915 hours, the two German battle groups moved out, preceded by combat patrols, after the final artillery salvo had been fired.

Kampfgruppe Kirchheim, which numbered *MG-Bataillon 2* among its forces, also had engineer assault detachments attached. Those were led by *Oberleutnant* Cirener, and they succeeded in eliminating a number of bunkers and field fortifications on the mountain.

Oberleutnant Muntau led his company—the *2./MG-Bataillon 2*—from the front. After Cirener had cleared the path for him, he succeeded in taking the north slope of the mountain at 2015 hours after an aggressively led final assault with machine guns and submachine guns blazing and hand grenades being tossed. The last remaining Australians on the mountain surrendered. When it was over, however, *Oberleutnant* Cirener was also among the fallen of that short, sharp engagement on the mountain.

The south slope of the mountain proved to be a different story. The German attack forces bogged down against the Australians in their bunkers and field fortifications. On the other hand, the ground gained was retained whenever the Australians launched immediate counterattacks.

In a continued assault, the main body of *MG-Bataillon 2* reached its initial attack objective, some 1.5 kilometers to the east of the *Ras el Madauar*.

In the sector of the other *Kampfgruppe*, the nighttime attack did not shape up so successfully. While the *I./Schützen-Regiment 115* of the *15. Panzer-Division* was able to achieve a rapid penetration along the Acroma–Pilastrino trail and

---

9. Translator's Note: Reverse-translated.

then also get to the trail crossroads at Point 187 (1.5 kilometers northeast of the *Ras el Madauar*), it soon became decisively engaged with enemy elements in the strongpoints.

When *Pionier-Bataillon 33*, also of the *15. Panzer-Division*, was sent forward to support the motorized infantry, it also became decisively engaged in the strongpoint fighting and suffered heavy casualties.

At 0200 hours, an assault *Kampfgruppe*—a regimentally-sized force consisting of *Kradschützen-Bataillon 15* and a battalion of motorized infantry— was committed. The motorcycle infantry were able to advance as far as Point 187. The motorized infantry, on the other hand, encountered strong resistance from the belt of strongpoints. All of the infantry officers were either killed or wounded.

At first light, the tanks of the *II./Panzer-Regiment 5* were committed in the attack sector of *Kampfgruppe Kirchheim*, enabling the infantry to advance again, after the tanks had engaged strongpoints S6 and S7 with direct fire and effectively silencing them. The infantry then stormed those strongpoints.

At 0830 hours, however, the fog that had blanketed the battlefield ever since midnight lifted, and the enemy artillery commenced pounding the German formations.

The battle group from the *15. Panzer-Division* was actually able to penetrate the outer ring of defenses and advance another 1.5 kilometers before its attack ran out of steam. The men then dug in where they were.

Kampfgruppe Kirchheim continued its offensive operations to the south, attacking in the direction of Fort Pilastrino, employing tanks and *MG-Bataillon 2*. The men and machines moved out after a *Stuka* attack. After a few hundred meters, the force ran into a minefield, effectively stopping the armored vehicles. The machine gunners continued the assault on their own, reaching the area 1 kilometer south of Giaida. There they received flanking fires from both the right and the left and were forced to dig in.

At 0900 ours, Rommel appeared in the area of the strongpoints. He ordered *Generalmajor* Kirchheim to continue the attack with the tanks. As Kirchheim went forward to carry out the new order, a messenger caught up with him with a countermanding order. He was ordered not to attack further east. Instead, he was directed to turn to the southeast and roll up the strongpoint defenses.

Rommel hoped that by opening up the Australians' defense line, he would pave a path for the *Ariete* Division to advance into the fortress.

Kirchheim started the flanking attack. Light *Flak* form *Flak-Bataillon 606* supported the engineers and forced them forward. Further supported by tanks, Strongpoints R4 and R5 could be taken.

British tanks then appeared. The tank-versus-tank engagement saw victims on both sides. The appearance of the enemy tanks delayed the remaining flank attacks. It was not until late in the afternoon that R6 could be taken; R7 fell the following morning.

Generalleutnant Paulus, who had ridden out to the front in the area of the breakthrough by *MG-Bataillon 2*, realized that the point of penetration stuck into the enemy's side and jutted far out ahead of the other German elements. Correspondingly, it was in danger of being cut off. He did not feel that a continuation of the attack promised any success, especially since the forces were exhausted and there was a sandstorm brewing. Rommel agreed and ordered the attack called off for 1 and 2 May.

The next day, Paulus presented the *DAK* with a memorandum, in which he stated that the forces of the *DAK* were not sufficiently strong to break the stubborn resistance of the enemy. For the *DAK*, the possession of Cyrenaica and the towns of Sollum and Bardia were of decisive importance. It was less important, he wrote, that the terrain in and around Tobruk was in German hands.

At that point, Rommel needed the permission of the Army High Command to continue the attack on Tobruk.

✠

After the motorcycle infantry were pulled back from their salient during the night of 3/4 May, it turned quiet around Tobruk. The remaining areas that had been taken from the enemy could be observed by him and were constantly under artillery fire. Despite that and the heat of the day, the plagues of flies, and the frosty cold of night, the soldiers held out. During the day, they had to perform their bodily functions in foxholes. The men rapidly became exhausted; the first cases of dysentery started to show up. The situation was unbearable. Rommel wrote in his diary: "Truly terrible conditions are present."

When Paulus left Africa on 7 May, he had formed a picture of the situation for himself. He later reported to *Generaloberst* Halder: "The problem in Africa is not Tobruk or Sollum, it's logistics."

This timeframe of the early fighting has not been covered much before. It is presented in detail here to show how much was accomplished with so little and also to demonstrate that this round of fighting was among the hardest the *DAK* experienced in the course of its campaigns.

Rommel stated essentially the same thing when he had the following entry made in the DAK daily logs on 4 May 1941: "The fighting for the *Ras el Madauar* will go down in the history of the *DAK* as some of its hardest."

The homeland is a long way away.

The 8.8-cm *Flak* gun, regarded as a "wonder weapon" in the desert by friend and foe alike. Killer of British tanks at any effective range.

The feared "Eighty-Eight" in action.

Hauptmann Johannes Kümmel, the "Lion of Capuzzo."

Panzers ready to advance. A *Panzer IV Ausf. E* with its short 75mm main gun and bolted-on supplemental armor is in the background.

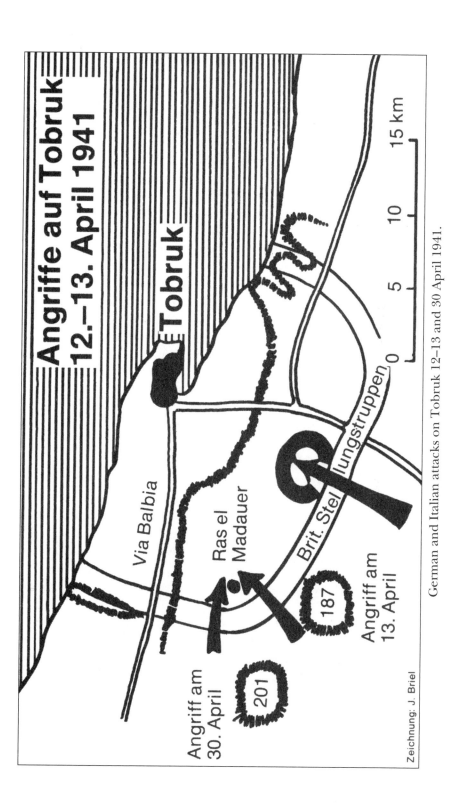

Angriffe auf Tobruk
12.–13. April 1941

Tobruk

Via Balbia

Ras el
Madauer

Brit. Stellungstruppen

187

201

Angriff am
30. April

Angriff am
13. April

15 km

10

5

0

Zeichnung: J. Briel

German and Italian attacks on Tobruk 12–13 and 30 April 1941.

CHAPTER 3

Battle at Sollum

SETTING THE STAGE: ASSAULT ON HALFAYA PASS

On 10 May, Rommel reiterated his previous directives for an aggressively mounted defense and constant reconnaissance to *Kampfgruppe von Herff* along the Egyptian frontier. Despite supply difficulties, the battle group moved more than 50 kilometers into Egypt on 12 May.

Halfaya Pass was left in the hands of a company of motorcycle infantry from *Kradschützen-Bataillon 15* and a battery of Italian artillery.

Early on the morning of 15 May, Brigadier Gott attacked the summit of Halfaya Pass. His forces were arrayed and employed as follows:

1. Along the coastal plain: A reinforced infantry battalion, which advanced against the foot of the pass and against lower and upper Sollum.
2. On the plateau: The 22nd Guards Brigade with 22 attached infantry tanks, which advanced against the pass and Capuzzo.
3. West of Halfaya Pass: The 7th Armored Brigade with 29 Cruiser tanks, armored cars, artillery, and antitank guns, advancing through Sidi Suleiman in the direction of Sidi Azeiz.

The three-pronged attack succeeded, and the entire pass and plateau were in British hands by the afternoon of 15 May. Only 12 Axis soldiers were able to escape from the pass.

At the same time, the strong enemy force advanced along the ridgeline from Habata to the northwest. Around Sollum, it pivoted north towards Fort Capuzzo, taking both. *Kampfgruppe von Herff* was gradually forced back to the north.

That same morning, *Oberst* von Herff had attempted to blunt the British attack with his 24 tanks, only 3 of which were *Panzer IV's*. They launched an immediate counterattack in the direction of the pass, but they were interdicted by British infantry tanks south of Capuzzo and forced north. The Italian battalion in Capuzzo was eventually overwhelmed after a hard fight, and pulled back to a small portion of the town. An immediate counterattack by some German tanks brought relief to the Italian forces and it was able to escape. The Germans then attacked with the motorcycle infantry and took back Capuzzo. During the fighting, the 1st Durham Light Infantry lost 29 dead and 64 captured.

Rommel immediately dispatched the *I./Panzer-Regiment 8* of the *15. Panzer-Division*, which had just arrived, to assist *Kampfgruppe von Herff*. The tanks were sent to El Duda. The tanks of the *Ariete* Division were sent to El Adem.

When Rommel discovered that the motorcycle infantry had retaken Capuzzo, he summoned *Oberst* Cramer, the commander of *Panzer-Regiment 8*: "Can you move out immediately with your 1st Battalion, Cramer?" When Cramer nodded in affirmation, Rommel continued: "Advance toward Sidi Azeiz with the 1st. I will give you a battery each of light and heavy *Flak*. Get things back in order there."

In the meantime, *Oberst* von Herff had also been attempting to retake Sidi Azeiz. He had his remaining 12 operational tanks from *Panzer-Regiment 5* attack three times. Each attack failed.

When it turned dark, von Herff moved back to the west, leaving behind only weak outposts. It was his intent to link up with the tanks rolling in from the west and attack again in the morning with the combined force. He radioed his intentions to Rommel.

Rommel had the following radioed back: "Enemy greatly overestimated. Otherwise, generally in agreement. Move out early through Sidi Azeiz to the south. The overall situation around Tobruk depends on the attack."

The two battle groups linked up west of Sidi Azeiz during the morning of 16 May. During the night, the enemy had pulled back to the south. The tank force, under the overall command of *Oberst* Cramer, advanced 15 kilometers to the south without encountering the enemy. A shortage of fuel forced him to halt.

Kampfgruppe von Herff reoccupied its old positions. Upper Sollum, which was still occupied by the enemy, was retaken.

That afternoon, a supply column arrived, bringing fuel for another 70 kilometers of operations for Cramer's tanks. Once refueled, he advanced against Sidi Suleiman. There was an engagement there against the 7th Armored Brigade. Due to a shortage of fuel, however, the fighting had to be broken off, and the German tanks returned to Capuzzo.

The British, for their part, also ceased fighting. They wanted to wait for more tanks to arrive before they continued offensive operations. It was only in Halfaya Pass that a strong contingent remained. It consisted of a reinforced battalion of the 22nd Guards Brigade, augmented by nine Mark II Cruisers. The British force was directed to hold the pass under all circumstances.

During he morning of 23 May, the *DAK* issued orders for *Operation "Skorpion,"* which had as its objective the taking of Halfaya Pass. The three-pronged attack started on the afternoon of 26 May. The three tank battalions under Cramer's command—reinforced by *Flak* and antitank guns—advanced east of Hill 206 to the southeast and pushed the enemy south of Halfaya Pass another 10 kilometers south. Two reconnaissance battalions, von Wechmar's 3rd and the 33rd, were consolidated into a *Kampfgruppe* under von Wechmar, which screened south and southwest of the tank force. The third group consisted of a reinforced motorized rifle battalion under *Hauptmann* Wilhelm Bach. The latter force advanced along the edge of the mountains, a portion along the upper plateau, and another portion in the flat land.

Oberstleutnant Knabe's motorcycle infantry formed the reserve of the assault force.

Bach's attack against the pass proper bogged down in the combined defensive artillery and small-arms fires of the enemy. Rommel ordered another attack the following morning with the commitment of the reserves.

At first light on 27 May, the motorized riflemen of Bach stormed ahead. They reached the *Wadi Qualada* and forced into cover for the second time in as many days by the strong enemy defensive fires. Machine-gun and artillery fire fixed Bach's forces. Bach summoned his messenger.

"Get the antitank guns forward!" he ordered the *Unteroffizier.*

When the 3.7-centimeter antitank guns were rolled up front, "Papa" Bach, as his men called the man who was also a minister, directed the guns into place. They were soon engaging the machine-gun nests and the identified artillery positions. But the enemy's fires were so strong that the antitank gunners were unable to get off accurate shots against their targets.

Hauptmann Bach raised himself up above the meager cover he had and looked at the enemy positions through his field glasses. He didn't waste too much time before dropping down again. A few seconds later, the area was raked with machine-gun fire.

Bach was able to orient the antitank gunners better. Finally, they were able to successfully engage the enemy position that was causing the most problem. When the enemy's fires abruptly died down, Bach jumped up and told his men to follow him.

Despite his 49 years, *Hauptmann* Bach led the charge at the head of his battalion. They followed him. One man yelled out the German battle cry of "Hurrah!" and he was soon joined by everyone else as the men assaulted into the enemy position.

At the same time, the motorcycle infantry were also attacking. They had been given the other side of the pass to take. *Oberstleutnant* Cramer's tanks provided support and took out the machine-gun nests and the artillery positions.

Halfaya Pass was back in German hands. It was 0615 hours, exactly one hour and forty-five minutes after the attack had been launched.

The victory came none too soon. Cramer's tanks were running on fumes. When the fighting was over, they were effectively immobilized. Only the motorized riflemen were able to mount up and pursue the withdrawing enemy.

The *DAK* then ordered the establishment of a strongpoint line running Hill 208 (referred to as Hafid Ridge by the enemy)–Hill 206–Halfaya Pass–coastal plain. The line was to be defended with all means available. It was ordered that all of the positions be improved; efforts were underway to supply them with reserves of water, ammunition, and fuel. The strongpoints were set up for an all-round defense. By 8 June, the Italian's *Pavia* Division relieved its comrades from the *Ariete*. By 12 June, it also relieved those elements of the *15. Panzer-Division* that were deployed in the sector. They were then held as corps reserves in the Acroma–El Adem area.

Rommel was of the opinion that the enemy was about to launch a new offensive. In the interim, he determined to make his defenses as good as possible, while attempting to address the nagging problem of supply. He directed an effort to build and improve a detour around the fortress of Tobruk.

In a remarkable feat, Italian engineer and construction battalions actually managed to construct a relatively good road—75 kilometers—around the fortress within a couple of months in the glowing heat of the African summer. The improved asphalt-surface road was anywhere from six to eight meters wide. It was hoped that logistics could flow better than ever before upon it.

What about the enemy, however? What were his intentions?

OPERATION "TIGER" AND PREPARATIONS FOR OPERATION "BATTLE AXE"

On 6 May 1941, a British naval convoy with the codename of "Tiger" passed the Straits of Gibraltar and steamed east through the Mediterranean on a course for Alexandria. Of the five large transports that were in the convoy, the freighter *Empire Song*, with 9,228 registered tonnage, hit a mine and sank. The remaining ships made it to Egypt. There were 238 tanks on board, some of which were in need of overhaul, as well as 43 fighters.

That convoy ensured that the British Commander-in-Chief, Wavell, had enough armored vehicles to start his planned offensive as soon as all of the tanks were operational. On 10 June, Wavell had the following radioed to the General Staff in London:

A portion of the Indian 4th Division, led by its commander, General Messervy, will advance between the sea and the steep slopes. A second Indian battle group will advance in the center of the attack sector against Halfaya Pass and be employed in the Capuzzo area.

The 7th Armoured Division, General O'Moore Creagh, will operate in the open south. It will take terrain to the west, go around Sidi Omar and then advance from the north into the rear of the enemy. The 4th Armoured Brigade of the division will be detached for other use and will support the 22nd Guards brigade in its attack on Capuzzo. After the mission is completed, it will return to the 7th Armoured Division.

It is our intention to meet the enemy in the south and defeat him with our armored main effort. A prerequisite is that the new Crusader tanks completely meet the demands of fighting in the desert.[1]

German signals intelligence, which intercepted practically all the enemy radio traffic during the weeks of May and June, determined an increasing number of signals facilities in the open desert after 10 June. On 14 June, it intercepted traffic from a divisional station as well as that of an armored brigade in the Habata area, 60 kilometers southeast of Sollum. When the codeword "Peter" was used on 14 June, the Germans knew the attack would start the next day.

In order to counter the British efforts, Rommel ordered the *5. leichte Division* to be ready to move no later than 0500 hours on 15 June. One battalion from *Panzer-Regiment 5*, augmented by a battery of light artillery, was sent forward to the Trigh Capuzzo area during the night of 14/15 June. From there, it was to advance along the desert trail to the area south of Gambut, where it was to screen the siege forces of Tobruk to the east.

The *15. Panzer-Division* was ordered to hold its positions and not to allow the fortress of Bardia to fall under any conditions.

What proved a formidable obstacle was the situation described in a report issued by the senior logistics officer of the *DAK* on 15 June: "The fuel situation is frightening. No large-scale movements can be conducted. Extreme concerns in the event of an attack."

During the night of 14/15 June, the standing armored patrols of the *15. Panzer-Division* reported the approach of large enemy formations, primarily armor.

The British and Commonwealth forces, under the command of General Beresford-Peirse, had started to move out in the afternoon. When the main bodies of two British divisions attacked at first light on the morning of 15

1. Translator's Note: This quote was reverse-translated from an unknown source.

June, the German soldiers were not surprised. The Indians advancing next to the sea and along and next to the *Via Balbia* were unable to advance, despite the support of the tanks of the 4th Armored Brigade. The 8.8-centimeter *Flak* on Halfaya Pass and the hills in front of it knocked out 11 of the 12 Matildas there. Six Mark II's followed, but four of them ran over mines and were immobilized. The 7th Armored Division, which was south of the Indians, moved past Point 206 and attacked Fort Capuzzo, taking it. The 7th Armored Brigade, which attacked against Hafia Ridge farther south, was met with withering fire from 8.8-centimeter *Flak*. Its vehicles turned off to the side and pulled back.

The English offensive came to a standstill, and the battle of attrition that Rommel had forced on his opponent cost him a large number of armored forces. Now that we have provided the overview, let us explore some of the smaller actions in detail.

FLAK ON HILL 208

The 1st *Oasis* Company of *Oberleutnant* Paulewicz had dug in on Hill 208, 30 kilometers southwest of Capuzzo, on 1 June. Italian engineers had prepared the position by constructing foxholes, machine-gun dugouts, and other redoubts by blasting holes in the rocky terrain. A platoon of 3.7-centimeter antitank guns was dug in, which had fields of fire to the east and southeast. Then the *3./Flak-Regiment 33* of *Oberleutnant* Ziemer was brought forward with its 8.8-centimeter *Flak*. Its four guns were also dug in and surrounded by walls of sandbags.

The *Flak* battery had been pulled out of its positions east of Bardia, where it had serving as a "fire brigade" for the individual formations. It had been with *Kradschützen-Bataillon 15* for 10 days at Sidi Azeiz, where it had helped keep British artillery at bay as well as fend off enemy tank attacks. When *Oberleutnant* Ziemer arrived at his new position, he saw to his satisfaction that the hill offered practically ideal fields of fire against approaching enemy forces to the east, southeast and south.

The outposts on Hill 208 heard the approach of many tanks even before daylight. Based on the direction, it could only be "Tommies." The alert was sounded. Two minutes later, the *Flak*, antitank guns, and the "Oasis" Company were ready to engage.

Gefreiter Huebner, a gunner on *Anton*, one of the 88's, was among the first to actually see the enemy: "Thirty tanks . . . massed . . . directly approaching us!" A few seconds later, the English preparatory fires commenced.

"Get ready!" *Oberleutnant* Ziemer yelled to the men of his battery. As soon as the four guns opened fire, however, the approaching tanks turned and disappeared in the dust clouds they had churned up.

"They're gone!" one of the crew of *Anton* shouted.

"They'll be coming back," *Unteroffizier* Heintze replied. And he was right. The enemy had been trying to figure out the exact location of the guns. Artillery fire preceded the next attack as well, with the rounds being well placed among the German positions. To the men on the hill, they thought the whole earth was exploding around them. They later found out that the British gunners had surveyed the hill extensively to allow them to better place their fires.

The enemy tanks appeared again at 1100 hours. This time the men counted 70 of them. Most of them were Mark II's.

Ziemer ordered his men to wait until the enemy had approached to within 1,000 meters.

When the rangefinders indicated 1,000 meters, the guns opened fire, practically simultaneously. The rounds raced towards the enemy. The first Matilda was struck. Over open sites, the German guns were able to completely penetrate the armor of what was a new tank for the British. Within a few minutes, the Germans knocked out 11 Mark II's without losing a single gun.

Then, suddenly, tanks appeared to the rear of the position. It appeared that the fate of the defenders had been sealed. But it turned out to be German tanks, to everyone's relief. They joined the battle and afforded the defenders on the hill a little relief.

It was afternoon before another group of tanks surfaced from out of the dust clouds. There was another thick cloud of dust behind it, which proved to contain yet another mass of armor. Their objective was, once again, Hill 208. Without that hill, the English could not be certain of not being attacked from the rear. The hill dominated the terrain and served as a cliff in the ocean, defiant against the breakers.

The 20 tanks of the second wave attacked Hafid Ridge directly, while the 40 tanks of the first wave passed the hill mass to the south. Once again, Ziemer did not give the order to fire until the tanks had closed to within 1,000 meters. The brilliant flash of the firing guns were mirrored a few seconds later by the equally brilliant sight of metal striking metal at enormous velocity. At the range the guns were firing, the report and the strike blended together into one dull crack. The first few tanks were knocked out. The 8.8-centimeter rounds penetrated through the fighting compartments of the tanks, usually killing the crews. Burning and glowing hot tanks littered the battlefield. When the ammunition went up in some of them, they were transformed into fire-breathing dragons.

All of a sudden, the enemy fire stopped. The enemy turned and hurriedly left the battlefield. As he fled, he lost another two tanks.

Two armored vehicles, perhaps confused in the tumult, turned and headed directly for the hill mass.

"Look! They're coming straight at us!" *Unteroffizier* Heintze alerted his comrades. He took one up in his sights, knocking it out barely 200 meters in front of the gun's position. The second tank continued to approach. It reeked of burned oil and cordite. The tracks rattled loudly. The steel monster was then in their position and rolled over one of the gun trails. It kept going, however, and did not stop in the position. Two crewmembers, who had been buried in their foxholes, were rescued.

It was quiet again for a while. Then, 10 enemy tanks showed up off to the flank. The *Flak* opened fire at 5,000 meters. When the enemy tanks had closed to 4,000 meters, the lead vehicle was hit and came to a halt. Then a second one was hit. The enemy was flabbergasted. The Germans were engaging them at ranges that were impossible to even conceive of!

The eight remaining tanks turned and disappeared in the evening twilight.

An hour later, one of the cannoneers on *Anton* identified a concentration of some 80 tanks at a considerable distance. The men around *Oberleutnant* Ziemer were not so sure they could hold out against that assault. The first batch started approaching Hill 208.

"Look!" one of the observers cried out excitedly, pointing to a narrow *wadi* that ran from the defensive position to the sea. German tanks were spilling out of the *wadi*. They were from *Panzer-Regiment 5*. They advanced rapidly in an effort to hit the enemy in the flank. The *Panzer IV's* in the middle of the group stopped to fire. The main guns cracked; hits could be seen in the distance. The remaining tanks continued to bound ahead on the flanks. Main guns fired; the sound of steel on target could be heard. The enemy pulled back. That evening, the tide had turned in the Germans' favor. The sharp edge of "Battle Axe" had been blunted. The British official history described the engagement at Hill 208 as follows:

> Operation "Battle Axe", which had started with such great expectations, failed because it was not possible to take the decisive Halfaya position and get past Strongpoint 208. The bravery and the firepower of the defenders were too great. The German 88 proved to be a deadly weapon against all of our tanks. The coordination between tanks and 88-millimeter *Flak* batteries that were employed far forward was a surprise for the British command and an important factor in its defeat.

Rommel's victory was a victory of his leadership, his forces, which fought in a superior manner, and his better weapons.

Let us now turn to the fighting at Halfaya Pass.

THE FIGHTING AT HALFAYA PASS

Early on the morning of 15 June, the riflemen of the *I./Schützen-Regiment 104* were in their forward positions when the enemy attacked on the high plateau. The alert had already been sounded when the first sounds of engines could be heard, long before the enemy could be seen.

When the alert signal sounded, *Hauptmann* Bach raced forward to the positions of the *Flak*, which were well dug in. As always, he was puffing on a cigar. Nothing seemed to upset him; he was unflappable.

"Let them get close," he told the *Flak* gunners, "every round needs to count."

By then, the enemy artillery had opened fire on the German positions. Shells rained down on the pass and exploded in the cliffs. Then the medium infantry Mark II's appeared, the Matildas. The riflemen took cover from the incoming artillery. When they looked up between exploding shells, they could see the silhouettes of trucks behind the tanks. Infantrymen were jumping down from them. Then, almost as if in peacetime, they formed up and marched behind the tanks.

"Fire!" the *Hauptmann* commanding the *Flak* barked.

The *Flak* fired rhythmically, and the few 3.7-centimeter antitank guns joined in. The sound of machine-gun bursts also joined the general cacophony. The first tank was hit by an 8.8-centimeter round and burst into flames. Its exploding ammunition flung open the crew hatches and sent tongues of flame skyward. The next Matilda had the turret knocked off of it.

The ear-deafening road of rapid-fire 2-centimeter *Flak* could then be heard, followed by the Italian battery of Major Pardi. The tall, dark-haired Italian stood upright next to his guns and acted as an observer. Bullets whizzed past him, but he appeared to be invulnerable.

The assault companies of the enemy ran forward *en masse*. Once they entered the killing zone and received the full brunt of the *Flak*, machine guns, and artillery, they were scattered and disappeared in the cover that nature provided to the right and left of the road.

At the foot of the pass, where the *I./Schützen-Regiment 104* was positioned, the attacking tanks ran into the minefield. One after another, five Matildas were immobilized with damaged track and running gear. Only one of the attacking tanks made it through, seemingly impregnable in the minefield. But when the tank commander figured out that he was alone, he had his vehicle stop. The tank started to move in reverse. It was then that it finally hit a mine. With a thunderous roar, one of its tracks was also torn from its running gear.

The *3./Schützen-Regiment 104* of *Hauptmann* Voigt, which had been positioned away from the battalion's main body, was also able to turn back the enemy. Halfaya Pass remained in German hands, despite the attacks of the 4th Tank Regiment and the Indian infantry brigade.

TANK VERSUS TANK

The English tanks that had not advanced past Hafid Ridge moved out to the north from west of Halfaya Pass early in the morning of 16 June with the main body of the 7th Armored Division. With a total of 300 armored vehicles, including many Mark II's, the force reached Capuzzo and Musaid. The minimally manned German strongpoints were swept away. From there, an armored battle group separated from the main body and headed far to the south in an effort to outflank the Germans. Those tanks encountered the positions of the *5. leichte Afrika-Division* with their lead elements. Despite heavy defensive fires, the English succeeded in getting through. The tanks then advanced on Hill 208, where they were turned back.

After the 7th Armored Division had assaulted and taken Capuzzo and Sollum, the motorcycle infantry of *Oberstleutnant* Knabe pulled back, in accordance with their orders. Fifty English tanks continued moving west rapidly. They were to take Bardia.

It was *Oberstleutnant* Tocki and his *Panzerjäger-Abteilung 33* that held up the British. He had a single 8.8-centimeter *Flak* at his disposal. Moving forward from Bardia, he had the gun set up when he saw the thick dust cloud that signaled the approach of the tanks. When the first tanks appeared from out of the cloud, Tocki gave orders to fire. The first round fired—at a distance of 2,000 meters—hit the lead tank between the turret and the hull and ripped the turret off the chassis. The sight picture for the next tank was taken up.

"Fire!" the gun chief bellowed. The next round hit the second tank and left it immobilized and smoking.

Then the third lance of flame left the barrel. It also hit and left another tank burning.

The British tanks stopped. They fired off the smoke pots they had with them and disappeared into the man-made smoke.

Tocki and the single gun had held off the enemy long enough for the *1./ Panzer-Regiment 8* to arrive. Led by *Hauptmann* Johannes Kümmel, the tanks advanced closer to the enemy force. *Major* Fenski, the battalion commander, had also brought up his 2nd and 3rd Companies on orders of *Oberst* Cramer, which proceeded to provide covering fire, wherever possible.

"Hannes" Kümmel stood in the open commander's hatch of his tank, observing. He felt he could observe better that way. Moreover, it allowed some air to get into the crew compartment, which could reach temperatures of 60 degrees (140 degrees Fahrenheit) if the hatches were closed. He saw the enemy tanks start to emerge from the thick veil. Main-gun rounds were whizzing past to both his right and left.

"Follow me and step on it!" he ordered.

They wanted to get under the enemy's fire. Kümmel dropped down his hatch and slammed it shut.

"Fire at will!" Kümmel directed his gunner.

Kümmel's gunner had already taken up a sight picture. He let the enemy tank get closer before he told the drover to stop. At 700 meters, the short-barreled 7.5-centimeter main gun was still capable of inflicting damage and knocking out enemy armor. One of the attacking Mark II's exploded when hit. The *Panzer III's* that were following their commander caught up with him, as well as the other short-barreled *Panzer IV* of the company. They started firing as well.

The tank engagements raged all around them. Tracks clattered, main-gun rounds slammed into steel. Explosions stood out among the sounds of battle.

"Hit . . . burning . . . must dismount!" one of Kümmel's platoon leaders reported.

"We'll cover you!" Kümmel radioed back. He had his driver back up to the stricken tank.

Two Mark II's were getting ready to put the finishing touch to the stricken *Panzer III*. Kümmel's gunner quickly took up a sight picture again. At 500 meters, the report of the main gun was indistinguishable from the sound of impacting steel on steel. The Mark II was penetrated from the side, the round killing the crew.

Another of Kümmel's *Panzer III's* took on the second Mark II. It hit the enemy several times before the final round was needed, although the first one had succeeded in jamming the enemy's turret.

At about the same time, both crews—the English and the German—dismounted from their stricken vehicles. The men of *Panzer-Regiment 8* saw two British tankers roll a burning German on the ground to extinguish the flames.

In the middle of the roar of battle, it was a sign of fairness and chivalry, which they would never forget. They only hoped they could repay the favor, if circumstances were different.

"Move out!" Kümmel ordered, when he heard his sister companies advancing on both the right and left. They headed straight into the enemy formation.

✠

"I can't get through," *Oberleutnant* Stiefelmeyer radioed, when his company bogged down.

Major Fenski radioed the regiment: "Battalion bogged down. Need relief attack."

The sonorous voice of *Oberstleutnant* Cramer responded: "2nd Battalion on the left flank!"

The regimental commander moved over to his 2nd Battalion and joined its lead elements. Faster and faster, they headed into the flank of the enemy. In the distance, Cramer could see that more and more tanks of the 1st Battalion were being lost.

Cramer ordered his 2nd Battalion to pick up the speed. The battalion rolled forward in an attack wedge. Soon, some 20 enemy tanks were in front of it. They were also trying to outflank the Germans and seek to decide the fight that way.

Cramer radioed Kümmel: "Turn and get the enemy in the flank!" Kümmel still had six operational tanks, including his and the other *Panzer IV*.

Kümmel executed the maneuver and rounds were being fired against the threat a few seconds later. Two, then three Mark II's were hit and set alight. Between the two *Panzer IV's*, eight enemy tanks were knocked out in a few minutes.

The company commander's action saved the regiment—perhaps even more. Cramer then wanted to decide the battle as well. He ordered his forces to turn east.

As Cramer's tank also started to turn, a main-gun round slammed into it. Cramer felt a hard blow to the head and a stinging pain in his arm. He had been wounded by shrapnel.

The engagement was broken off. The enemy had been stopped, Bardia remained in German hands, and the battered *Panzer-Regiment 8* was able to roll back to its assembly area. Kümmel had lost half of his tanks. The remaining companies had been hit just as badly.

Although the *DAK* did not know it at the time, the enemy decided to call off his offensive.

✠

Rommel decided to shift his main effort in order to grab the initiative for himself and force the enemy to dance to his tune. The thoughts of the Commanding General are contained in his diary entry of the time: "Frequently, shifting the main effort can decide a battle, when it comes as a surprise to the enemy."

During that round of fighting, *Panzer-Regiment 8* lost some 50 tanks out of the 80 it had had initially. Some of them could be repaired and returned to operational status, however, since they did not fall into the hands of the enemy. When Rommel discovered that *Panzer-Regiment 5* had likewise defeated the enemy in a dramatic armored engagement, he went to the *5. leichte Division.*

As always, he wanted to take advantage of the situation. He ordered *Generalmajor* von Ravenstein, who had replaced *Generalmajor* Streich at the helm of the division at the beginning of June, that he was to move rapidly into the area northeast of Sidi Omar and continue the attack from there on Sidi Suleiman.

At 0430 hours on 17 June, the reinforced *Panzer-Regiment 5* moved out to attack. The enemy's resistance was broken, and the regiment advanced into the area around Sidi Suleiman, where it then screened. Contact was established there temporarily with *MG-Bataillon 2,* but the enemy attacked from the southern flank a short while later with tanks and artillery, and the machine gunners were forced back to Sidi Omar.

Because of the strong enemy armored forces in the south and the heavy presence of enemy artillery, von Ravenstein decided to have the non-armored elements of his division organize for the defense in and around Sidi Omar, oriented primarily to the south and southeast.

✠

Generalmajor Neumann-Silkow, who had assumed command of the *15. Panzer-Division,* encountered elements of the 7th Armoured Brigade at Bir Ghirba. Those forces were covering the British flank at Capuzzo. The enemy was overcome by the employment of mobile 8.8-centimeter *Flak,* whose effective range of out to 2,000 meters had a sort of shock effect on the enemy, and the follow-on aggressive employment of armor. The division then continued its advance past the frontier fence with Egypt and headed in the direction of Alam Abu Dihak. While the division was on the move, its signals intelligence intercepted British radio traffic in which a withdrawal from the area of Sollum–Musaid was ordered.

Major General Messervy issued the order on his own initiative just before 1100 hours. General Wavell and Beresford-Peirse, who were at the command post of the 7th Armoured Division at the time, endorsed the order.

That signaled the end of "Battle Axe." Wavell flew back to Cairo, where he sent a message to the General Staff in London: "I regret to inform you that Battle Axe has failed."[2]

The Western Desert Force pulled back to its original lines of departure.

Rommel ordered the immediate pursuit of the withdrawing British forces with the objective of interdicting and destroying them. The effort failed due to logistical problems. It was not until 18 June that a pursuit was launched. By then, most of the enemy forces where back where they had started.

Churchill was shocked. On 17 June 1941, he wrote in his diary: "Everything fell apart on 17 June."

Four days later, he sent a letter to Wavell in Cairo in which he laconically stated: "I have come to the decision that public interest is best served by General Auchinleck being appointed Commander-in-Chief of the Army in the Near East in your place."

Churchill sent a letter to Auchinleck as well: "You are assuming command at a time of crisis . . . You need to give your special attention to the situation at Tobruk, the introduction of enemy reinforcements in Libya and the fact that the Germans are primarily occupied with the invasion of Russia at the moment. You must certainly realize how important these problems are."

The war in the desert reached a temporary stalemate.

---

2. Translator's Note: Reverse-translation here and in the remaining English quotations in this section.

CHAPTER 4

The *Luftwaffe* in Africa

AIR COMMAND "AFRICA" AND ITS FLYING FORMATIONS

On 15 February 1941, *Oberstleutnant* Harlinghausen of the *X. Flieger-Korps* arrived in Africa with the headquarters of the *DAK*, which had just been formed. He was to be the senior liaison officer for the *Luftwaffe* and had overall supervisory responsibility for any flying formations dispatched to Africa to support the *DAK*.

But just five days later, the Air Force High Command created Air Command "Africa"[1] with a commander and headquarters staff. Air District VII in Munich was charged with establishing the new headquarters.

The actual commander was *Generalmajor* Fröhlich. His operations officer was *Oberstleutnant i.G.* Ernst Knapp, who, in turn, was assisted by *Oberleutnant* Böß. *Oberstleutnant Ritter* von Voigtländer was the intelligence officer. Although the *Fliegerführer Afrika* reported tactically to the *X. Flieger-Korps*, he was ultimately responsible for all of the air operations that took place in the African theater.

The first elements that arrived in Africa belonged to *Zerstörergeschwader 26*[2], The *III./ZG 26* had the 7th, 8th and 9th Squadrons as part of the group. *Major* Kaschka commanded the force of *Bf 110 C's*. The twin-engined fighter-bombers were based at Castel Benito, Sirte, and *Arco dei Fileni*. The *II./ZG 26* was based in Bengasi.

At the same time, two groups of *Stukas* were also based in North Africa, one at Castel Benito and one at Sirte. They were equipped with the *Ju 87 B* and were part of *Stukageschwader 3*.

Eventually, elements of the *II.* and *III./Kampf-Lehr-Geschwader 1*[3] also arrived.

These relatively meager air elements had to support Rommel's surprise maneuvers in the spring of 1941. It was not until later that the air elements were augment by additional forces and fighters.

---

1. Translator's Note: *Fliegerführer Afrika.* In German, this can refer to the person who commands the organization or the organization itself. Unless the reference is directly to the commander, the more general reference will be used.

2. Translator's Note: 26th Destroyer Wing.

3. Translator's Note: 1st Bomb Wing (Instructional). Despite its designation, this was a combat formation.

The special climatic conditions in the desert proved a challenge to the aviators from the very beginning. While it was possible to keep the aircraft airborne by means of the addition of special filters and their regular "desanding," it was not possible to reduce the wear and tear on the crews as a result of the heat and the dust. The maintenance personnel often measured temperatures of up to 70 degrees (158 degrees Fahrenheit) under the cabin roofs. That proved particularly problematic for the aircrews of fighters and reconnaissance personnel, since they tended to fly in the heat of the day, whereas the *Stukas* flew when it was marginally cooler, early in the morning or in the evening.

The transport of the aircraft and aircrew to Africa went through Italy and then to Tripoli. The senior *Luftwaffe* officer in Rome, *Generalmajor Ritter* von Pohl, directed those operations. The ground personnel and support equipment were shipped by sea from Naples. There were also groups of *Ju 52's* used to transport urgently needed logistics to Africa, primarily fuel.

Generalmajor Fröhlich moved his command post to Sirte from Castel Benito in March. *Reichsmarschall* Göring had given Fröhlich the following directive: "As the Air Commander 'Africa,' it is your job to command and employ all of the elements of the *Luftwaffe* being sent to that theater for operations—*Flak* as well as flying personnel—and support the Army formations fighting there to the greatest extent possible."

In some cases, Fröhlich received orders directly from Göring, as was the case for special sorties against the Suez Canal and Cairo.

For the advance of the *DAK* on 31 March, Fröhlich received instructions to support it with both of his *Stuka* groups, as well as using the destroyer group in a fighter-bomber role.

Early on the morning on 31 March, *Generalmajor* Fröhlich flew from his headquarters in Sirte to his forward headquarters at the En Nofilia airfield. He personally briefed the men heading out on their first sorties.

Over the next few days, the *Stukas* and destroyers supported the ground fighting. Enemy positions that were in the way of the advancing *DAK* were eliminated through *Stuka* attacks. Other positions were eliminated through sorties launched by entire squadrons. The headquarters of Air Command "Africa" had to be moved forward further to the east practically every day during that hectic period. It was not until the airfield at Derna was reached that the aircrews and ground personnel got a break.

On 14 April, Sergeant Ellis of the RAF's 73rd Squadron shot down three *Stukas* that were flying sorties against Tobruk. That afternoon, the same squadron shot down another three *Stukas* out of the 20 flying.

That same afternoon, Rommel informed Fröhlich that "from now on, we cannot advance east at the same tempo as we have been."

On that day, there were still no German fighters in Africa who could take up a more equal fight with the British Hurricanes. The first *Bf 109 E's* landed at the Ain el Gazala airfield on 18 April. They were from the *1./Jagdgeschwader 27*.[4] The group was brought up to full strength—three squadrons—within three days. The group was commanded by *Hauptmann* Eduard Neumann, who had seen fighter operations as early as the Spanish Civil War. Commanding the squadrons were *Oberleutnant* Redlich (1st), *Hauptmann* Gerlitz (2nd), and *Oberleutnant* Homuth (3rd). Within the group were two officer candidates who would later make a name for themselves: Hans-Arnold Stahlschmidt and Hans-Joachim Marseille.

The *Bf 109 E's* started flying sorties almost as soon as they arrived. On the first flight out, *Oberleutnant* Redlich and *Leutnant* Werner Schroer encountered Hurricanes over Tobruk. Redlich shot down two and Schroer claimed the remaining one. Later that day, *Unteroffizier* Sippel shot down another Hurricane.

During his second sortie in Africa, Schroer was shot down by an English pilot. Schroer was able to bring his aircraft down and make a belly landing. He escaped the aircraft before it went up in a ball of flame.

From that point forward, the British bomber forces, which had appeared over German strongpoints and bombed with apparent impunity in the spring, became a rare sight. One of the shot-down bomber pilots said the following to Fröhlich at the end of April: "Every day without German fighters is a good day!"[5]

For the English bomber crews, the "good" days in Africa were over. Nonetheless, the Germans also suffered losses. For instance, after *Oberfeldwebel* Espenlaub reported a "kill" on 21 April, *Leutnant* Schroer was shot down for the second time, this time being slightly wounded. *Unteroffizier* Sippel was killed in an aerial duel.

The *Luftwaffe* stepped up its attacks on Tobruk. On 22 April, 30 *Stukas*, 12 *Bf 109's,* and 12 Fiat G 50's of the Italian Air Force flew sorties against Tobruk. On that day, Lieutenant Denis of the 73rd Squadron shot down three of the *Bf 109's*. That same day, the Germans obtained some relief when the 3rd Squadron of fighters finally arrived at Gazala.

The 23rd of April was marked by dogfights over Tobruk again. Lieutenant Commander Weld, the commander of the 73rd Squadron, was killed. *Oberleutnant* Redlich shot down two Blenheim medium bombers, with *Oberleutnant* Fanzisket and *Leutnant* von Moller each accounting for two Hurricanes.

---

4. Translator's Note: The 1st Squadron of the 27th Fighter Wing.

5. Translator's Note: Reverse-translated from an unknown source.

That day also marked the first victory in Africa for officer candidate Marseille. He shot down a Hurricane from head on. He barely escaped the four other Hurricanes by quickly pulling back on the stick and turning off. When he took off again later that afternoon, he was hit 30 times in the cockpit and engine, which immediately quit. The *Oberfähnrich* was able to guide the machine down and make a successful belly landing. Once again, Marseille had to turn away from the enemy. Two rounds penetrated the cockpit area and missed him by only a few inches. Lieutenant Denis was the pilot who almost extinguished Marseille's career before it had begun.

That evening, *Oberfähnrich* Stahlschmidt was sitting outside his tent on the edge of the *wadi*, looking into the sky that had been swept clear by a light wind from the east. He was writing a letter to his mother and told her that he had just seen his first shooting star in Africa.

When Stahlschmidt heard something, he looked up: "Who's there?"

"I am, the oldest *Oberfähnrich* of the *Luftwaffe*," Marseille responded from the darkness. He then stepped forward into Stahlschmidt's view.

"Have a seat, Jochen!" Stahlschmidt told his friend. They started to talk about the war and the chances they had in Africa. Marseille was of the opinion that they would be successful if their soldiers' luck held out.

"So, you want to be a big eagle, Jochen?" Stahlschmidt asked.

Marseille did not hesitate: "A big one, Hans!" He bent forward and slapped Stahlschmidt on the shoulder. "Haven't you ever dreamed of that? Everyone does. Whenever I lay awake at night, I go through a dogfight like it should be, at least the way I think it should be. I see myself in the middle of a bunch of them, firing, hitting with every burst, but not being hit, because I'm in the middle of them."

"So, a sort of young Siegfried?" Stahlschmidt replied, referring to the hero of the German fable, a touch of sarcasm in his voice. "Boy, that would be great!" he continued, when he noticed his young friend was quite serious.

Over the next few minutes, Marseille told his friend how he envisioned a dogfight.

"Our machines are the base point, Hans, which everyone needs to master. You must be able to shoot in any position. From a left turn or a right . . . from a roll . . . from upside down, if necessary. That's the only way to develop your own tactics. It's an attack tactic that needs to be a series of incalculable und unpredictable lightning-fast actions for the enemy over the course of the entire dogfight. You can never attack the same way twice. Only by doing that can you survive and be victorious. You have to break open the enemy's ring and then shoot him down from the inside out."

Stahlschmidt never forgot what his friend said. It was for that reason that he was also not surprised when Marseille used those tactics for the first time.

On 28 April, a Blenheim from the 45th Squadron flew into the fighter airfield at Tobruk. The pilot had been instructed to pick up five personnel from the fortress, who were needed elsewhere. Among them were a wing commander, a squadron leader, and a priest. Marseille, who was flying an air cap over Tobruk, saw the machine as it prepared to take off. He dove down and set it alight barely 20 meters above the water. The Blenheim exploded upon contact with the water.

Marseille curved off, pulled off to the side, and disappeared.

When Rommel started his attack on Tobruk early on the morning of 1 May, 20 aircraft from the two *Stuka* groups headed out to support the attack. Eight *Bf 109's* flew as escort. *Oberleutnant* Homuth led the group of fighters that provided cover at a lower altitude; Marseille was in charge of the upper group. Marseille was already recognized for his uncanny eyesight. After the *Stukas* had finished their mission, Homuth saw a British reconnaissance aircraft over Acroma. When he turned towards it with his flight, he saw six Hurricanes over the fort at the same altitude he was—4,000 meters. The Hurricanes had started to climb in order to have "altitude" on the Germans for an attack. The British did not see Marseille's flight. From an even greater altitude, Marseille dove straight down and fired at one of the Hurricanes, striking it. The stricken aircraft spun down towards the desert below. Homuth shot down two of the enemy, of which one parachuted to safety. The second aircraft attempted an emergency landing at Tobruk.

✠

On 7 and 8 May, the *II./KG 26* flew bombing missions on the Suez Canal. On the first day, one bomber was lost; on the second day, two *He 111's* were shot down. *Oberleutnant* Pfeil was killed; *Oberfeldwebel* Kleinschmidt was reported as missing.

✠

In May, additional flying formations were sent to Africa. Two more *Stuka* groups arrived, although one of them was only sent on a temporary basis. The *I./JG 53* also arrived, followed later by a group from *Jagdgeschwader 77* from Sicily. The two provided "assistance" until the rest of *JG 53* could arrive. On a case-by-case basis, a group of *Ju 88's* was also made available for employment for long-range targets.

The *Stuka* and destroyer groups were based at Derna. The fighters were at Ain el Gazala, and the *Ju 88's* at the Benina airfield outside of Bengasi.

The immediate future was filled with alternating bomber and fighter sorties on both sides. On 20 May, the British introduced a new bomber squadron to Africa, the 14th. During its first mission on the Capuzzo–Tobruk road, the Blenheims encountered a group of German fighters. Five of the medium bombers were shot down.

The British fighter force, which had come under considerable pressure, received reinforcements on 21 May. Six Hurricanes from the 229th Squadron and seven from the 223rd Squadron took off from the deck of the aircraft carrier *Furious* off the coast of Gibraltar and headed for Malta. With them was a Fairey Fulmar. After refueling on Malta, they continued on to Egypt. They were sent to support the 247th and 73rd Squadrons.

At the same time, the 24th Squadron of the South African Air Force arrived from the south. That squadron was outfitted with "Maryland" bombers.

Starting from Africa, British bombers in Africa were sortied to Crete to bomb German airborne and mountain forces that had invaded the island on 20 May. Many bombers were lost over the island, and it was a relief for the *DAK* when the RAF had to divide its energies like that. Although British fighters scored seven "kills" on 31 May over the island—as opposed to only one of their own—the additional air effort could not change the outcome. The island fell into German hands.

The 45th and 55th Squadrons had to be withdrawn from African service at the end of May. The Beaufighters of the 272nd Squadron, based on Malta, flew in to take their place on 31 May. Based at Abu Sueir, the fighters flew escort duty for a convoy steaming into Tobruk on 1 June.

The arrival of the *7./JG 26* signaled the last of the expected German fighters in Africa. The squadron flew the *Bf 109 E7*, which had a mounting for a 300-liter drop tank and, with the later versions, a slightly more powerful DB 601N engine. The squadron commander was *Oberleutnant* Joachim Müncheberg, who was already a recipient of the Oak Leaves to the Knight's Cross to the Iron Cross at that time.

✠

On the morning of 2 June, a steamer was sighted off the coast. A flight of four fighters from the *2./JG 26* was scrambled to intercept it. One of the pilots was Stahlschmidt. After a few minutes, Stahlschmidt and the flight commander, *Leutnant* Kothmann, sighted the craft.

"Let's take a closer look!" Kothmann radioed. The aircraft approached more closely and Stahlschmidt dipped his nose to get a better look. Both aircraft circled the ship that displayed neither a flag nor signs of life.

Suddenly, however, there were muzzle flashes. Machine-gun salvoes headed in the direction of Stahlschmidt. He continued to descend. When the bridge of the 200-ton ship came into view, he depressed the firing button. The rounds slammed into the ship's superstructure. Kothmann then dove and strafed the ship. The small steamer did not register any effect.

"I'm going lower!" Stahlschmidt exclaimed. After describing a wide arc, he dove down towards the deck of the ship. The ship's bridge again came into his sights. Stahlschmidt depressed the trigger and rounds from the two 2-centimeter cannon were sent on their way. The stern of the ship lit up. A bright-red lance of flame shot skyward and then spread rapidly over the ship.

Stahlschmidt cut a tight turn so as to see better. He saw at least a dozen figures drop a boat into the waters. They then rowed crazily to get away from the ship and head to shore. Two minutes later, a powerful explosion rent the air. The ship was literally lifted out of the water. When the cloud from the detonation lifted somewhat, there were nothing but pieces of wreckage to be seen in the water.

Two hours later, 14 members of the crew were taken prisoner. They stated they had had ammunition for Tobruk on board. After the war, however, it was determined that it had been a raiding party consisting of eight English and four Greeks. The leader of the group, a small, wiry officer with a golden earring by the name of Chessney was an adventurer of the old school.

Marseille, who greeted his friend upon his return, stated dryly that he must have hit a sterno stove in the ship's galley. It was Stahlschmidt's first "kill," and instead of an aircraft, a ship was painted on the tail of the aircraft.

The next day, Stahlschmidt and Kothmann steered a course out to sea again. A launch had been sighted with 18 men aboard. Flying close to the surface, the two fighters guided the boat to shore. The men were from a shipwreck. With the men previously taken prisoner, the two fighter pilots were then given credit for a total of 32 prisoners.

✠

During the British summer offensive, the men of the *Luftwaffe* units flew almost constantly. Squadrons and flights took off daily to Sollum and Bardia, to Capuzzo and Sidi Azeiz, to Suli Suleiman and beyond, as far as Mersa Matruh.

Fighter encountered fighter. Both sides attempted to wrest victory through lengthy dogfights, lightning-like strikes, and low-level attacks. Stahlschmidt had a dogfight that lasted 35 minutes. The enemy's fire came dangerously close to his cockpit. Finally, Stahlschmidt got on his opponent's back. When his counterpart attempted to escape by turning, he crossed Stahlschmidt's sights. Stahlschmidt fired and dark smoke started to stream behind the British aircraft. The British pilot did not give up, however. He raced on and attempted to escape by flying through a *wadi* that led into Sollum Valley. Stahlschmidt dove. The *Bf 109* slipped down and into the flak of the enemy. Stahlschmidt's thumb pressed the trigger. Both cannon and both machine guns hammered away at the same time; 2-centimeter and 7.92-millimeter steal-jacketed rounds slammed into the aircraft's flank. The Hurricane dissolved in a bright-red star of flame, and the remnants of the aircraft crashed into the cliffs of Halfaya Pass.

For the first time, *Oberfähnrich* Stahlschmidt waggled his wings as he circled over the airfield. His ground crew, which had already uploaded the aircraft eight times that day, tossed their arms into the air in jubilation. It was 15 June 1941.

✠

A few days later, the first P-40 Tomahawks arrived in the desert; they had two .50-caliber and four .30-caliber machine guns. The aircraft were assigned to the 250th Squadron. The Curtiss-Wright aircraft would give the German fighters a bit more of a challenge in the future.

On 17 June, Marseille, who had finally been promoted to *Leutnant,* shot down two Hurricanes. *Leutnant* Heinz Schmidt accounted for two more and *Oberfeldwebel* Förster and *Feldwebel* Mentnich each scored one "kill" apiece.

In the four days of fighting around Sollum, 32 British fighters had been shot down. Twenty-five of them were at the hands of Messerschmitt fighter pilots. After the war, Major General Playfair wrote: "The heavy losses in fighters were traced back by Air Marshall Tedder to, on one hand, insufficient training and a lack of experience and, on the other hand, to the fact that the fighter patrols had been ordered to form a thick, seamless air cap over the ground forces, which were too weak in places."[6]

✠

The first sortie of *Hauptmann* Müncheberg was on 20 June, when he shot down a Hurricane to the southeast of Buqbuq. From that point forward, things only looked up for Müncheberg, just as was the case with Marseille and Stahlschmidt. *Leutnant* Schroer was also making a name for himself, with numerous "kills" credited to him. On 15 July, Müncheberg was almost shot

---

6. Translator's Note: This quote was attributed to *History of the Second World War, the Mediterranean and the Middle East.* Reverse-translated.

down from the ground, when a Tommy standing on the road shot off the left earpiece of his flight helmet with a rifle round! At the time, Müncheberg wrote to a friend that the P-40's were appearing more and more often and that the planned upgrade to the *Bf 109 F* in August could not come soon enough. The new version of the fighter was capable of reaching 600 kilometers an hour.

At the end of July, the *7.JG 26* was sent back to Sicily. That ended Müncheberg's operations in Africa, although he would be active in the skies above Malta.

✠

On the British side, there were some changes in leadership and organization. Air Vice Marshal Collishaw was replaced by Air Vice Marshal Sir Arthur Coningham. The 253rd Squadron was formed, a special-purpose formation consisting of a fighter squadron, a reconnaissance squadron and a bomber squadron.

On the Italian side, the *Regia Aeronautica* in Africa was built up with two squadrons—the 153rd and the 157th—which was equipped with Macchi MC 200's. In general, however, the Italian air force in Africa was equipped with a variety of aircraft that were inferior to both their German and British counterparts. Despite that disadvantage, the pilots participated fully in the fighting and were able to score considerable success, albeit at considerable loss, as well. When some Macchi 202's arrived, the Italians finally had an aircraft the equal of the *Bf 109 F2* (tropical).

✠

During that summer, Stahlschmidt became one of the most successful German fighter pilots. When 10 Martin A 26 "Maryland" attack aircraft struck German forces on the ground, Stahlschmidt was able to shoot down one of them. When the fighters were released from air cap duties that day, there was a dogfight with some 20 Hurricanes above Buqbuq, on the far side of Halfaya Pass. *Feldwebel* Förster spotted them first. They were flying well below the Germans but far ahead of them. Stahlschmidt maxed out his throttle. The Germans quickly approached the mass of British aircraft. Soon, Stahlschmidt's sights were filled with the silhouette of a Hurricane. The enemy fighter was swept aside with the first burst. It turned nose down and slammed into the desert, glowing wildly upon impact.

Two minutes later, Stahlschmidt, halfway flipped over and making a tight turn, approached his next opponent. Stahlschmidt heard a warning from a wingman, and he turned in the nick of time, as bullets raced past his cockpit.

He dove almost vertically, with the result that the next burst from the enemy also shot harmlessly through the desert skies.

Stahlschmidt's burst hit home, however, and the Hurricane started to burn. A minute later, his wingman saw the impact in the desert, which confirmed the second "kill" of the day.

In addition to the fighters, the bomber pilots bore a heavy burden during the summer fighting. Their targets were Mersa Matruh and Tobruk. One time, when *Hauptmann* Mahlke, the commander of the *III./Sturzkampfgeschwader 1*, was reporting to *Generalmajor* Fröhlich, the Air Commander "Africa" asked him what the best course back from Tobruk was.

Mahlke showed him on the map: "That's the course I always take!"

Surprised, the general officer noticed that the course was over a long stretch of terrain that was heavy with antiaircraft defenses: "Why do you fly a long stretch over *Flak*-heavy areas?"

The brash bomber pilot answered immediately: "So we can have more of it, *Herr General!*"

Mahlke, one of the bravest pilots to ever sit behind the controls of a *Ju 88*, flew his aircraft, christened *Jolanthe*, every day to Tobruk, where he bombed the harbor or the roads. He would dive through a wall of antiaircraft fire and drop his bombs, on target and skillfully.

✠

The "destroyer" crews were also a band of brothers. When a *Bf 110 C* had to make an emergency landing in the desert, its wingman also landed and took the stranded crew aboard. The single aircraft, at that point with a "crew" of four, made it safely back to its base.

When asked whether that might have been a risky undertaking, the pilot responded: "We leave no one behind!" After a pause, he continued: "I'd rather go to the dogs than be accused of leaving a comrade behind to die a miserable death in the desert."

✠

An attack by 27 Fiat G 50's of the 20th Group against the airbase of the South African 1st Squadron at Sidi Barrani ended in the death of 6 of the Italian pilots. Nevertheless, Lieutenant Colonel Mario Bonzano, who led the attack, reported that 12 aircraft were destroyed on the ground and a number of other ones damaged.

The Italians repeated an attack on an enemy airbase on 6 September. The 33rd Squadron was hit, with one Hurricane destroyed and two badly damaged.

A third attack was launched on 7 September. That time, the Italians' success was greater than the previous two missions combined. Twenty-two MC 200's of the 153rd group and 15 G 50's of the 155th Group attacked the airfield. *Bf 109's* joined the attack. Seven Tomahawks went up in flames. Five Hurricanes of the South African forces were also destroyed.

The attack was repeated that afternoon. Within 24 hours, the British lost 21 aircraft there.

The British air formations around Sidi Barrani were ordered to evacuate the following day and move back to Sidi Haneish. They were ordered to Sidi Barrani only if they needed to refuel.

✠

A heavy blow was delivered to the German and Italian air forces on 14 September. On that day, 12 *Ju 87's* flown by Italian crews from the 209th Squadron headed out to attack Sidi Barrani in support of a German advance in that area. When they lost contact with their escorts, they got lost and 10 aircraft had to make emergency landings in the desert, widely scattered. Eight of the *Stukas*, together with their crews, fell intact into the hands of the enemy.

By the same token, the 14th of September was also a good day for the *Luftwaffe*. The *II./JG 27* arrived, which was equipped with the *Bf 109 F4*, the latest version of the fighter. The *Bf 109F* was superior in top speed and climb to the latest version of the Spitfire so was more than a match for the Hurricane and the P-40. The group commander was *Hauptmann* Lippert, who had already received the Knight's Cross to the Iron Cross and was an experienced fighter pilot from the Spanish Civil War. His squadron commanders were *Oberleutnant* Rödel (4th Squadron), *Oberleutnant* Düllberg (5th), and *Oberleutnant* Strößner (6th). There were a number of successful fighter pilots among the groups ranks, and they would soon make a name for themselves in Africa as well.

✠

The 24th of September was an important day for *Leutnant* Marseille, who was able to employ his special brand of aerial tactics successfully for the first time.

The 20 aircraft of the *I./JG 27* encountered some 20 Hurricanes over Halfaya Pass. Nine of the Hurricanes were flown by South African pilots.

Diving out of the evening sun, the German fighters, including *Leutnant* Marseille, *Oberleutnant* Homuth, and *Oberfeldwebel* Kowalski, hit the mass of British fighters. The English formation dispersed. Following in a tight left curve, Marseille fired on a Hurricane from a distance of only 40 meters, setting the British fighter on fire and on its way to the ground. The British then formed their feared defensive circle. Marseille climbed above it and then dove almost vertically right into the middle of it. Catching his machine and pulling up, he peppered a Hurricane and climbed steeply.

Ten minutes later, the defensive carousel turned and one Hurricane turned out of the circle and flitted off to the west. Marseille dove again and quickly reached the single machine by dint of greater speed. His first burst was a direct hit.

Earlier in the day, Marseille had shot down another hurricane, so he was able to book four victories that day: 20 to 23.

✠

At the end of September, there were so many *ghiblis* of such intensity that there was barely any flying weather. It was not until 3 October that the *II./JG 27* was able to launch a larger mission. When it returned, it had another four "kills" to its credit. Lieutenant Lacey of the RAF shot down the first *Bf 109 F* near Sidi Barrani that day, however.

On 6 and 7 October, *Oberfeldwebel* Schulz shot down two Hurricanes and two Tomahawks, making a name for himself in the annals of the air war over Africa.

✠

At the end of October, the British had further reinforced their air force in Africa. The 260th Squadron was moved from Palestine to Egypt. On 29 October, the machines of the 94th Squadron appeared in the desert. That squadron had made a name for itself in the Battle of Britain against German bombers and fighter-bombers. The 24th Squadron of the South African Air Force was the first bomber formation in Africa to receive the Douglas Boston III.

✠

During the summer and fall, *Generalmajor* Fröhlich had wanted to move his forces to the area between Tobruk and Bardia. Those efforts failed for a number of reasons. On the one hand, it would have meant an almost untenable lengthening of the supply route, a problem which will be addressed in detail in the next chapter. Additionally, the *DAK* was concerned that having the air bases so far forward would make them susceptible to commando raids and air attacks.

As a result, Derna remained the main air base. Fröhlich maintained his headquarters there. He personally spent most of his time at his advanced headquarters at Gazala. He was closer to the action there and could make decisions faster. His command post was in an underground Arab burial site and safe from being bombed. During the day, the men performed their duties outside. Meals were also frequently taken outside as well. Whoever visited the headquarters was an invited guest at the next meal, where Fröhlich himself was often to be found, sharing the table with a clerk from the staff or one of his pilots.

Once fall passed, the rainy season came. It was a bad time for flying personnel. Nevertheless, the war on the ground continued and preparations were made on both sides.

The elegant lines of a *Bf 110C Zerstörer* (Destroyer). A relative failure as a long-range escort fighter in the Battle of Britain, the *Bf 110* was a success in Russia and Africa, where it was employed as a reconnaissance aircraft, fighter-bomber, and, ironically, a long-range fighter escort. In this instance, it is escorting *Ju 52* transport aircraft.

Ungainly and anachronistic, the exceptionally rugged and reliable *Ju 52* was the backbone of the *Luftwaffe* transport units. It was nicknamed *Tante Ju* (Aunt *Ju*) by the ground troops it supplied and evacuated when they were wounded.

The characteristic "geodetic" construction identifies this burned-out aircraft as a British Wellington.

The exposed *DB 601* inverted V12 engine of a *Bf 110C* that was shot down by antiaircraft fire.

A *Bf 109E* of *I/JG 27* with the pilot and ground-crew at readiness. The *109* is painted in European camouflage, although it does have the white Mediterranean theater fuselage band and has been fitted with a tropical air-filter.

CHAPTER 5

Logistical Problems of the
Deutsches Afrika Korps

SETTING THE STAGE

Supplying the *DAK* with its constant need for rations, fuel, weapons, and ammunition proved to be extraordinarily difficult and constantly insufficient from the very beginning. A sea dominated by the enemy lay between the sailing ports of the transports and their destination harbors. The enemy employed three submarine flotillas in the Mediterranean, and their effectiveness was enormous.

There were approximately 80 ships available in North African, Mediterranean, and Italian ports to meet the supply needs of the *DAK* at the start of the German engagement in Africa. Most of the ships were in the latter ports. Initially, they had to supply "only" two divisions and a few special-purpose formations. They needed to transport the supplies, personnel, and equipment to the port of Tripoli and unload them there. They then had to be loaded onto trucks and transported to the front. As the German and Italian forces advanced to the east, the distance to the front became longer on an almost daily basis.

The senior quartermaster officer for Africa was *Oberstleutnant Graf* Klinkowström. He organized his logistics support forces into three supply columns, each with a lift capacity of 360 tons. There were also a few Italian truck elements available to transship the materiel from Tripoli to the supply depots around the city. The logistics officers of the *5. leichte Division* and the *15. Panzer-Division* had their columns pick up the supplies from there and take them to a depot that was established nearer to the front at the *Arco dei Fileni*. The light division needed 320 tons daily just for its needs.

Above and beyond that, there were the needs for water, which had to be brought forward in tanker trucks. In order to get the monthly 9,000 tons needed for the light division from Tripoli, some 670 kilometers away, it would have required a far greater capacity than ever existed. Every column that made the round trip to the *Arco dei Fileni* required 6 days in all for the journey. That meant that the one column of vehicles that was available to the light division was only able to bring forward 1,600 tons of the 9,000 required.

For that reason, coastal water traffic, consisting of vessels of all sizes and capacities, was quickly organized and employed. That helped somewhat.

With the shift of the front to the area around Tobruk and then Bardia, the distances to the front from the main port of supply climbed to 1,500 kilometers and beyond. The quartermaster had most of his lift capacity organized to go to Bengasi, where it would then be loaded onto coastal craft for the continued trip to Derna.

The coastal waterway traffic was constantly disturbed by submarine and RAF activity, however. It was only the Italian submarines, which set course for Africa from lower Italy that made it without a problem. They would bring 80 tons of tank main-gun ammunition or 140 tons of fuel.

The first two convoys made it through with personnel unscathed, but next one saw a German steamer with 5,608 registered tonnage lost. From January to May 1941, 11 German supply ships with a total freight capacity of 42,000 registered tons were lost.

The first really heavy blow to the German supply effort was delivered by Force "K"—four destroyers—on the evening of 16 April. Near the island of Kerkennah, the British force encountered an Axis supply convoy consisting of the freighters *Adana, Aegina, Arta* and *Iserlohn*. The Axis force was escorted by three Italian motor-torpedo boats. All four freighters were sunk and more than 3,000 *DAK* soldiers swam in the waters of the Mediterranean for their lives. The Italian vessels fought in an exemplary fashion under Commander Cristofaro and were able to sink the British destroyer *Mohawk*. The Italian boats spent the rest of the night fishing shipwrecked German soldiers from the waters and calling for help. In all, some seven motor-torpedo boats, two hospital ships and a few amphibious aircraft were involved in the rescue operations.

The rescue effort was able to pick up 1,248 German soldiers. The rest were claimed by the sea. It was a heavy blow to the *DAK*.

✠

The Italian submarines *Atropo* and *Zoea* took fuel from Taranto to Derna in two operations. A single torpedo would have turned those boats into a flaming hell.

On 1 May, the steamers *Larissa, Arcturus,* and *Leverkusen* were lost. The first ship mentioned ran into a mine, while the remaining two were sunk by British submarines.

Vessels carrying Italian forces were also lost. During a troop transport to Tripoli lasting from 22 to 25 May, which was conducted by four large freighters, which were escorted by two destroyers and three motor-torpedo boats, it was intended to bring 8,500 Italian soldiers to Africa.

Two cruisers and three destroyers were responsible for the long-range screening of the convoy. Despite that, the submarines form Malta were able to infiltrate. The *Upholder* of Lieutenant Commander Wanklyn sank the 17,879 registered ton *Conte Rosso*. Of the 2,500 soldiers on board, 820 went down with the ship.

A few days previously, the Italian freighter *Birminia* had reached Tripoli safely. In the bowels of the10,000-ton ship was ammunition for the *DAK*, including a number of 10-kilogram bombs, which were crated in bundles of 10. During the offloading, one of the crates was dropped and it went off. As a result of sympathetic explosions, all of the remaining ammunition went up, ripping off the deck of the ship.

Korvettenkapitän[1] Meixner, the German harbor commander, and *Hauptmann* Otto, who would later become the senior logistics officer for Africa, raced to the pier. The Italian auxiliary cruiser *Citti di Bari*, which had been loaded with fuel, had also gone up. There were some 70 killed and 88 wounded in all.

Meixner then discovered that another two ships at sea that were inbound and due to arrive in the next 24 hours were carrying the same deadly cargo. He had them anchor in the roads. The anchors were not allowed to be dropped. Instead, they had to be lowered by hand into the water to avoid any shaking of the cargo. The Commander-in-Chief of the *Luftwaffe* was asked what should be done. Göring replied that the ships should be taken out to sea and sunk. Of course, that was easy for him to say when the bombs were desperately needed at the front.

Meixner did not have the ships blown up. Instead, he put out a call for volunteers, who carefully opened the ammo crates on board the ships and checked to make sure the safety switches were properly mounted. Those that were properly mounted could be offloaded into the lighters and taken ashore. The first three crates had no problems. The fourth crate, however, had dislodged its safety devices. Captain Reinen, a captain who had been stranded in Tripoli when his ship had been sunk, volunteered to go aboard the ship with an explosives expert to attempt to disarm the bombs. On the first day, they succeeded in defusing six of them, one of which would have been enough to blow up the entire ship because of all the other munitions on board.

In five days, 22 bombs were defused. Reinen and his assistant remained in the bowels of the ship by themselves. Eventually, both of the ships were saved.

---

1. Translator's Note: Lieutenant Commander.

Kapitän Reinen became the first merchant marine captain to receive the Iron Cross, First Class. *Oberleutnant* Krüger, who replaced the explosives expert when he was called away, also received the same decoration.

✠

On 3 June, two Italian convoy ships were sunk by British bombers. The Italian submarines *Zoea, Corridoni,* and *Atropo* brought additional fuel to Bardia. The journeys by those submarines must be considered among the most dangerous of the entire war.

Of the two convoys that set out for Africa in the middle of July, a ship was sunk in the first convoy by the P 33 of Lieutenant Whiteway-Wilkinson. The attack by the submarine *Unbeaten* on a ship of the second convoy missed by a hair.

On 22 July, the *Preußen* was sunk south of Pantelleria by British air attacks. Two hundred Germans went down with the ship. In addition, 6,000 tons of munitions, 1,000 tons of fuel, 1,000 tons of rations, 320 vehicles of all types, and 3,000 mailbags were lost.

The bombers that flew those attacks were based on Malta. The submarines of the British 10th Flotilla were based in Malta's harbor. They would lie in wait at the forced crossing points. Malta was a thorn in the flesh of the Axis forces in Africa.

Despite all those losses, around 25,000 tons of munitions, 32,000 tons of fuel and 18,000 tons of rations were offloaded in Bengasi alone from April to December 1941.

From June to the end of October, 40 ships were lost at sea. After the arrival of the *15. Panzer-Division* in July, the monthly supply requirements for the Army rose to 30,000 tons, with a further requirement for 20,000 tons in reserve. In addition, the *Luftwaffe* needed 8,000 tons. For the offensive planned in November, it was estimated that 24,000 tons would be needed in Tripoli and 35,000 tons in Bengasi. The situation at sea continued to worsen, however. The negative trend ran from October through December. The lack of supplies for the *DAK* took on menacing dimensions. In October, around 50,000 ton of supplies were sent to Africa. Of that amount, approximately 63% was sunk. Of the 37,000 tons that were loaded on ships in November, only 23% reached their ports of call. All the rest was sunk from the air or by submarines.

Despite the almost superhuman efforts of the German and Italian sailors and the coastal waterway traffic, the needs of the *DAK* for its attack on Tobruk were only 40% met.

CHAPTER 6

The Great Winter Battle

The fighting in North Africa had come to a stalemate around Tobruk. The German forces east of Tobruk had advanced as far as Sollum. By then, the *15. Panzer-Division* had arrived in its entirety into the theater.

Rommel, who was promoted to *General der Panzertruppe* on 1 July, after Hitler had ordered it on 19 June, had formed *Panzergruppe Afrika* with the approval of the Italians. The headquarters of the new command took up its work on 1 August. *Generalleutnant* Crüwell assumed command of the *DAK* in September. He had come to Africa after serving with distinction in the Soviet Union.

Despite the start of the Campaign in Russia on 22 June 1941, a third division was being introduced to Africa. The first elements of the *Afrika-Division z.v.B.* started arriving in the middle of July.

The Germans prepared as best they could for a new offensive.

✠

Sir Claude Auchinleck, the new British commander in the desert, had also taken advantage of the summer break in operations. The British 8th Army was created on 26 September. General Sir Alan Cunningham was its first Commander-in-Chief. He established his headquarters in the desert, and he had two corps at his disposal: the XXX Corps with the 7th Armoured Division, the South African 1st Infantry Division, and the 22 Guards Brigade; and the XIII Corps with the New Zealand 1st Infantry Division, the Indian 4th Infantry Division, and a battle group of armor that was equipped with Mark II tanks. The 4th Armoured Brigade was the field army's standing reserve. That brigade was armed with the new "Stuart" light tanks that had been provided by the USA under provisions of the Lend-Lease Agreement. By the end of October, the British forces in the field had 300 Crusaders, 300 Stuarts, 168 infantry tanks, 34,000 trucks, 600 artillery pieces, 80 heavy antiaircraft guns, 160 light antiaircraft guns, 200 antitank guns, and 900 mortars at its disposal.

The Commanding General of the XXX Corps was General Vivian Pope, an armor expert who had been employed up to that point in the War Department in the procurement of armored weaponry. When he was killed in a fatal aircraft crash on 5 October, he was replaced by Major General Willoughby Norrie, who had previously been the commander of the 1st Armored Division. At the time of his appointment to corps command, he was promoted to Lieutenant General. Lieutenant General Godwin-Austen became the Commanding General of the XIII Corps.

The British were busy hatching offensive plans of their own. Operation "Crusader" intended for the XXX Corps to advance across the frontier between Maddalena and Sidi Omar to occupy jumping-off positions for the offensive at Gabr Saleh, 50 kilometers to the west. It was intended for the corps to remain there to see what Rommel's armored forces would do. At the same time, the XIII Corps was to bypass the German positions along the border to the right, with the intent of fixing the German forces there. The 4th Armoured Brigade was to advance between the two corps. It had a two-fold mission: to protect the flank of the XIII Corps and to stand by as reinforcement for the XXX Corps.

The basic intent was to involve the *DAK* in an armored battle that would lead to its destruction. Once that was done, the Tobruk garrison would be relieved after the forces there attempted their own breakout, which would be ordered by General Norrie.

To provide the front-line forces with water, a 250-kilometer-long water line had been built, featuring seven pump stations and nine reservoirs. A German air attack directed against the line at Fuka succeeded in destroying a good portion of it, however. The water that had been collected there flowed into the desert. It would take the British until the middle of November before they could get the water line working again.

✠

At the time, *Panzergruppe Afrika* consisted of the *DAK* and a number of Italian elements. The *DAK* consisted of the *15. Panzer-Division,* the *21. Panzer-Division,* which was the new designation for the *5. leichte Division* effective the beginning of August, and the Italian's *Savona* Division. The Italian contribution consisted of two corps, the XXI Corps of General Navarrini (*Trento, Bologna, Brescia,* and *Pavia* Divisions) and the XX Armored Corps of General Gambarra (*Ariete* Armored Division and the *Trieste* Division). Replacing Gariboldi in overall command of the forces in Africa was General Ettore Bastico.

The *Trieste* Division did not arrive in theater from Italy until the middle of September. The Italians relieved the XX Corps from its reporting responsibilities to Rommel and placed the corps under the direct command authority of Bastico.

During July and August, the two German armored divisions were moved back to tent encampments along the sea between Bardia and Marsa Belafarit, some 40 kilometers east of Tobruk, to conduct battlefield reconstitution. The *15. Schützen-Brigade* of the *15. Panzer-Division*, which had been in position along the *Ras el Madauar* in the heat of the summer, was relieved by elements of the *Afrika-Division z.v.B.*, which started to arrive.

The reported sick cases within the *DAK* rose to 10,000 in August and then to 11,000 in September. That was out of a ration headcount strength of 48,500 men. Those were serious illnesses and diseases: dysentery, malaria, and diphtheria. Skin and leg ulcers were not uncommon.

In Germany, the General Staff had anticipated the attack on Tobruk to take place sometime in the first half of September. When the loss of ships took on frightening proportions staring in September, *Panzergruppe Afrika* had to report that the attack on Tobruk would be decisively delayed if there were no relief with regard to the supply convoys.

As early as July, the Germans also identified through aerial reconnaissance that the enemy was getting stronger and stronger. The reports in August only confirmed the buildup. At the end of August, the *Luftwaffe* reported the discovery of four large supply depots in front of the German lines, specifically in the areas of Bir Khireiqat, Bir Diqnash, and Bir Habata.

Rommel ordered the *DAK* to raid the dump at Bir Khireiqat on 27 August and take off with its supplies. If that could not be done, it was to be destroyed. Rommel later expanded that directive at the beginning of September to destroy the elements of the 7th Armoured Division that were positioned behind the depot. The mission was handed to the *21. Panzer-Division.*

OPERATION "SUMMER NIGHT'S DREAM"

During the night of 13/14 September, a battle group composed primarily of the tanks of *Panzer-Regiment 5* rolled forward from their attack positions. Led by *Oberst* Stephan, they advanced rapidly to the area around Deir el Hamra, 56 kilometers southeast of Sollum. Enemy groups that appeared were chased off with a few rounds, and several enemy tanks were knocked out.

In all, there were three battle groups. The second one, led by *Major* Schütte, had the following forces: the reconstituted *MG-Bataillon 8*, the attached *Panzerjäger-Abteilung 602*, the *I./Artillerie-Regiment 33*, and a platoon of *Fla-Bataillon 606*. It also advanced rapidly, reaching the *Quaret el Ruweibit*. It was engaged by British armored cars there. The antitank guns and the *Flak* elements moved forward, engaged the armored cars and knocked out two of them. At that point, the British reconnaissance forces pulled back to the east through the desert.

The third battle group was led by *Major* Panzenhagen. It consisted primarily of the *III./Infanterie-Regiment 347* of the *Afrika-Division z.v.B.*. Panzenhagen's force advanced along the southern flank of the attack wedge. While both of the first two battle groups were eventually held up, Panzenhagen's force continued to advance.

In the afternoon, enemy armored cars appeared in front of Panzenhagen's men. Shots were exchanged, and a few of the enemy armored cars were hit. The Germans took some casualties in the form of wounded.

That night, Panzenhagen had his forces form a "hedgehog" position in the desert. His precaution proved judicious, when enemy infantry, supported by armored cars, attacked a few hours later. The enemy was turned back by bursts of machine-gun fire and a few *Flak* salvoes. A second attack at 0200 hours was also turned back. The next day, the battle group was ordered back to its lines of departure. The entire attack proved to be a jab into thin air.

✠

During October, Rommel continued to receive reports and indicators that the enemy's offensive was just around the corner. But Rommel did not give any credence to those reports, since the reconnaissance information yielded by his forces on the ground did not indicate that.

At the beginning of October, Rommel felt that the enemy situation offered him opportunities for his forces. He also knew that the situation would become worse for him over time. Consequently, he reported to the Army High Command on 4 October that he intended to attack Tobruk in the first half of November. The Italian Supreme Command agreed with his proposal, although the Italian High Command in Africa was still hesitant. On 26 October, the attack order for Tobruk was issued.

It was intended for the *DAK* to attack along the southeastern portion of the Tobruk front after a thorough artillery preparation. The XXI Corps was to attack to the left, although the *DAK* would be the main effort. The battalions of the *Afrika-Division z.v.B.* were to cut a path through the enemy's fortifications, with the *15. Panzer-Division* passing through and into the depths of the enemy's defensive system. The initial attack objective was the fork in the road 8 kilometers south of the city. It was then to advance through Fort Solaro and on to the coast.

It was intended for the attack to start sometime between 15 and 20 November. Although Rommel asked for Gambarra's XX Corps to be released to him, the Italians refused. The Italian High Command in Africa only agreed to have Gambarra's division advance in the direction of Bir el Gobi–Bir Hacheim. That meant that the Italian corps would only screen the attack on Tobruk from the south.

On 1 November, Rommel flew with several staff officers to Rome to brief the Supreme Command on details of the planned attack.

On 6 November, the German Armed Forces High Command agreed with Rommel's intent "to conduct an attack on Tobruk, as soon as sufficient air forces are available." Rommel was given authority to coordinate with the *X. Flieger-Korps* for the best time to attack and get the Italian High Command to agree. The intended D-Day was to be reported to the Army High Command.

On 10 November Gambarra's *Ariete* and *Trieste* Divisions moved out in the direction of Bir Hacheim and Bir el Gobi. Although Rommel could not directly use those forces, his southern flank was relatively secure and he assured Gambarra that "a great weight had been lifted from him."

On 13 November, the Radio Intercept Detachment Southeast determined the South African 1st Infantry Division was south of Sidi Barrani. There was no special meaning given to that information, however.

Starting late in the evening of 15 November, the formations of the *Afrika-Division z.v.B.* started to relieve the formations of the *Bologna* Division in place along both sides of the coastal road. At the same time, the German division was attached to the XXI Corps.

During the night of 15/16 November, the *21. Panzer-Division* rolled into its staging areas south of Gasr el Arid, 15 kilometers south of Gambut. A hour before midnight, British bombers attacked Bardia, the command post of the *DAK.* The coastal road and the former assembly areas of the *21. Panzer-Division* were also bombed. In the staging areas, *Aufklärungs-Abteilung 3 (mot.)* and *Aufklärungs-Abteilung 33 (mot.)* were attached to the *21. Panzer-Division.* The two reconnaissance battalions were consolidated for the attack and placed under the command of *Oberstleutnant* Wechmar.

Kampfgruppe Wechmar was given the mission of conducting a reconnaissance-in-force deep into Egypt, advancing along a line running Maddalena–Sidi Omar and going as far as a line running Bir el Chamsa–Bir Habata, some 100 kilometers southeast of Sidi Omar.

On 16 November, German artillery moved to better support the attack against the southeastern portion of Tobruk. Because a *ghibli* blew in, its movements were well hidden.

Kampfgruppe Wechmar had advanced as far as the frontier fence and reported the advance of enemy patrols through the fence on both sides of Maddalena and in the south in the direction of the *Trigh el Abd.* Tanks were also observed among the enemy forces advancing, with the result that the *21. Panzer-Division* sent Wechmar some antitank guns.

The sandstorm continued unabated through all of 17 November. The aerial reconnaissance on both sides was prevented. German radio intelligence noted that the enemy had gone to complete radio silence. That was a troubling sign.

The heat of the day signaled an approaching storm and a horrendous storm—at least for Africa—burst over the areas of operations that evening. There were cloudbursts all over Cyrenaica and in Marmarica and deep into the desert. The airfields, especially those at Ain el Gazala and Tmimi, were turned into seas of mud, making them unusable for several days. Long stretches of the coastal road had been washed out; camps sites and command posts that had been established in the *wadis* were washed away when the dried-out riverbeds were filled to overflowing. German soldiers and their Italian comrades drowned in the desert. Lightning flashed through the night. At Gambut and at Halfaya Pass, tents and radio vehicles were washed away; guns flooded. The radio silence was broken: "Flood . . . flood!"

The German word *Hochwasser* meant more than just flood that night, however. Unfortunately for the Germans, it had also been chosen as the code word to launch the attack. No one was sure what was meant when it was heard in conjunction with the unusual and violent weather. The reconnaissance soldiers of *Kampfgruppe Wechmar* remained alert, however, and continued to report enemy movements in the direction of the *Trigh el Abd*. The British attack—Operation "Crusader"—was underway.

At the same time, another British operation was underway that bears closer scrutiny.

COMMANDO RAID AGAINST ROMMEL AT BEDA LITTORIA

During the night of 14/15 November, the British submarines *Torbay* and *Talisman* neared the bay on the Cyranaican coast in order to land a commando party under the overall command of Colonel Laycock. The commando party had received the mission to "strike the brains and nervous system of the enemy army at the critical moment."[1]

This meant, of course, Rommel and his headquarters. It was intended to either take him prisoner or kill him 12 hours before the start of Operation "Crusader."

This operation had been planned by the senior special operations commander in Britain, Admiral Sir Roger Keyes. Preparation had been taken in London at the special school for commando training. Out of 100 volunteers, 53 remained after the initial round of testing. Major Geoffrey Keyes, a son of the admiral, had selected the men.

When the commando group attempted to row to shore from the *Torbay*, the small boat capsized again and again in the heavy swells. After a struggle, the men, including Keyes, who had since been promoted to Lieutenant

---

1. Translator's Note: This quote was reverse-translated.

Colonel, and Captain Campbell, who was selected because he spoke not only German but also Arabic, made it ashore.

Colonel Laycock, who set out from the *Talisman* with his party, had a rougher time of it that night. Two soldiers drowned and only seven made it to the coast from the rest. The remaining men had to be hauled back on board. That meant that effectively only half of the raiding party made it ashore. Colonel Laycock remained behind on the beach with three other commandos to maintain contact with the submarines, which were supposed to pick the men up again. Keyes and Campbell headed inland with the rest of the raiding party, where they linked up with Lieutenant Colonel John Haselden, one of the leading figures of the Long-Range Desert Reconnaissance Group. Haselden, who had already spent several months behind German lines disguised as an Arab, briefed the commandos. He gave them the cardinal direction in which they had to march if they wanted to reach Rommel's headquarters at Beda Littoria. He also provided the commandos with three Arab guides, just as a precautionary measure.

They did not take off until the night of 15/16 November. The next night, they reached the dunes near Beda Littoria. They identified the buildings from the aerial reconnaissance photos, as well as the cypress grove, which was a distinguishing feature. According to reports from agents and local Arabs, in the middle of the grove was a large rectangular stone building in which Rommel lived and worked and, above all, also slept.

What the British did not know was that the building had only served a temporary function as a headquarters for Rommel while the new *Panzergruppe Afrika* was being established. It was only in August of 1941 that Rommel actually stayed there. The building was currently being used by the senior logistics officer for Africa and his staff. The smaller buildings around the large one were marked with signs indicating "Commander," "Operations Officer," "Logistics Officer," and "Intelligence Officer," but they were all references to the staff of the quartermaster. At the end of August, Rommel had moved on to Ain el Gazala and then, a short while later, to Gambut.

When the heavy downpour ensued late in the evening of 17 November, the men of the raiding party breathed a sigh of relief. "This is going to work!" Keyes said to Campbell, who nodded in agreement.

Keyes directed six men to the front entrance of the main building and three to the rear. He had Sergeant Terry be in charge of taking out the German guards at the front. At 2400 hours, the men began the raid.

The commandos moved noiselessly through the night. The heavy rain abetted their silent movements.

When Terry attempted to slit the sentry's throat, the German turned away suddenly, since he heard a noise. Terry was discovered and a shrill alert sounded through the night. The commandos did succeed in blowing up the generator, thus extinguishing all lights, however.

The commandos stormed the main building. A wild firefight ensued. *Feldwebel* Lentzen and *Unteroffizier* Kovacic, who were sleeping in the arms room, grabbed their weapons when they heard the firing. When Lentzen threw open the door to the arms room, Keyes tossed in two hand grenades. Kovacic was killed, but Lentzen was only slightly wounded. He fired his side arm. Hit, Keyes backed up. Campbell was hit in the leg. *Leutnant* Kaufholz, a liaison officer who had been sleeping upstairs, ran to the door of his room with his pistol when he heard the firing. He saw Keyes below and also fired at him, hitting him again. Campbell fired his submachine gun, cutting down the German officer. As he was falling, however, he managed to get off another round, which hit Campbell in the shin. Campbell collapsed, screaming in pain.

The commandos who had been at the back entrance found it barricaded. While they decided what to do, one of the commandos fired at a German who was jumping through the window of an outbuilding. *Oberleutnant* Jäger, hit 11 times, collapsed to the ground, dead.

The salvoes outside led the commandos inside to the conclusion that fighting had also erupted there. They attempted to flee. The group that had been at the rear also departed.

That signaled the end of the operation. Four German soldiers had been killed. Lieutenant Colonel Keyes had been killed as a result of the combined fires of Lentzen and Kaufholz. Campbell was taken prisoner and his smashed leg was saved by a German surgeon in Derna.

The remaining commandos hid out with the Arabs, since they feared being caught if they took a direct route to the coast and the waiting submarines.

Most of the commando group was eventually discovered among the Arabs by the Germans. Only Sergeant Terry was able to make it back to English lines with two of his comrades.

Rommel stopped the commandos being treated as such, since Hitler's orders in that regard would have meant certain death for them. Lieutenant Colonel Keyes was buried with military honors at the Beda Littoria cemetery along with the four dead Germans.

"THE CRUSADERS ARE COMING!"

Early in the morning, the British rolled out with complete radio silence. When the first reports arrived from *Kampfgruppe Wechmar*, Rommel thought it was only a reconnaissance-in-force.

Rommel had just returned from Rome and was in the midst of the planning for his own offensive when the British armored armada with 1,000 vehicles headed out on 18 November. The XXX Corps advanced in the south in a wide arc with its two divisions and the 22nd Armoured Brigade. Once it reached the area around Bir el Gobi, it turned north. Its general axis of advance was towards Tobruk.

The XIII Corps with its two divisions and the 1st Armored Brigade advanced north of the other corps and directly on Sollum. Its left wing, which went around Bardia in a wide arc, headed for the sea. From the oasis at Girabub, mobile forces advanced into the rear of the Axis forces. They were given the mission of interrupting the German and Italian supply lines.

Initially, Rommel discounted the concerns of *Generalleutnant* Crüwell. When *Generalmajor* von Ravenstein also reported enemy armor to his front that evening, the leadership of *Panzergruppe Afrika* had to concede that an English offensive was under way. The stream of armor and motorized formations had pushed back the reconnaissance screening line between Bir el Gobi and Sidi Omar.

By evening of that day, it was certain that the enemy was moving out with 1,000 armored vehicles, some 100,000 soldiers, and about 1,000 aircraft, with the aim of wresting victory and delivering a decisive blow to the Axis forces.

By the morning of 19 November, Rommel had still not taken up the battle. Correspondingly, General Cunningham, had the 22nd Armoured Brigade advance on Bir el Gobi, where the *Ariete* Division had set up its field fortifications. The British attack was turned back by the Italians.

The 4th Brigade of the 7th Armoured Division advanced with its 3rd Royal Tank Regiment 20 kilometers east of Gabr Saleh towards *Kampfgruppe Wechmar*, which had to pull back to the northwest into the area around Gasr el Arid.

The 7th Brigade advanced without enemy contact almost as far as the airfield at Sidi Rezegh. It was there that its main force, the 6th Royal Tank Regiment, encountered German forces. It was *Infanterie-Regiment 361* of the *Afrika-Division z.v.B.*, which had just arrived there. The regiment consisted of a good number of former French Foreign Legionnaires, who were battle-hardened soldiers.

The Italians' "Young Fascist" Division, which was encircled around Bir el Gobi, did not surrender an inch of ground. The *Ariete* Division, which was near by, knocked out five British tanks that afternoon.

Rommel discovered from the aerial reconnaissance of the missions launched by Air Command "Africa," which were finally able to get off the ground after three days, that the enemy was advancing between Maddalena and Gasr el Abid in roughly brigade strength. Rommel had *Schützen-Brigade*

15 of the *15. Panzer-Division* alerted and had an armored battle group from the *21. Panzer-Division* conduct a reconnaissance-in-force in the direction of Gasr el Abid.

The *Kampfgruppe* from the *21. Panzer-Division* consisted of *Panzer-Regiment 5*, supported by the division's light artillery battalion and a heavy battery of *Flak*. The battle group moved out from south of Gasr el Abid to the south, where it encountered the reinforced 4th Armored Brigade northeast of Gabr Saleh.

Transitioning from a movement to contact, the 120 tanks of *Oberst* Stephan attacked, with both battalions engaged a short while later. Catching the enemy by surprise, the Germans knocked out tanks, trucks, and personnel carriers. The enemy pulled back to the south through the *Trigh el Abd*, hotly pursued by the Germans. Of the Stuart light tanks that attempted to hold up the Germans, 23 were knocked out and an additional 20 suffered battle damage. The Germans lost only three tanks. The enemy attack at that location had been stopped.

✠

Oberst Mickl, the commander of *Schützen-Regiment 155* of the *Afrika-Division z.v.B.*, was given command of a *Kampfgruppe* consisting of his regiment, *Afrika-Regiment 361,* and *Panzerjäger-Abteilung 605.* British armored cars appeared in his sector on both sides of Sidi Rezegh. From the few armor-defeating weapons on hand—mostly outmoded 3.7-centimeter antitank guns—he knocked out some of the enemy forces and forced the remainder back.

At 1635 hours, Air Command "Africa" reported enemy tank and truck columns advancing to the northwest from the area around Girabub. Their lead elements were only about 30 kilometers south of Bir el Gobi. It was then that the scope of the British offensive was realized.

Von Ravenstein recommended to Crüwell on the evening of 19 November that the armored forces of both the *15.* and *21. Panzer-Division* be combined to strike and eliminate the enemy armor. *Oberstleutnant i.G.* Bayerlein passed the recommendation, which had been approved by Crüwell, on up to Rommel. Rommel, in turn, gave Crüwell complete operational freedom on 20 November. His only comment: "Crüwell, you need to eliminate the enemy in the areas around Bardia–Tobruk–Sidi Omar before he is in a position to break through our siege positions around Tobruk. If that is the case, all the efforts of the past few months will have been in vain."

Crüwell decided to attack the enemy armor that had been sighted in front of *Aufklärungs-Abteilung 3 (mot.)* first. That was the enemy force that most threatened the German positions around Tobruk, because it had advanced the farthest north.

The *21. Panzer-Division* was directed to advance on Sidi Omar north of the *Trigh el Abd.* The *15. Panzer-Division* was ordered to advance across the *Trigh Capuzzo* to Sidi Azeiz, whereupon it would then turn towards Capuzzo itself.

That same evening, General Cunningham had ordered the 7th Support Group to link up with the 7th Armoured Brigade. He ordered the South African 1st Infantry Division to attack Bir el Gobi, which was being stubbornly defended by the "Young Fascists," the next morning. To the north, the 22nd Armoured Brigade was engaged. Cunningham's reserve, the 4th Armoured Brigade, was held at Gabr Saleh.

The *21. Panzer-Division* encountered nothing but empty space in its attack on Sidi Azeiz, since the King's Dragoon Guards, as well as the 3rd Royal Tank regiment, had pulled back form there. Pursuing the enemy, the *21. Panzer-Division* an out of fuel at Sidi Omar. Von Ravenstein requested his division be supplied from the air with fuel.

The *15. Panzer-Division*, which moved out during the morning of 20 November from the area around Gasr el Arid, rolled in a broad arc as far as Sidi Azeiz. In the area northeast of Gabr Saleh, it encountered the British 4th Armored Brigade.

Once again, tank engagements ensued. The battle raged back and forth until the fall of darkness. The German armored tactics again proved to be superior. Using quick jabs and maneuvers by leaps and bounds, the two tank battalions of *Panzer-Regiment 8* knocked out 55 of the enemy's 165 tanks. Coupled with its previous losses, the British brigade had an operational strength of only 68 tanks at the end of 20 November.

The New Zealand 2nd Infantry Division, which was only 10 kilometers away from the tank battle, had a number of armored vehicles in support of it and it could have made the difference in the outcome, but the commander of the 4th Armored Brigade had turned down its offer of support.

During the evening of 20 November, the BBC broadcast the following: "The 8th Army has started a large offensive in the western desert with its 75,000 magnificently equipped soldiers. It is intended to eliminate the German-Italian forces in Africa with it."[2]

Since the position of the British forces in the area around Sidi Rezegh could be consolidated that day, Major General Gott, the commander of the 7th Armoured Division, ordered his 7th Support Group, under Brigadier Campbell, to be prepared to advance on Tobruk. Working through General Cunningham, he arranged for the forces of General Scobie in the fortress to attempt to break out on 21 November.

2. Translator's Note: This quote was reverse-translated.

By doing so, the British deviated form their original plan, which was to find and defeat the armored forces of the *DAK* in battle. They had barely engaged them, let alone eliminated them.

General Cunningham was of the belief—a belief confirmed after the war—that the fighting of his 4th Armoured Brigade against the *15. Panzer-Division* had been *the* armored engagement and that the main forces of the *DAK* had been eliminated. He was reinforced in his beliefs by the disruption of radio communications, which did not allow any messages to get through.

That same night, the South African 5th Brigade was ordered in the direction of the ridgeline at Sidi Rezegh.

During the night of 20/21 November, Rommel issued his own orders to the *DAK*: "Attack on 21 November from the area 25 kilometers west of Sidi Omar in the direction of Belhamed against the rear of the enemy forces advancing on Tobruk." Five hours later, he had a supplemental order issued: "Situation is serious! Move as quickly as possible!"

Around that time, the 7th Armoured Brigade had established contact with the 7th Support Group, thus establishing the prerequisites for continuing the attack on Tobruk.

In Tobruk proper, Major General Scobie had assembled four British battalions and an armored brigade for the breakout attempt. The objective was El Duda, some 7 kilometers north of the ridgeline north of Sidi Rezegh, which was the objective of the 7th Armoured Brigade.

The breakout attempt succeeded. Although half of the British tanks were lost and the 2nd Battalion of the "Black Watch" lost three quarters of its personnel in assaulting the German *"Tiger"* Strongpoint, the British succeeded in cutting a 6-kilometer-wide corridor in the siege front and advanced a fair distance in the direction of El Duda.

Approximately two hours after the start of the breakout attempt, Brigadier Campbell advanced with the 6th Royal Tank Regiment and a reinforced battalion of the King's Guards. He succeeded in reaching the ridgeline and establishing a narrow sector there. Eight hundred German soldiers were taken prisoner for a short while. When the 6th Royal Tank Regiment continued to advance on El Duda, the link-up point, however, it was stopped and almost completely wiped out.

Brigadier Davy ordered the two remaining battalions of the 7th Armoured Brigade to the southeastern sector, where the British forces were being threatened. One of the battalions, the 7th Hussars, encountered German tanks and antitank guns there. The battalion commander was killed and most of his vehicles went up in flames within the space of a few minutes. The 12 tanks remained on the battlefield, either immobilized or completely destroyed.

The situation at Sidi Rezegh had become dangerous for the British.

✠

For the fight against the 7th Armoured Brigade and the 7th Support Group, the soldiers of the *Afrika-Division z.v.B.* were available in the north. To the south was the *Bologna* Division. Both forces were supported by general headquarters artillery, which was located in a favorable position.

Under the command of *Major* Ryll, the Foreign Legionnaires of the *II./Infanterie-Regiment 361* were in the center of the bitter fighting. They turned back the enemy's attacks twice, during which they eliminated three enemy tanks by means of demolitions. They were able to stop a penetration to the north and the northeast.

Elements of the *DAK* rolled into the rear of the enemy on 21 November. The main forces of the *DAK* had disengaged from the enemy during the early-morning hours, leaving behind only strong rearguards that were oriented to the south and southeast. The rearguards were reinforced with antitank guns and heavy *Flak*. The main body had moved out along a broad front , attacking to the northwest in the direction of Belhamed (objective of the *21. Panzer-Division*) and Sidi Rezegh (objective of the *15. Panzer-Division*).

The 100 enemy tanks that tried to block the *DAK* were pushed back through a series of advances and flanking attacks. By noon, the *DAK* reached the ridgeline southeast of Sidi Rezegh. When tanks from the 7th Armoured Brigade attacked from the flank in an effort to stop the German advance, 30 of their number were knocked out.

When evening fell, the *15. Panzer-Division* took up hedgehog positions around Sidi Muftah, while the *21. Panzer-Division* established an all-round defense south of Point 175.

The soldiers of the "Young Fascist" Division at Bir el Gobi held out admirably again for another day against the assaulting enemy forces.

During the night, Rommel reorganized his armor. *Generalleutnant* Crüwell succeeded in disengaging the *15. Panzer-Division* unnoticed from the enemy and recommitting it against the British deep flank in the east. The *21. Panzer-Division* left the positions it had taken along the ridgeline and marched north of the *Trigh Capuzzo* into the area around Belhamed–Zaafran. But the supply columns were unable to reach the reorganized forces in time, and it took until 1000 hours before the uploading of ammunition and refueling could be completed.

Crüwell ordered *Oberstleutnant* Cramer to take his *Panzer-Regiment 8*, encircle the enemy's 4th Armoured Brigade, and destroy it.

At noon on 22 November, Rommel personally directed the operations of the *21. Panzer-Division* against the enemy forces positioned around Sidi Rezegh.

When *Panzer-Regiment 8* encountered the enemy, the latter withdrew. Cramer ordered his tanks to pursue. The pursuit lasted the entire afternoon. When it turned evening, it appeared the enemy had escaped, but Cramer ordered the pursuit to continue. Cramer summoned *Major* Fenski, a battalion commander: "Fenski, take the lead with your battalion. As soon as you encounter the enemy, report. At the same time, attempt to get the enemy to fight."

Three minutes later, the *II./Panzer-Regiment 8* rolled forward and assumed the lead. Standing in his open hatch, Fenski could barely see his hand in front of his face. Despite that, he had his tanks move forward at a walking pace and tightly concentrated.

It was 1830 hours when his advance guard ran into a large concentration of armored and wheeled vehicles. *Major* Fenski searched the area with his night-coated binoculars. He was unable to discern any suspicious movements.

"Reform . . . 1st, go around to the left . . . 3rd, to the right. 2nd . . . follow me!"

Major Fenski rolled forward into the midst of the enemy with his one company while the other two companies conducted the outflanking maneuver.

"Turn on your lights . . . fire white pyrotechnics!"

The brilliant light of the headlights and pyrotechnics transformed the dark desert and illuminated it with streaks of flickering light.

"Take prisoners!" Fenski ordered, as he saw some of the Tommies attempt to escape. A handful of enemy tanks started up in an effort to escape the trap. A burst of machine-gun fire and a main-gun round from the battalion commander's tank convinced the British tankers to give up the effort.

When four tanks attempted to escape, they were greeted by the fires from the waiting companies. Two British tanks were set alight; the other two surrendered. The light from the burning tanks heightened the ghostly spectacle.

The German tank commanders dismounted and, armed with their crew submachine guns, took the English prisoner. In all, there were 18 officers and 160 enlisted personnel. It was the entire headquarters of the 4th Armoured Brigade and the 8th Hussars. Thirty-five tanks and armored cars were captured, in addition to several radio and command and control vehicles.

After contact had been established with *Schützen-Regiment 155* and *Afrika-Regiment 361*, the men rested in the area they had reached.

On that day, the *21. Panzer-Division* west sent west by Rommel towards the "Axis" Road. *Panzer-Regiment 5*, reinforced by a heavy battery of *Flak*, headed out at 1300 hours. Once at the "Axis" Road, it swung south and rolled past Abiar el Amar, 3 kilometers west of Sidi Rezegh, towards the foothills and then turned east towards the airfield, where the 7th Support Group was positioned. The enemy initially stopped the tank regiment by means of its large antitank contingent and artillery, but the Germans eventually forced their way through, even though they were also defending against attacking tanks from the 7th and 22nd Armoured Brigades. The Germans took the airfield as it started to turn dark. The enemy lost 19 tanks and a number of artillery pieces during this round of fighting. *Panzer-Regiment 5* lost 10 tanks.

Exploiting the opportunity, *Schützen-Regiment 104* mounted up, advanced to the foothills, and took them.

The English forces from Tobruk had received orders to expand their area of penetration by advancing in the direction of El Duda, taking the ridgeline, and eliminating all enemy armor there. But those forces failed on 22 November as well when they encountered the legionnaires of *Afrika-Regiment 361* on Hill 175. *Oberst* Grund, the regimental commander, and his two battalion commanders, *Oberstleutnant* Harder and *Major* Ryll, were forward in the trenches with their men, inspiring and rallying them where necessary.

The British forces attacked the hill again on 23 November. The positions of the *II./Afrika-Regiment 361* seemed to be singled out for particular attention. *Major* Ryll's adjutant, *Leutnant* Eisfelder, fell by his side when hit in the head. The attacking enemy tanks were engaged by legionnaires with Molotov cocktails. Soldiers of the 2nd Battalion climbed aboard abandoned enemy tanks and charged the enemy with them, causing complete surprise and confusion among the enemy's ranks.

Despite the heroic defense, the battalion was overrun. Around 1500 hours, *Major* Ryll was hit in the right elbow by a round from a 2-centimeter gun. A finger on his left hand was shattered, and his right arm was paralyzed by a grazing round. Two of the four company commanders were killed and one was badly wounded. In all, the battalion lost 300 men in its effort to maintain its sector on the hill.

On the same day, *Oberst* Grund and *Oberstleutnant* Harder were also badly wounded. Despite those losses, the regiment had contributed significantly to the fact that the fighting on *Totensonntag*[3] on that 23 November was settled in favor of the *DAK*. On the evening of 23 November, the enemy pulled back, worn down and exhausted, from the positions of *Afrika-Regiment 361* he had taken.

That 23 November was also marked by an additional heavy blow to the *DAK*. After Crüwell left his command post at Bir el Giaser with his immediate

---

3. Translator's Note: Sunday of the Dead. A Protestant feast day in which the dead are commemorated. It takes place on the Sunday before the 1st Advent.

battle staff to go to the location of the *15. Panzer-Division*, the operations staff was supposed to follow 45 minutes later. When it moved out around 0630 hours, it ran into the New Zealand 6th Brigade, which was resting along the *Trigh Capuzzo*. The German headquarters element was scattered after a short, sharp firefight. It lost almost all of its radios and communications signals instructions, along with 200 officers and men.

At 0730 hours, the *15. Panzer-Division* moved out to the south. When it encountered vehicles of the enemy that were oriented to the northwest a short while later, it launched a surprise attack on them. Twenty British tanks, which then attacked from the east in an effort to roll up the German flank, were held at bay with the antitank guns of the *15. Schützen-Brigade*. *Panzer-Regiment 8*, which was deployed along a broad front and in the lead, turned west and continued to eliminate the enemy's concentration of vehicles. *Generalmajor* Neumann-Silkow, the division commander, recommended to Crüwell that the attack be continued westward. Crüwell, who was riding along with the attack in his captured British armored car, christened *Moritz*, decided instead to support the *Ariete* Division around Bir el Gobi and the "Young Fascist" Division in Bir el Gobi. The division reorganized and continued its attack to the southwest. At 1235 hours, its lead armored vehicles encountered tanks from the *Ariete* Division 12 kilometers northeast of Bir el Gobi.

Individual formations of the XXX Corps then attempted to fall on the back and flanks of the *DAK*. Since those operations were conducted in a piecemeal fashion, they were turned back time and again, with the enemy suffering heavy losses.

At the same time, the *21. Panzer-Division* was undergoing difficult defensive fighting against the 7th Armoured Division. The *Pavia* Division held back another breakout attempt from Tobruk, even though it was supported by 60 tanks.

After reaching the *Ariete* Division, the combined forces of the *DAK, 15. Panzer-Division,* and *21. Panzer-Division* needed two and one half hours to turn around, reorganize, and continue its attack north.

Panzer-Regiment 5 was arrayed on the right in the attack formation, *Panzer-Regiment 8* in the middle and the *Ariete* Division on the left. Following behind *Panzer-Regiment 5* was *Regimentstab z.b.V. 200*[4] with *Kradschützen-Bataillon 15* and *MG-Bataillon 2*. Following behind *Panzer-Regiment 8* was *Schützen-Regiment 115*. The formations moved out ay 1530 hours. The enemy responded with heavy artillery fire from more than 100 guns and antitank-gun fires from self-propelled mounts. The German grenadiers, who had mounted the armored

---

4. Translator's Note: 200th Regiment (Headquarters-Special Purpose), which was a headquarters staff formed for taking command and control of *ad hoc* battle groups.

vehicles, were being decimated. The attack of the *Ariete* Division bogged down, and the *15. Panzer-Division* suffered heavy losses from flanking fires from the northwest.

At 1530 hours, Crüwell ordered the *21. Panzer-Division* to attack with its motorized rifle formations to the north. The reinforced *15. Panzer-Division* fought its way into an 8-kilometer-wide and 10-kilometer-deep area of the British lines.

Around 1700 hours, the *I./Panzer-Regiment 8* reached the airfield at Sidi Rezegh. *Major* Fenski had been killed, however, and *Oberstleutnant* Cramer narrowly escaped being captured or killed when he ran into an enemy artillery position far in the enemy's rear. Despite being hit several times, he was able to get back to the main body of the *I./Panzer-Regiment 8.*

Hauptmann Kümmel, who had assumed acting command of the battalion after the death of Fenski, advanced into heavy concentrations of enemy armor. The situation became critical for the battalion, until the sister battalion of *Hauptmann* Wahl was able to press through the enemy defenses and link up with Kümmel, giving him some breathing room.

The fighting was not decided until the motorized infantry could be brought up, however. In order to do that, the *II./Panzer-Regiment 8* had to turn around, move back through the enemy, and pick them up. Three company commanders—*Oberleutnant* Wuth, *Leutnant* Adam, and *Oberleutnant* Körner— were killed in the dramatic fighting. Four German tanks were immobilized or destroyed on the battlefield. It was largely thanks to the *3./Flak-Regiment 33* of *Hauptmann* Fromm that those movements succeeded. The *Flak* was able to knock out enemy armor in critical moments.

While the 2nd Battalion was going back, the 1st Battalion continued to move forward. Kümmel led his formation from an open hatch. He led his force by means of hand and arm signals since he had lost his radio. He was finally able to hammer his way through to the airfield, where he then established contact with the *21. Panzer-Division,* attacking from the north.

There were some 100 enemy vehicles scattered over the battlefield. More than 2,000 prisoners were taken. *Oberstleutnant* Cramer's tankers had eliminated 32 tanks, 18 antitank guns, and 3 batteries just in the area of the airfield alone. They also took 400 prisoners.

The fighting on *Totensonntag* was over. The enemy had lost another large formation. The South African 5th Brigade no longer existed.

As a result of those blows, many British historians think that General Cunningham lost his nerve. Cunningham asked to speak to Auchinleck. That same evening, the British Commander-in-Chief arrived at the headquarters of the 8th Army. Air Marshal Sir Arthur Tedder was with Auchinleck. The latter ordered Cunningham to continue "the offensive without delay."[5]

Rommel had the following radioed to the German Army High Command on the evening of 23 November concerning his intentions for the following day:

> Intentions for 24 November:
> a. Complete the destruction of the 7th Armoured Division.
> b. Advance with elements of my forces on Sidi Omar, with the intent of attacking the enemy along the Sollum Front.

That those intentions were not easy to realize is demonstrated in the losses the *DAK* took. *Panzer-Regiment 15* had only 11 *Panzer II's*, 16 *Panzer III's*, and 2 *Panzer IV's* operational; *Panzer-Regiment 8* had 18 *Panzer II's*, 36 *Panzer III's*, and 7 *Panzer IV's*. In all, the two regiments lost 72 tanks the previous day.

Because the battlefield fell into the hands of the enemy on 25 November, the German losses were predominately total losses, since the vehicles could not be recovered. The British, on the other hand, could fall back on the 200 some tanks they had in reserve in depots south of Saleh. Thus, the German victory at Sidi Rezegh was one for which too high a price ultimately had to be paid.

ADVANCE AND RETREAT

Early on the morning of 24 November, Rommel went with his battle staff to the *15. Panzer-Division* and ordered *Generalmajor* Neumann-Silkow to prepare to attack. *Oberstleutnant* Westphal, the Operations Officer of *Panzergruppe Afrika,* remained behind at the main headquarters. Rommel had assured him that he "wanted to complete the destruction of the rest of the enemy" and cut off the British retreat route to Egypt. He said he would return by the evening, at the latest.

Rommel instructed Westphal to remain behind, because he was taking *Generalmajor* Gause, the Chief-of-Staff, with him. Westphal was to keep an eye on the Tobruk front. Rommel instructed Westphal that it was imperative to maintain the siege ring around Tobruk.

Westphal interjected: "It's dangerous to go so far east of Tobruk with the *DAK*." He continued: "On the one hand, the enemy may try another large-scale breakout attempt. On the other hand, it is known that the New Zealand 2nd Division is approaching from the east."

"Most of that division is still north of Sollum," Rommel countered. "It can't take part in any fighting around Tobruk today."

---

5. Translator's Note: Reverse-translated.

Rommel pulled all of the motorized forces from out of the siege ring. Only the non-mobile forces remained behind, under the direct command of *Generalmajor* Böttcher, the corps artillery commander.

Initially, Rommel, who had arrived at the location of the *15. Panzer-Division*, ordered an advance guard formed under Cramer. It was to move in the direction of Sidi Omar and interdict the withdrawing enemy. Cramer could not head out, however, until after the tanks had been resupplied. Rommel then went on to the *21. Panzer-Division*, which he reached at 0600 hours. Crüwell reported on the successes of the previous day and further recommended that the enemy be pursued. He further suggested advancing in the area between the *Trigh Capuzzo*[6] and the *Trigh el Abd*, clearing it and scooping up any enemy spoils of war.

Instead, Rommel ordered the *DAK* to attack in the direction of Sidi Omar, with the objective of relieving pressure on the Sollum front. The orders directed *Schützen-Regiment 115* and *Afrika-Regiment 361* to look after the spoils of war, with the aim of replenishing their depleted stocks of motor vehicles.

The divisions were ordered to move out at 1000 hours. It was intended for the *21. Panzer-Division* for form the lead element, with the *15. Panzer-Division* trailing.

A report was received from *Aufklärungs-Abteilung 33* that strong enemy forces were west of Bir Sciafsciuf, with elements advancing west. The *15. Panzer-Division* was initially directed against those forces, but the orders were then amended for the division to go around them to the left and prepare to conduct a pursuit.Gambarra's Italian corps, which had been subordinated directly to *Panzergruppe Afrika* the previous evening, was directed by Rommel to follow the *DAK* in the direction of Sidi Omar with the *Ariete* Division.

The *21. Panzer-Division* started its attack at 1030 hours. The advance guard was formed by the 30 tanks of *Panzer-Regiment 5* that were still operational. When the enemy resistance stiffened along the left flank, the tank regiment was forced to orient in that direction.

Rommel, with the corps and division staffs, moved past *Panzer-Regiment 5* to the south with all of the wheeled elements. The tanks were left behind. Moving rapidly, that group reached the frontier fence at Gasr el Abid around 1600 hours. From there, Rommel had the forces move past the Sollum front to the east and into the area southeast of Halfaya Pass. When it turned dark, the *21. Panzer-Division* was stretched out for a distance of 70 kilometers.

The *15. Panzer-Division*, on the other hand, marched along a shallow front and set up an all-round defense 25 kilometers south of Sidi Omar that evening.

---

6. Translator's Note: Trail, e.g. (as used here) The Capuzzo Trail and the Abd Trail.

It was 1700 hours when Crüwell received orders from Rommel that he was to take his forces and those of Gambarra's corps and eliminate the enemy forces east of the Sollum front. The plan was to encircle the enemy with the *21. Panzer-Division* from the east, the *15. Panzer-Division* from the south, and the Italian forces from the west. Both of the armored divisions were to drive the enemy into the minefields in front of the German strongpoints. *Aufklärungs-Abteilung 33* was directed to advance to Habata. Its mission was to take the foothills of the mountains that rose from the sea there and block the retreat route, as well as the lines of communication, for the 8th Army.

Both of the tank regiments moved out separately to attack Sidi Omar on 25 November. *Panzer-Regiment 5* ran into elements of the Indian 7th Brigade. In the tank engagement that followed, *Panzer-Regiment 5* suffered heavy losses. *Oberstleutnant* Stephan was killed. *Major* Mildebrath assumed acting command of the regiment.

At the same time, *Panzer-Regiment 8* encountered strong enemy forces, but it was able to defeat them in bitter fighting.

Aufklärungs-Abteilung 33, which moved ahead in accordance with its orders to interdict the British supply point at Habata, was identified on its approach by English aircraft, subjected to terrific aerial punishment and effectively stopped.

Rommel then attempted to have the *15. Panzer-Division* bypass the enemy. The motorized elements of the division moved rapidly to the west around Sidi Omar. As it was executing that movement, 20 British tanks attacked, of which 16 were knocked out. It was elements of the 7th Armoured Brigade, which suffered considerable losses, although it succeeded in inflicting damage on *Panzer-Regiment 8* as well.

By the time it was evening, Rommel had reach the *Trigh Capuzzo* west of Sidi Azeiz and taken 30 kilometers of terrain, but his effort to encircle the British had failed. The attacks of *Panzer-Regiment 5* against Sidi Omar had not succeeded. Of the 12 tanks the regiment had left, only 2 were operational by that evening.

The *Ariete* Division was involved in a heavy firefight with the South African 1st Brigade at Bir Taieb el Esem, 20 kilometers southeast of Bir el Gobi. The South Africans were joined by the 4th Armoured Brigade. The Italian armor and antitank forces, which fought bravely, succeeded in driving back the Commonwealth forces.

That evening, the *Ariete* Division disengaged from the enemy, as ordered, to continue its march in the direction of Sidi Omar.

That evening, on a day which had not gone well for Rommel, *Oberstleutnant* Westphal attempted to reach Crüwell from Tobruk. In the radio message, Westphal indicated that Böttcher's forces had turned back an attack by New

Zealanders that had been supported by two battalions of tanks. Westphal further asked for a situation report from the Sollum front and what Rommel's intentions were.

Generalmajor von Ravenstein, whose *21. Panzer-Division* was embroiled in heavy fighting in the area around Sidi Rezegh, started to hear alarming reports from his supply forces. The supply columns were stretched for 20 kilometers along the *Via Balbia* and exposed to the enemy. Von Ravenstein summoned *Hauptmann* Briel, the commander of *Fla-Bataillon 606*: "Briel, get to the supply point immediately and straighten things out there. You have complete authority to do what is necessary."

Briel asked for that authority in writing, which proved to be a prudent precautionary measure. A short while later, he headed out with some *Flak* from Sidi Rezegh for the *Via Balbia*. Once there, he saw a New Zealand formation approaching from Bardia, moving along the edge of the mountains parallel to the road and headed straight for Tobruk.

The lead elements then turned off and down from the mountains and headed straight for the train elements.

Oberleutnant Franz was in their path with a single 2-centimeter *Flak*. He opened fire. The surprised enemy, not expecting resistance, moved back to the mountains, continuing west until the next mountain cut-off at Gambut. Briel, who was familiar with the terrain, then took his forces and raced towards the next cut-off in order to interdict the enemy. On the way, he was joined by train elements and 8 tanks. He also picked up a 21-centimter howitzer, commanded by *Wachtmeister* Wolf.

After the war, Briel told the author that he used those weapons to form a hedgehog position around the White House at Gambut. All of the weapons were aimed towards the mountain cut-off, "where the enemy had to appear. He came as expected."

It was the main body of the New Zealand 2nd Infantry Division. The Germans drove the New Zealanders back, and they continued their march in the mountains towards Tobruk.

CRISIS SITUATION AROUND THE SIEGE RING OF TOBRUK

Kampfgruppe Böttcher, which was in positions on both sides of Belhamed and south of the *Via Balbia*, was attacked almost without pause on 25 November. The infantry brigades of the New Zealand 2nd Infantry Division, supported by tanks, were attempting to break through. *Generalmajor* Böttcher was able to turn back those attacks with his artillery and *Schützen-Regiment 115* and *Afrika-Regiment 361*. But the situation worsened by the hour along the siege ring.

When the New Zealanders attacked again after the onset of darkness, they were able to take Balhamed in the course of the night. Early in the morning of 26 November, a portion of the Tobruk garrison, supported by 50 tanks, broke out once again. A crisis arose when El Duda fell.

It was only through a bitter and bravely conducted immediate counterattack by the *Bersaglieri* of the *Trieste* Division that the positions in the north could be held.

During the afternoon of that decisive 26 November, another breakout group from the fortress—that one with 30 tanks—succeeded in getting though the siege ring and establishing contact with British forces at Belhamed. The motorized and light infantry of the siege forces then knocked out 26 enemy tanks and wiped out most of the breakout force, forcing the remainder back into the besieged city.

Despite that setback, the British retained a narrow corridor and maintained contact between the New Zealanders and the Tobruk garrison.

When all efforts to reach Rommel on 26 November failed, Westphal acted on his own initiative. He needed to call back the *DAK*, if he did not want it to be lost. His radio message to the *DAK* basically stated that all previous orders were to be ignored and that the forces were to return to Tobruk as soon as possible. The message made it to the *21. Panzer-Division*, and *Generalmajor* von Ravenstein's *21. Panzer-Division* hammered its way through the New Zealanders along the *Via Balbia* back to the west. When von Ravenstein ran into Rommel, the latter was dumbfounded. He initially suspected some sort of radio deception maneuver on the part of the British. But when he appeared at his headquarters in El Adem during the evening of 26 November, he knew that Westphal had functioned as the "operational conscience of the field army." That he had been correct in his judgment was proven when Rommel submitted Westphal for the Knight's Cross to the Iron Cross. The pressing situation outside of Tobruk had forced Westphal's hand.

✠

Over the next few days, the fighting in the desert raged back and forth. To cover all of the operations would exceed the scope of this book, but a few will be covered to be illustrative of the unique aspects of fighting in the desert.

✠

During the afternoon of 28 November, the *15. Panzer-Division* was committed against the airfield at Sidi Rezegh. On the way to the airfield, the New Zealand main dressing station was overrun. Nine hundred German prisoners were released from temporary captivity. In the field hospital was also Colonel Kippenberger, who had been wounded during the night of 25/26 November. He had led the New Zealand 4th Brigade against Belhamed.

✠

During the evening hours of 28 November, *Generalmajor* von Ravenstein had gone to see *Generalleutnant* Crüwell at his command post to report that the division was inbound. When von Ravenstein left to go to the command post of the *15. Panzer-Division*, where an orders conference for the *DAK* was to be held, he ran into machine-gun fire when he arrived at the designated point at first light on 29 November.

The commander's staff car went up in flames. Von Ravenstein and his escorts jumped out. The driver was wounded. The vehicle had rolled right into the middle of a well-camouflaged New Zealand position. General Freyberg, the New Zealand commander, greeted his prisoner cordially and invited him to breakfast.

✠

After Rommel discussed the pressing logistical concerns of the forces in the field with General Bastico during the evening of 30 November, both men sent urgent requests to Rome. On that day, the *21. Panzer-Division* had only 21 operational tanks, the *15. Panzer-Division* 39. In contrast, Major General Gatehouse's 7th Armoured Division had 120 tanks, despite the fact that the 8th Army had already reported the loss of some 814 armored vehicles to Cairo.

The radio message sent by Rommel to the *Führer* Headquarters on 2 December had the following content:

In uninterrupted heavy fighting from 18 November to 1 December 1941, 814 tanks and armored cars of the enemy have been destroyed and 127 aircraft shot down. The large amount of spoils of war in weapons, ammunition and aircraft cannot be estimated yet. The number of prisoners exceeds 9,000, including 3 generals.

No decision could be reached in the fighting of the next few days. The last large armored engagement of that round of fighting in the desert war was against a large concentration of enemy armor at Bir el Gobi. The "Young Fascist" Division, which had defended magnificently there, was attempting to link up with the *DAK*. The fighting against the British Guards Brigade started. Shortly after the engagement started, the 7th Armoured Division joined in. Those forces were then joined by a breakout group from Tobruk that contained elements of the 70th Infantry Division. Those forces got as far as a line running El Duda–Belhamed. *Panzergruppe Afrika* no longer had the combat power to effectively counter those forces, especially when Gambarra's corps refused to join in. Gambarra had thrown in the towel; he had radioed Bastico that his men were too exhausted to participate in the murderous fighting.

The fighting continued on 7 December. *General* Neumann-Silkow was killed. *Oberst* Menny assumed temporary command, until *Generalmajor* von Vaerst could arrive.

✠

While the defenses west of Tobruk were maintained, the *DAK* and the motorized Italian forces disengaged during the night of 7/8 December. Elements of the non-motorized Italian XX Corps and the *90. leichte-Division* had been moved out ahead of time, with their lead elements already in Gazala.

Kradschützen-Bataillon 15 served as the rearguard all the way back to the Gazala Line. Once there, the withdrawal continued.

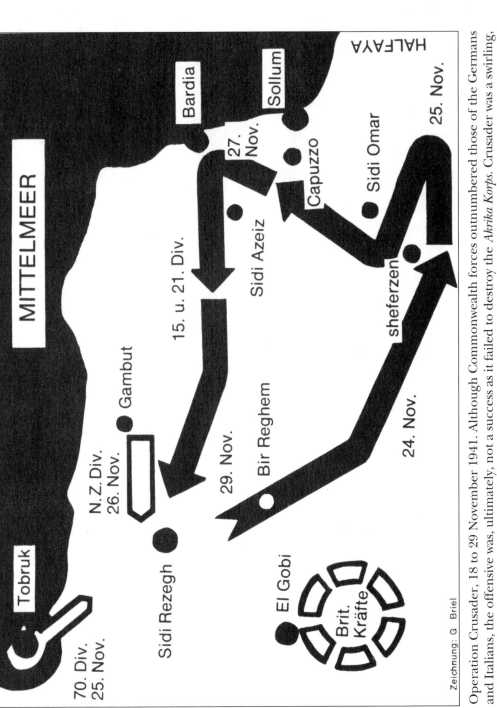

Operation Crusader, 18 to 29 November 1941. Although Commonwealth forces outnumbered those of the Germans and Italians, the offensive was, ultimately, not a success as it failed to destroy the *Afrika Korps*. Crusader was a swirling,

Zeichnung: G Briel

The heavily armored British Matilda Mark 2 infantry tank. Relatively impervious to the standard German antitank guns, only the famous "88" could knock it out at long range.

A somewhat dazed crew-member of the Matilda shown above is taken into captivity. Note the *P 08 Luger* at lower left.

A destroyed British Crusader tank. Great things were expected of this vehicle but it was a disappointment, being mechanically unreliable and still mounting the inadequate 2-pounder main gun.

A 20-mm *Flak 38* antiaircraft gun, here in use in the ground combat role. Note the white "kill rings" on the barrel.

The fighting around Tobruk was often fierce, with constant attacks and counterattacks. Members of the *Afrika Korps* find some respite in a rock dugout.

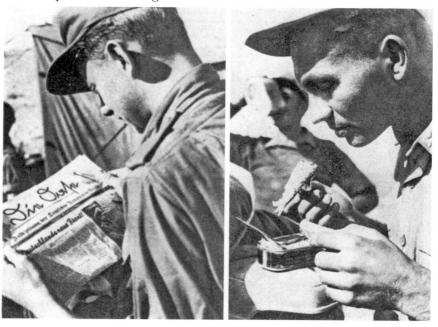

Life in the desert: In addition to newspapers from home, many front-line newspapers were produced—such as this copy of *The Oasis*; German rations were adequate but somewhat repetitive and unimaginative.

Adequate hydration was a constant problem in the searing heat. The supply of water took priority over almost everything else. Note the tropical "pith helmet"; heavy and awkward, it was soon replaced by the more comfortable and practical visored, cotton field cap as shown in the previous photographs.

Warning, mines! Massive minefields were widely used by both sides.

CHAPTER 7

Between Two Offensives

THE PURSUIT

General Auchinleck replaced General Cunningham with General Ritchie as Commander-in-Chief of the 8th Army. At that point, it was incumbent upon Ritchie to stick like glue to the withdrawing divisions of the Axis forces and defeat them. To do that, he needed to employ his fastest large formation, the XXX Corps.

Instead, Ritchie had that corps eliminate the enemy strongpoints along the border and the coastal area near Halfaya. He ordered his XIII Corps to take up the pursuit. As reinforcement, he attached the 7th Armoured Division to it.

General Godwin-Austen ordered his New Zealand 5th Brigade and his Polish brigade to attack the Italian forces and hold them up, while he took the 7th Armoured and Indian 4th Infantry Division to the south in an effort to outflank Rommel.

The Indian 4th Infantry Division wound up fighting elements of the Italian XX Corps, however, and the efforts of the 7th Armoured Division to bypass the *DAK* also proved fruitless.

When the Indian 5th Brigade ran into elements of the *15. Panzer-Division* on 15 December, it was badly battered. It lost more than 1,000 men taken prisoner. According to the Official History, the British bomber fleet, which was in a position to decisively influence the German withdrawal, "did not drop a single bomb for three days on German forces that were located southwest of Gazala and would have offered good targets."[1]

Nevertheless, the pressure exerted by Ritchie's forces was so strong that Rommel decided on 16 December to abandon the Gazala Line and pull back further. In Italy, those in power were distraught. It appeared as though Rommel was also headed for an inglorious end. General Cavallero immediately flew with *Generalfeldmarschall* Kesselring from Rome to Africa to plead with Rommel not to pull back. They met at Giovanni Berta. In hard discussions, Rommel succeeded in convincing Cavallero that the retreat from Gazala to Mechili was necessary. When aerial reconnaissance reported the advance of strong British columns along the southern flank, Rommel issued orders to pull back further to the west.

---

1. Translator's Note: Reverse-translated.

At 2300 hours on that memorable 16 December, Count Cavallero met once again with Rommel at the latter's command post. With him were Kesselring and the Italian generals Bastico and Gambarra. They demanded that Rommel rescind his retreat order.

"The loss of Cyrenaica will have terrible political consequences for the *Duce*," Cavallero swore.

"We cannot give up the airfield at Derna," Kesselring chimed in.

"Nothing changes. My orders have been issued and already partially executed. If we do not want to sacrifice the entire *Panzergruppe* to the enemy, then the only thing possible for us is to fight our way back during the night through the enemy, who is already behind us with some elements. I am faced with the question: Stay here, whereby the *Panzergruppe* and I will be offered up *and* Cyrenaica *and* Tripolitania will then be lost, or to start a withdrawal this evening, fight my way through Cyrenaica and reach the area around Agedabia and, at least, hold Tripolitania. The last course of action can be my only decision."

Late in the evening, the Italian motorized corps, which had been placed under the command and control of Crüwell, was on the move. The infantry divisions marched on foot; some lucky soldiers were trucked.

By 22 December, Beda Fomm and Antelat were reached.

The fact that Rommel had won the day in the decision on whether to withdraw was the salvation of the Axis forces in Africa. The British Official History notes: "If general Rommel had not remained by his decision, then the Axis forces would have undoubtedly been eliminated . . . He deserves the highest praise for completely grasping the situation *and* refusing to deviate from his decision, once it had been made."[2]

The fact that the withdrawal went smoothly was in large measure due to the efforts of *Kradschützen-Bataillon 15*. At the start of the withdrawal, it had 500 men. Within four weeks, it had lost 400 of them. The new battalion commander, *Major* Ehle, was able to mold his men into a band of brothers, who almost always succeeded in holding back the enemy and allowing the foot soldiers to escape.

Agedabia was reached on Christmas Day. There was a battle there two days later. The 8th Army attempted to expel the Germans with the 1st and 7th Armoured Divisions attacking from the front, while the 22nd Armoured Brigade attempted to maneuver south to outflank. The motorcycle infantry of *Major* Ehle and elements of *Aufklärungs-Abteilung 33* succeeded in stopping the enemy initially, while the German armored forces and heavy weapons positioned themselves. The 22nd Armoured Brigade, fully equipped, advanced from El Haseiat. The battle raged for three days.

---

2. Translator's Note: Reverse-translated.

The 8.8-centimeter *Flak* of *Major* Hecht were the first weapons to claim victims. *Flak-Regiment 135* was in its element. The enemy tanks were being taken out at a distance of 2,000 meters, long before they could get off a single effective round.

When the enemy tanks closed on the German positions and the tanks of the 22nd Armored Brigade also started coming in from the south and southwest, Crüwell committed his 60 remaining tanks in an immediate counterattack. They knocked out 37 of the 22nd Armoured Brigade's 90 tanks, while losing only 7 of their own in those dramatic engagements. Another attempt by the British resulted in the loss of an additional 23 tanks, while the Germans again lost only 7. In all, some 136 enemy tanks were counted scattered along the German front when the fighting was over.

The British divisions that had attacked frontally pulled back to the northeast. Rommel used the opportunity to pull his forces back in an orderly and disciplined fashion to the positions at Marsa el Brega, after New Year's was celebrated at Agedabia. For the first time in the desert, the German national anthem could be heard being sung from position to position.

✠

On 12 January 1942, *Panzergruppe Afrika* and the Italian formations were ready to conduct the defense from their positions at Marsa el Braga.

THE FIGHTING ON THE "ISLANDS" IN THE SAND

Excluded from the withdrawal of *Panzergruppe Afrika* were the German and Italian forces manning the strongpoints at Sollum, Halfaya Pass, and Bardia. They were like islands in the stream behind the British lines. On 30 December, the 8th Army went after Bardia first. Supported by artillery, air, and naval gun power, the enemy attacked with strong armored forces on 30 December. The town fell three days later, on 2 January 1942.

Sollum, which had been occupied by the Germans since 21 November, was held until 12 January 1942 by a few companies of *Oasen-Bataillon z.b.V. 300*.[3] After a terrific preparatory barrage on 11 January, the enemy attacked *Hauptmann* Ennecerus and his 70-odd men. The British did not succeed in penetrating the defenses until the next day. Ennecerus had to call off the fight, since he ran out of ammunition. After holding out for 56 days, the men of the Oasis Battalion finally left a living hell.

The German defenders at Halfaya Pass continued to hold out under *Major* Bach. After the British took Lower Sollum, drinking water started to become

---

3. Translator's Note: 300th Oasis Battalion (Special Purpose).

scarce in addition to rations. Rommel was aware of the precarious situation and ordered *Ju 52's* to fly in supplies. On the second night, the aircraft were shot down and it was deemed too dangerous to attempt aerial resupply.

In the middle of January, General di Giorgis pulled the rest of his *Savona* Division from the lower western positions to the pass, where Major Pardi's artillery battery was still assisting the Germans.

Major Bach sent an emissary to the South Africans, who accepted the surrender of the Germans under honorable conditions. On 17 January, the last defenders of the pass formed up to surrender. The last Axis bastion east of Marsa el Braga had fallen.

CHAPTER 8

The Path to Tobruk and El Alamein

THE LOGISTICS SITUATION

On 5 January 1942, a German-Italian convoy made it through to Tripoli. Among the large number of logistical items brought were 50 tanks and 20 armored cars.

Rommel, who considered himself anything but through, took the arrival of the convoy as a good omen. He was already toying with the idea that he might be able to launch a new attack while the enemy was still weak. *Oberstleutnant i.G.* Westphal supported him in those thoughts: The enemy had not yet closed up; his supplies had not caught up; he had not been able to launch a massed attack; and, finally, he was ill-prepared to defend against a new offensive.

On 13 January 1942, Rommel had made up his mind. He announced the following during the evening staff meeting: "We're going to attack again!" He based his intention on the following: "If we allow the 8th Army to rest until February, then he will have been so heavily reinforced that nothing will be able to stop him. We cannot wait. Instead, we need to spoil the enemy's plans."

The 10th Submarine Flotilla in Malta, which had caused such problems during the previous fall, was being increasingly successfully combated by *Luftflotte 2* on Sicily. German *U-Boote*, which had been employed in the Mediterranean starting in the fall, became an increasingly dangerous opponent for the British surface fleet as well.

All of that contributed to the fact that more and more materiel was making it to Africa for the Axis.

Rommel had the plans made for his attack kept under the tightest of wraps. Clever propaganda about the potential for a continued retreat by *Panzergruppe Afrika* attempted to lull the enemy into a false sense of security. British agents reported the Rommel was getting ready to move. In Rome, of course, that possibility filled the Italians with horror. On the British side, Auchinleck was not completely convinced. He ordered increased reconnaissance of the Germans.

On 19 January, additional transports arrived in Tripoli. Rommel then had 111 tanks available, with an additional 28 being held in the rear as a reserve. The Italian XX Corps (Motorized) was able to report 90 operational fighting vehicles.

Rommel had outbuildings burnt down in Marsa el Brega during the evening of 20 January. Ships were blown up in the harbor; the British agents' reports followed, one after the other.

When all of those reports had been digested, even Auchinleck came to believe that Rommel was at the end of his rope.

But things looked quite a bit different on the morning of 21 January. Rommel's order-of-the-day was read aloud to the men of *Panzergruppe Afrika* that morning:

German and Italian Soldiers!
You have difficult fighting against a numerically superior enemy behind you. But your morale remains unbroken. At present, we are numerically superior to the enemy forces facing our front. To eliminate that enemy, the field army is moving out to attack today.

I expect that every soldier will give his all during the upcoming decisive days.

Long live Italy! Long live the greater German *Reich*! Long live the *Führer*!

THE ASSAULT BEGINS

It was 0600 hours on 21 January when Rommel headed out with his battle staff from the command post of *Panzerarmee Afrika*. The field army received the new designation at 0530 hours, when the directive redesignating it was received from the *Führer* Headquarters in Rastenburg.

Rommel went to *Kampfgruppe Marcks*, which had received orders to strike the first blow through the enemy's defensive ring. The Italian XX Corps (Motorized) was then to follow through.

At the same time, the *DAK* "took to the horizon" in a wide outflanking maneuver to the south to reach its designated jumping-off positions. It was to advance along the *Wadi Faregh* to the northeast to hit the enemy in the rear.

When Rommel arrived at the command post of *Kampfgruppe Marcks*, which was comprised of elements from the *90. leichte-Division* and the other two armored divisions, *Oberstleutnant* Marcks reported his forces ready to move.

"What are you waiting for, then, Marcks?" Rommel stated after the report. "Don't lose sight of the fact that your objective is Agedabia."

"We're rommeling again!" the motorcycle infantry and mounted riflemen said to one another as they started to move out.

The light armored cars were in the lead. Tanks followed so that any resistance could be quickly eliminated. When the first enemy tanks appeared, they were knocked out by the Germans. The *Kampfgruppe* then poured into the enemy positions. A field battery was overrun at El Giofia. By 1100 hours, *Kampfgruppe Marcks* had punched through the enemy positions.

In the meantime, Rommel had gone on to the XX Corps. He gave General Zinghales, the new corps commander and an acknowledged armor expert, the green light to advance. The Italian armor quickly rolled through the gap in the enemy's lines.

Exactly 24 hours after breaking through the British positions at Marsa el Brega, *Kampfgruppe Marcks* was in Agedabia. The fighting to take the city lasted an hour, before it fell to the German battle group.

Rommel ordered Marcks and the Italians to continue advancing on to Antelat, another 60 kilometers further east in the desert. The vehicles bogged down in the soft sand, however.

Shortly after *Kampfgruppe Marcks* had arrived at Agedabia, *MG-Bataillon 8* also arrived. From there, it was directed forward along the Antelat Trail to the area around Hseir el Aunami, 15 kilometers west of Saunau. It occupied positions there and oriented to the south and southeast. The *3./MG-Bataillon 8*, reinforced by two platoons from the *2./Panzerjäger-Abteilung 39*, took up positions some 800 meters further forward on high ground. Just as it arrived there, 20 British tanks attacked. Four Mark IV's were taken out by one of the antitank-gun platoons.

A short while later, the machine-gun battalion moved out again, this time to support the attack of *Panzer-Regiment 5*, which had 25 tanks and two 8.8-centimeter *Flak* in support, on enemy-occupied Saunau.

Just outside of Saunau, the Germans ran into a British force of some 100 tanks. In the hard fighting that following, during which the enemy continuously fired smoke to escape from the sight of the Germans, 32 enemy tanks were knocked out. The machine gunners prevented the enemy from conducting a flanking maneuver. Rommel appeared and ordered the attack to be continued to the northeast. The force moved out across the rolling terrain in the direction of the deep depression, where the water point at Saunau was located. When the tanks reached the edge of the depression they saw some 50 enemy tanks, two batteries of artillery, and a number of trucks at the water point below them.

Orders were dispatched. The machine gunners were to go into position along the ridgeline. The tanks were to attack the depression by swinging out to the west.

When the fighting started, 10 of the British tanks made it to the ridgeline, where they were engaged by the antitank guns of the *2./Panzerjäger-Abteilung 39* and turned back. The next wave succeeded in overrunning the position, however, taking three guns under its tracks. They also destroyed the prime movers with their on-board machine guns before they left at high speed.

When an unsuspecting British truck convoy rolled into the depression during the morning of 24 January to get water, 5 of the trucks were set alight and another 12 captured.

The *3./MG-Bataillon 8* remained behind at the water point to secure it. The rest of the machine-gun battalion followed the tanks south towards Maaten el Grara. It was intended for them to relieve *Kampfgruppe Marcks* there. Rommel had given the battle group the following orders: "Advance though Saunau to the southeast towards Abd el Grara. From there, continue on to Giof el Mater and attack the eastern flank of the British 1st Armored Division."

In addition to *Kampfgruppe Marcks*, *Kampfgruppe Warrelmann* had also been sent initially to Agedabia. *Major* Hinrich Warrelmann, the commander of *MG-Bataillon 2* of the *15. Panzer-Division*, had a battle group consisting of his battalion, the attached *II./Panzer-Artillerie-Abteilung 33*, and a company from *Kradschützen-Bataillon 15*. When his force was in Agedabia and refueling, Rommel showed up: "Warrelmann, don't refuel . . . attack!"

"If we want to attack further, *Herr General*, we have to refuel first!"

"Good . . . when you're done, continue east. Forty kilometers from here is the desert fort of Antelat. Take it and hold it. There's going to be a big battle east of Agedabia."

That meant that two battle groups were being sent in the direction of the fort: *Kampfgruppen Marcks* and *Warrelmann*. Warrelmann's force took off in the evening, reaching the fort two hours later. The fort had been abandoned by the enemy. Warrelmann's men set up an all-round defensive position. As it turned light, Warrelmann saw combat and combat-support forces of the British passing by all around him. When two English fighters tried to land on the trail at Antelat, they were shot down by machine-gun fire.

During that phase of the fighting, Warrelmann received a report that additional English aircraft were at the airfield, less than a kilometer away. He dispatched a company of motorcycle infantry to check out the report. The enemy was waiting with a company of reconnaissance vehicles. The eight enemy aircraft parked there were fired upon and set on fire.

An enemy tank attack during the afternoon of 22 January was turned back. *Major* Warrelmann did not allow his men to open fire until the enemy had closed to within 100 meters. Within a short period, eight English tanks were ablaze. The enemy pulled back.

That afternoon, Warrelmann's 4th Company hit the flank of a large British convoy. It cut the convoy in half, capturing seven armored cars and taking a number of prisoners. On 23 and 24 January, he repeated his flank thrusts, in the end, garnering more than 1,800 prisoners. On the evening of 24 January, Warrelmann received orders from the *DAK* to move out against Msus the next morning at 0530 hours. Once there, he was to rejoin the *DAK*.

On the way to Msus, *Kampfgruppe Warrelmann* encountered a concentration of enemy armor consisting of 20 vehicles. Warrelmann had his forces deploy and his antitank guns take up position. The artillery also went into position.

After several enemy tanks were set alight, the enemy turned off in the direction of Msus.

Increasing its speed, the battle group pursued but started taking fire from a battalion of English self-propelled guns. After the Germans returned fire, it also pulled back.

When the battle group reached the high ground outside of Msus, a British formation with 12 tanks and a number of other vehicles approached it from the rear. The artillery turned around, went into firing positions, and engaged the enemy. When they received fire, the English turned off to the east.

A few minutes later, the patrol that Warrelmann had sent out returned. The patrol leader reported a large concentration of armor 6 kilometers away. Warrelmann immediately sent out a company to conduct a reconnaissance in force. When they reached the halt area of the tanks, which had wanted to go to Msus to refuel but had been unable to reach it, the company discovered the tanks abandoned. The *Kampfgruppe* added another 30 vehicles to its tally.

At the Msus airfield, the battle group captured 12 aircraft and a large supply dump.

Just as the battle group set up for the defense, three tanks and two armored cars approached rapidly. It was not the enemy, however; it was Rommel. He received Warrelmann's report and corrected him: "You didn't knock out 24 tanks, Warrelmann; it was 26!"

A third *Kampfgruppe* had been formed under *Oberst* Geißler, the commander of *Schützen-Regiment 115*. It moved out on 21 January after the sun went down. It reached Agedabia the next morning and immediately moved on ahead in the direction of Saunau–Antelat with some of its elements. In the process, it managed to cut off a portion of the British 1st Armoured Division and force 1,000 soldiers to surrender. It also captured 117 tanks and armored cars, 33 guns, and a number of other vehicles.

Oberst Geißler later described the pursuit the following day in vivid terms:

> On 23 January, the *DAK* marched inexorably forward as far as the trail crossroads at Msus. Moving rapidly, our formations rolled north along a broad front . . . It was a wild ride; a breathtaking competition with the withdrawing enemy. Looking through the clouds of dust, you could see English columns parallel to you and heading in the same direction. Soldiers were hanging on the vehicles like bunches of grapes; they wanted to go back, too.
>
> While the English moved back to Mechili, a strong enemy force succeeded in reaching Bengasi and stopped there. The field army headquarters therefore decided to take Bengasi first and clear all of Cyrenaica of the enemy.

Kampfgruppen Marcks and *Geißler* were employed against Bengasi. *Kampfgruppe Geißler* was able to take Maraua, which was stubbornly defended by the enemy, on the morning of 29 January.

✠

Kampfgruppe Marcks, which had received orders on 24 January to advance on Msus in a flanking maneuver from the west while the *DAK* and the Italians would attack from the east, moved out on 25 January to conduct that attack. Rommel, who had just been promoted to *Generaloberst*, appeared at the location of the battle group as it was moving out and gave Marcks some typical Rommel advice: "Exploit, Marcks, exploit!"

Two hours later, Marck's men encountered enemy tanks, which were knocked out. *MG-Bataillon 2*, which had been attached, engaged English infantry who got in the way and mowed them down. When English defensive fires started landing heavily in the middle of the battle group, Rommel appeared.

"Take your faster forces and head for Msus. When the enemy pulls out to finish you off, fall back and draw the British tanks into the *Flak* and antitank guns that we are establishing behind you."

That was typical of Rommel. A few minutes later, the mobile elements of *Kampfgruppe Marcks* headed out in the direction of Msus. The enemy started registering his fires on Marck's men. When Marcks gave the order to turn around just outside of Msus and the battle group described a wide arc to the west, the English defenders in Msus started to pursue. The enemy's tanks and armored cars fired as they moved. A German motorcycle and a personnel carrier went up in flames.

The battle group moved back through the 8.8-centimeter guns of *Flak-Regiment 135*, which had been brought forward. When the enemy had approached to within effective range, the *Flak* and the antitank guns opened up. After three quick salvoes, seven English tanks were ablaze. The remaining ones turned around, although some of them were caught by the far-reaching *Flak* as they attempted to escape.

"Follow them . . . get on them!" Rommel commanded.

The *Kampfgruppe* then advanced forward rapidly, raced through the partially manned positions of the enemy, and reached Msus just as the British set the fuel tanks ablaze and thick clouds of smoke wafted skywards.

Msus was taken. Despite the loss of the fuel, large supply dumps were captured. More than 600 vehicles, 127 guns, and a large number of other vehicles were captured. In the maintenance facility at Msus, 50 English tanks were taken intact.

"Keep going, Marcks!" Rommel directed, after the *Kampfgruppe* had refueled and taken on more ammunition. "Your next objective is Bengasi. Assault directly via El Rhegima and Benina."

Rommel placed *Aufklärungs-Abteilung 3 (mot.)* at Marck's disposal. He also promised Marcks the use of *Kampfgruppe Geißler*, as soon as the latter had taken Maraua.

An hour after the battle group headed out, a tremendous *ghibli* started up. The sand blew across, over and under the columns. *General der Panzertruppe* Rommel, who was moving with the battle group, moved to its head. He assumed the duties of guide with a sure instinct, just as he had so many times before. Then, on top of everything else, it started to rain. The motorcycles and personnel carriers got stuck in a broad *wadi*. It was not until the ground became more rocky that the battle group was able to pick up speed again.

Ridotta Rhegima was reached during the morning of 28 January. By 1600 hours of that day, Benina had been taken. The Bengasi airfield was taken by surprise. When the battle group reached the eastern outskirts of Bengasi, it received fires from Indian formations.

In the ensuing fight, the command vehicle of *Oberstleutnant* Marcks was shot out from under him twice. The enemy was trying to hold up the advancing Germans as long as was needed to blow up all of the supply dumps in Bengasi and Coefia. But the effort proved fruitless, and a portion of the Indian brigade that was defending later marched off into captivity.

On the radio in Cairo the next day, the following was heard: "General Rommel, a rapscallion among the modern generals, has pulled another rabbit out of his hat of tricks."[1]

On 30 January, *Kampfgruppe Marcks* took Barce and Tocra. Advancing further, after having helped out *Kampfgruppe Geißler* at Maraua, the motorcycle infantry rolled into Cirene, followed by Giovanni Berta.

The Indian 5th Brigade put up a fight at Martuba. The engagement lasted three hours before the enemy took flight; Marcks immediately had his forces pursue. Er-Rzem was bypassed and Tmimi taken. All of Cyrenaica was in the hands of the Axis forces. It had taken Rommel 17 days to take back all that he had lost in a long-lasting and slow withdrawal.

On 5 February 1942, *Oberstleutnant* Marcks personally received the Knight's Cross to the Iron Cross from Rommel. In receiving the award, Marcks stated: "Behind this symbol are blood, tears, and destruction. At the same time, however, bravery, trustworthiness, and the selfless sacrifice of many men."

During those days, Rommel had visited almost all of his formations that were in the front lines. After the British 1st Armoured Division had been effectively destroyed, he took a trip over the battlefield in a Fieseler *Storch* to get an overall impression. He was greeted by heavy antiaircraft fire during the flight. Shrapnel pierced the thin skin of the light utility aircraft. Rommel kept his head and even gave the pilot advice on how best to avoid the antiaircraft fires. *Oberstleutnant i.G.* Westphal, who was with him, saw a flight of Hurricanes above the aircraft. Fortunately for the Germans inside, they did not spot the small aircraft. Rommel appeared to be invulnerable.

Panzerarmee Afrika set up its positions in front of the British Gazala Line. It needed an operational pause to rest and replenish its ranks before it could continue the offensive.

On 15 February, Rommel and Westphal flew to Rome to brief Mussolini. From there, they flew on to Rastenburg, where they also briefed Hitler.

But Hitler was not interested in Africa. The first winter in the East had badly battered the German Army; his disappointment in the fact that the colossus of the Soviet Union had not fallen was too great.

Rommel asked for more divisions: "Six German motorized divisions, including three armored divisions, and we will sweep the enemy from the African continent."

Hitler avoided answering the request.

Rommel then asked that Malta be removed from the equation, so that the worst threat to the German-Italian supply route could be eliminated. Hitler also avoided answering that question.

---

1. Translator's Note: Reverse-translated.

Westphal, who had an audience with Jodl on 18 February, discovered that all eyes were fixed on the Soviet Union in the Armed Forces High Command as well. Africa had become a secondary theater of war, since the war against the Soviet Union had reached a decisive point and the enemy still showed no signs of being eliminated.

Rommel and Westphal flew back to Rome. Rommel then attempted to win over *Il Duce.* He proposed the taking of Malta and another offensive, with the primary objective of taking Tobruk. Although Mussolini lent an attentive ear, the Italian dictator was ultimately powerless to sway his German counterpart

THE LOGISTICS QUESTION BECOMES EVER MORE PROBLEMATIC

Through conservation and the large quantities of materiel that had been captured in Mechili, the employment of the Axis forces in Africa was guaranteed prior to the winter battles. The constant demand meant that the stockpiling for the attack on Tobruk could only be 40% complete by November 1941. As the result of draconian measures, it was possible for *Panzergruppe Afrika* to hold out against the British winter offensive for the first two weeks.

During those two weeks, the losses in shipping rose to 60%. Only that fact that Italian submarines docked with their dangerous supplies at Derna and Bardia prevented a disaster. In addition to Italian transport vessels, the German freighters *Maritza* and *Procida* were lost to Force K at the end of November. At the beginning of December, the stockpiles had been exhausted. The few means left were barely sufficient to enable the withdrawal to the west. Since the losses in tanks, ammunition and equipment could not be replaced, strongpoints such as Sollum, Bardia, and Halfaya Pass fell to the British in their offensive.

Through 31 December 1941, Italian submarines conducted 13 supply runs. The submarine *Milo* made three such journeys, receiving the honor of the busiest boat. The submarine *Carraciolo* was caught by the British destroyer *Farndale* off the African coast and sunk.

The Italian convoy, which was underway from 29 November to 2 December from Brindisi to Africa, was caught by Force K and decimated. The next convoy was conducted by warships. The cruiser *Luigi Cadora* took fuel to Bengasi and took 900 prisoners back to Italy. The motorboat *Sebastiano Venier,* which had taken supplies to Africa, started the return trip to the European mainland with 2,000 English prisoners on board. The British submarine *Porpoise* sank it. It was thanks to the Italian hospital ship *Arno* that 1,800 of the prisoners could be saved.

The British submarine *Upright* sank two Italian freighters in January.

At the beginning of January 1942, the Italian submarine *St. Bon*, which was taking fuel to Tripoli, was sunk by the British submarine *Upholder*.

The next three convoys, however, provided the impetus for Rommel's new offensive planning. They arrived between 3 and 6 January at Tripoli. These were followed by five more convoys from 22 to 25 January. A further convoy—*K 7*—also reached Tripoli safely.

For the time being, Rommel had fewer logistical nightmares to worry about than previously.

MALTA IN THE CROSSHAIRS

During the spring of 1942, the German combat pilots based on Sicily increasingly flew missions against Malta. At first, it was just a few machines, but they appeared over Malta eight times a day. The *Ju 88's* were escorted by the Messerschmitts of *Hauptmann* Wilcke's *III./Jagdgeschwader 53*. Once again, *Major* Mahlke's *III./Stukageschwader 1* also participated, just as it had done in the first assault on Tobruk.

By the middle of April, the bombing campaign over Malta had reached its apex. After destroying most of the airfields, the fighters and destroyers attacked the fighter base at Ta Kali and completely destroyed it. After four days of intense bombing, the airfields at Malta could not be used.

Following those attacks, continuous runs were launched against a convoy that had steamed out of Alexandria for Malta. *Supermarina*, the Italian high command for its navy, launched a number of submarines against it and ordered Admiral Parona, the responsible surface naval officer, to launch an attack against the convoy, preferably with at least three cruisers and four destroyers. Admiral Iachino, with his naval fleet based in Tarento, was also employed. He had the battleship *Littorio* within his command, as well as four destroyers. That force was joined at sea by an additional two destroyers.

The strong naval escort the convoy enjoyed prevented the Italian vessels from sinking any freighters. Nevertheless, as a result of the long-lasting naval engagement, the convoy did not reach Malta until daybreak. That was the time for the *II. Flieger-Korps* to shine. Ship after ship was bombed. Of the 25,900 tons of cargo on board, only 5,000 tons made it ashore.

The third phase of the bombing of Malta started at the end of March. The port of La Valetta was in the crosshairs of the German aviators, with the docks and loading areas being bombed. The attacks lasted through all of April. Until 28 April, Malta was eliminated as a naval and air strongpoint. At that time, the island was deemed ready for an operation that had been in the planning for some time: *Operation "Herkules,"* the aerial conquest of the island by airborne forces.

General der Flieger Student, the Commanding General of the German airborne corps, went to Rome at the beginning of April to consider the conquest of Malta. He was joined there by *Generalmajor* Ramcke, a senior airborne officer, who was in Italy to assist the Italians in forming their own airborne division, christened the *Folgore* Division.

In Student's first plan, he placed responsibility for the operation squarely on the shoulders of the Italians. Colonel General Count Cavallero, the Italian Chief-of-Staff, was to coordinate all of the operations. Mussolini had already promised the support of the entire Italian fleet.

The airborne forces of Student were to jump in as an advance guard to secure a bridgehead for the island. The majority of the forces would then be brought in by ship and air, protected by the Italian fleet.

For the transport of heavy weapons, such as the *Panzer IV*, for instance, there were 12 *Me 323 "Gigant"* transporters, each with six engines. In addition, there were 100 *Go 242's* and 1,000 *DFS 230* gliders.

The buildup and debarkation of the earmarked forces was to take place on Sicily. The *II. Flieger-Korps*, together with the Italian Air Force, would overwatch the air space over Malta and attack any approaching naval vessels.

In the middle of all of his planning, Student was summoned to the *Führer* Headquarters by telegram. When he arrived there, *Generaloberst* Jeschonnek, the *Luftwaffe* Chief-of-Staff, informed him that he would have a difficult time of it with Hitler the following day, since *General* Crüwell had just had an audience with Hitler, informing him that the fighting morale of the Italian forces was poor.

Student presented his plan the following morning. Hitler asked several questions, which the airborne general was able to answer satisfactorily. Then Hitler stated what he thought of the plan: He considered it as thoroughly executable. There was just one snag, however: "Good, Student, that the bridgehead is formed by your forces. I guarantee the following, however: When the attack starts, the British fleet in Alexandria will set sail. The forces stationed at Gibraltar will also come. Then you'll see what the Italians will do. They all turn back to their harbors, the warships as well as the freighters. And then *you* will be all alone on the island with your paratroopers."

Student tried to counter that that eventuality had also been foreseen and that *Generalfeldmarschall* Kesselring had promised the employment of the *Luftwaffe*, so much so that the area outside of Malta would become the grave of the British fleet. But Hitler remained adamant. His decision: "The attack on Malta will not take place in 1942. Instead, it will take place later."

Winston Churchill, who had informed the new governor of the island, Lord Gort, that he would have the "sad duty of turning Malta over to the enemy,"[2] would have been able to breathe easier had he heard that conversation.

The German summer offensive in the Soviet Union, which was about to get underway, also took away the air formations that had made Malta and the warships and convoys in the Mediterranean hold their breath. *Kampfgeschwader 77* was personally directed to the east by Hitler. The *I./Kampfgeschwader 54* was moved to Eleusis, near Athens. The *Stukas* of the *III./Stukageschwader 3*, the destroyers of the *III./Zerstörergeschwader 26* and the night fighters of the *I./ Nachtjägergeschwader 2* were dispatched from Sicily to Africa to support Rommel if he went over to the offensive in the summer from the areas he had recently taken in the spring. In addition, the *III./Jagdgeschwader 53* was also sent to Africa. The continued air operations in Africa will be covered in a subsequent chapter.

MR. CHURCHILL'S WISH

General Auchinleck attempted to get his 8th Army back up to full combat power after the loss of Cyrenaica in the early spring. He needed to be able to withstand any further German advances and, at the same time, prepare for offensive operations of his own. But he needed time for that, and it was time that he did not appear to have an abundance of. On 2 May 1942, Churchill sent him radio traffic in which he pressed for an attack to commence shortly. He closed with the words: "We believe that an effort to drive German forces out of Cyrenaica in the coming weeks is not only extremely necessary for the security of Malta, on which so much hangs, but also offers the only hope of deciding a battle as long as the enemy is relatively weak and does not have sufficient amounts of logistics of all types available."[3]

Based on that guidance, Auchinleck sent a telegram to the Chiefs of Staff in London in which he outlined the overall situation in Africa and emphasized the risks that would surface from a new attack before the complete reconstitution of the 8th Army.

Churchill's answer on 8 May had the following as its main argument:

We are in full agreement that you would do the right thing, despite the risks mentioned by you, if you would attack the enemy and involve him in a large battle, preferably in May and the sooner the better . . .

2. Translator's Note: Reverse-translated.

3. Translator's Note: Reverse-translated, as are all of the originally English passages in this section.

In the process, you undoubtedly have to take into consideration
the fact that the enemy himself may intend to attack you at the
beginning of June.

Auchinleck could read the handwriting on the wall, and corresponding
plans were quickly drawn up. General Ritchie, the Commander-in-Chief of
the 8th Army, briefed on 16 May that his attack objective was the destruction
of the enemy's armored forces in the Gazala–Tobruk–Bir Hacheim area. That
would be his first step in retaking Cyrenaica.

The British defensive positions stretched from the coast at Ain el Gazala
some 60 kilometers south to Bir Hacheim, which served as the southernmost
defensive bulwark of the Gazala Line. Between those two localities was a series
of strongpoints, with gaps of up to 20 kilometers in between.

General Auchinleck, who visited Ritchie's headquarters on 20 May, was
asked what he thought Rommel might be up to. Auchinleck recommended
placing all of the 8th Army's armor on both sides of the *Trigh Capuzzo*, because
Rommel, "in all likelihood," would conduct a feint against Bir Hacheim so as
to then attack with the majority of his armored forces, the *DAK*, in the middle.
Moving though the minefields, the armor would then turn north so as to "to
surround the northern portion of the defensive blocking position and attack
Tobruk."

Ritchie, as well as his commanders, thought differently. General Norrie
was of the opinion the German attack would come in the north. Ritchie, on
the other hand, was almost certain that "Rommel, the clever fox, [would]
bypass Bir Hacheim to the south." For that reason, he positioned his armored
reserve, the 1st Armoured Division, in the middle of his defensive positions
west and southwest of El Adem. He directed the 7th Armoured Division even
further south.

In the end, Ritchie would be proven right.

PANZER-ARMEE AFRIKA PLANS ITS NEXT MOVES

Rommel was in one accord with his commanders when he thought he needed
to attack before the enemy did. On 20 May, he released an attack order for
Panzer-Armee Afrika:

The opening phase of the attack will be marked by a frontal attack
by the Italian divisions in the Gazala position. These divisions will
attack the British 50th [Infantry] Division and the South African [1st
Infantry] Division. Around the clock, efforts will be made to deceive

the enemy into believing large concentrations of armor are in the north. To that end, tanks and [other] vehicles will move in circles.

The intent is for the British armored formations to close up close behind their infantry formations.

By daylight, all movements of the motorized forces will be in the direction of the Italian infantry. It will not be until darkness that the motorized group will move to its actual staging areas.

The motorized group consists of the *DAK,* with the *15.* and *21. Panzer-Division,* the Italian XX Corps (Motorized), with the *Trieste* and *Ariete* Divisions, and the *90. leichte-Afrika-Division,* which is attached to the Italians. In turn, the *90. leichte* will have all three of the divisional reconnaissance battalions attached to it.

The start of the advance is 2200 hours. It will go around Bir Hacheim. From there, the *DAK* and the Italian XX Corps will advance via Acroma to the coast, in order to interdict the lines of communication and eliminate the British divisions in the Gazala position, as well as the British armored formations assembled there.

The *90. leichte* advances with its three attached reconnaissance battalions into the El Adem–Belhamed area and prevents the garrison of Tobruk from withdrawing and well as the bringing up of reinforcements from the Acroma area. In addition, the British are to be separated from their supply depots that they have established in the area east of Tobruk.

Following the rapid destruction of the 8th Army in Marmarica, the rapid taking of Tobruk is planned.

FRONTAL ATTACK AND "HORIZON" MOVE

On the morning of 26 May 1942, the fire plan of the corps artillery was executed against the forward British positions. When the opening preparation was shifted further to the rear, *Ju 87's* and *Ju 88's* arrived and dove on Tobruk, El Adem, Bir Hacheim, and the other "boxes" the British had constructed. At Gambut, 60 *MC 202's* attacked the British airfield and damaged a number of aircraft based there.

Four Italian divisions—*Sabratha, Trento, Brescia,* and *Pavia*—attacked. Assaulting with them were the men of *Oberst* Menny's *Schützen-Brigade 15* of the *90. leichte-Afrika-Division,* which had been detached from the division to support the Italians.

The soldiers of the former *Afrika-Regiment*—now redesignated as *Panzergrenadier-Regiment 361*—advanced rapidly and were soon among the British strongpoints.

The attack by *Panzer-Armee Afrika* had started. But for the enemy, he was still uncertain whether the German operations were part of a deception campaign or the real thing.

After the onset of darkness, the *DAK* and the XX Corps (Motorized) set out from their staging areas around North Segnali towards the southeast. The *15.* and *21. Panzer-Division* were in the middle, with the *90. leichte-Afrika-Division* on the right and the Italian corps on the left. The advance moved rapidly, and the mighty armada of armor soon found itself in a gigantic cloud of dust. The tanks of the lead divisions were churning up the fine sand. The 10,000 tracked and wheeled vehicles that followed made it many times worse. The desert, which was usually silent at night, echoed with the reverberations of thousands of engines and the grinding of tracks. The formation moved, tightly concentrated, navigating by compass. The drivers were practically blind. They were guided by the tank commanders standing in the open hatches, who shouted down directions. Guides sat on the fenders of the vehicles. There were collisions and near misses. The damaged vehicles were pulled off to the side, and the advance continued.

As it turned day, the armada had made the turn past the fortress of Bir Hacheim. The reconnaissance battalions moved ahead. Broadly dispersed, the tanks of the armor regiments followed. Behind them were the artillery and the headquarters staffs. Bringing up the division rear were the motorized riflemen, the engineers, the antitank forces, the *Flak* elements, and other divisional troops.

Moving between and up front with the divisions was the headquarters of the *DAK*, which had been under the command of *Generalleutnant* Nehring since March.

In all, 560 tanks of *Panzer-Armee Afrika,* including those of the *Ariete* Division, were rolling north and northeast through the morning haze. For the first time since it had arrived in Africa, *Panzer-Regiment 8* had all of its authorized equipment and was rolling together with all 150 tanks. Each of the two battalions moved in an inverted wedge that was 3 kilometers wide and 1.5 kilometers deep. *Oberstleutnant* Teege was the regimental commander.

Suddenly, a report: "Tanks ahead!"

From 3 kilometers away, the tanks appeared from out of a depression. Teege informed his battalion commanders to be prepared to engage. It was formations of the British 4th Armoured Brigade, which had just been equipped with the U.S.-built "General Lee" medium tank.

Teege ordered his formations to move out, with the 1st Battalion attacking frontally.

The German tanks started rolling to within range. Before they could get there, they were engaged by the longer 75-mm main guns of the General Lee's.

"Move under it! Get Closer!" *Hauptmann* Kümmel ordered his battalion. The German tanks rolled forward, but they were stopped.

"We need artillery!" Kümmel radioed back to the battalion. The request for artillery support was passed up the line.

To the left of *Panzer-Regiment 8*, *Panzer-regiment 5* had also rolled into combat under its new commander, *Oberst* Gerhard Müller. In advancing, one of the battalion commanders, *Major* Martin, received a direct hit.

Oberstleutnant Teege had his *II./Panzer-Regiment 8* make a broad sweep around the side of the enemy force. While Kümmel's men distracted the enemy with their fires and their constant changes of course, the 2nd Battalion succeeded in flanking the enemy, catching him by surprise when it opened fire. The first few Lee's went up in flames; others were immobilized. At the same moment, Kümmel had his tanks advance. They advanced into the maelstrom and stopped to open fire at a distance of only 600 meters. At that range, the German main-gun rounds also penetrated the frontal armor. Fires blazed. One after the other of the enemy tanks was set alight. The 8th Hussars, the steel core of the 4th Armoured Brigade, lost 16 Lee's there before pulling back.

At that moment, the staff car of the division commander, *General* Gustav van Vaerst, pulled up. Vaerst was standing in the open-topped vehicle. *Leutnant* Max Keil, the acting commander of the *1./Panzer-Regiment 8* called out: "Where to, *Herr General?*"

Before Vaerst could answer, his adjutant replied: "There . . . where Rommel is!"

Soon thereafter, the men could hear Rommel's voice on their radios: "Close up and follow me!"

The joint German-Italian force continued north. The *90. leichte-Afrika-Division*, minus the detached *Schützen-Brigade 15* but with the attached three reconnaissance battalions, steered a course directly for El Adem.

All of the formations were advancing full speed ahead and it appeared that Rommel's gambit had paid off, when 60 British tanks attacked from the east. They rolled right into the flank of the *15. Panzer-Division*. The division's tanks were far ahead, however, and could do nothing to stop the British armor. A panic started to break out.

Nehring, who was with *Oberst* Wolz, the commander of *Flak-Regiment 135*, suddenly saw himself surrounded by retreating soldiers. Wolz immediately employed his 8.8-centimeter *Flak*. Widely dispersed, the guns were moving across the open terrain that was devoid of cover or concealment. They stopped whenever an enemy tank appeared, and fired from the still-limbered guns. Soon, the battlefield was covered with the smoking wrecks of Lee's. The enemy artillery started to reply, and it was only a matter of time before they would be able to register on the exposed guns. Wolz broke off the engagement. He had bought time and stopped the enemy flanking maneuver. He sent his guns forward to rejoin the main combat elements of the *DAK*.

When the guns rejoined the corps headquarters, they were soon busy again. Dispersing at an interval of 150 meters, they went into position. It was not a moment too soon, because the first tanks of a group of 35 started to appear from out of the thick dust at a distance of approximately 1,500 meters. The first salvo from the *Flak*, shattered four of the enemy's number. The remaining halted and then pulled back.

At that decisive moment, *Major* Gürke, the commander of the *I./Flak-Regiment 43*, appeared, bringing with him the six guns of his 2nd Battery. They were inserted into the improvised line to the left. Half an hour later, the *3./Flak-Regiment 43* also showed up as reinforcement. It was brought forward by the field army's adjutant, on Rommel's direct orders. With the additional guns, the Germans had a established a *Flak* "front" of nearly 3 kilometers. For the first time in history, antiaircraft weapons would help decide a major engagement.

The enemy attacked with his tanks again. When he had closed to within 1,200 meters, the *Flak* opened fire. Sixteen guns fired as one. The Lee tanks that received direct hits blew apart. Others were immobilized and then destroyed for good with the next salvo. As it turned dark along the front, there were 24 knocked-out British tanks left behind on the battlefield.

The 4th Armoured Brigade was effectively destroyed. It had been intended for it to block any advance of the Germans.

The *DAK* and the Italians continued to advance, parallel to the Gazala Line. The *21. Panzer-Division* reached Acroma on 28 May and was on the *Via Balbia* with its lead vehicles. Soon, patrols were standing at the Mediterranean.

By the 29th of May, a crisis situation started to develop for the Germans. Bir Hacheim, the southernmost outpost of the British defenses, which was manned by 4,400 Free French under the command of General Pierre König, had not fallen. Worse, tanks of the 1st Armored Division were approaching it from the east. The German forces east of the Gazala Line were being threatened with encirclement. Nehring, as well as Gause, Bayerlein, and Westphal, all recommended the Axis forces turn west, break through the British lines, and re-establish their lines of communications. The forces east of the Gazala line were running out of water and fuel. Even the wounded could not be evacuated. The situation only looked to get worse over the coming days.

With a heavy heart, Rommel agreed and decided to try to turn west through a gap in the Gazala Line that had yet to be reconnoitered.

While searching for that gap, the *DAK* ran into the desert fort of Got el Ualeb, which was manned by the British 150th Brigade. Operating on a reversed front, the *DAK* had to attack it from the east and take it. During the attack, the headquarters of the *DAK* was strafed. Nehring was not wounded, but his staff car was hit by shrapnel. The effort to take the fort at the first attempt failed. In addition to the 2,000 soldiers, there were some 80 Mark II's of the 1st Armored Brigade in support. The gap in the minefield, which had been created by the *Trieste* Division, was under constant artillery fire.

At the same time, the British Guards forces in the Knightsbridge strongpoint were fighting desperately against the reconnaissance forces attached to the *90. leichte-Afrika-Division.*

Because the German efforts did not seem to be going well, Ritchie radioed Cairo that Rommel was weakening. Auchinleck radioed back: "Bravo, 8th Army! Finish him off!"[4]

At Got el Ualeb, the Germans readied their second assault. *Panzer-Regiment 5* rolled out; when it finally withdrew, 12 of its tanks had been knocked out by the British antitank gunners. *Kampfgruppe Kiehl*, which was the next formation in the meat grinder, also attacked and failed, taking heavy losses in the heavy enemy defensive fires.

Nehring then ordered the *III./Schützen-Regiment 104* committed on the advice of his Chief-of-Staff, Bayerlein. The battalion had been the former *Kradschützen-Bataillon 15. Generalmajor* von Bismarck received the directive and went forward to conduct a leader's reconnaissance with *Major* Ehle, the battalion commander. In the middle of their reconnaissance, they were staffed by British fighters. Ehle was wounded and *Hauptmann* Reißmann assumed acting command of the battalion. He had the thankless mission of taking Got el Ualeb. Later on, he commented about the mission: "Everything hinged on getting ready in a hurry, moving forward rapidly, and keeping things going as quickly as possible."

At 0430 hours on 1 June, the battalion stood ready with a number of engineer, artillery, and *Flak* attachments. *Oberst* Crasemann, who had assumed acting command of the division from the wounded *Generalmajor* van Vaerst, wanted to launch an immediate attack, but the supporting weapons were slow to close up.

After the artillery finally arrived and opened its fires, the battalion attacked, mounted up, at 0715 hours. The battalion remained mounted until it had reached the half-way point to the desired point of penetration. When the men had approached to within 300 meters, they could identify the enemy positions behind the rolls of barbed wire. The enemy opened his fires. The men dismounted and worked their way forward in leaps and bounds.

---

4. Translator's Note: Reverse-translated.

Protected by 2-centimeter *Flak*, the engineers cleared two lanes for the two attack groups.

The penetration succeeded at 0800 hours, thanks to the platoon of *Oberleutnant* Köppe of the *11./Schützen-Regiment 104*. The company advanced further and reached the high ground, where it was able to bring its antitank guns forward. The enemy proceeded to place heavy machine-gun, mortar, and small-arms fire on the hill. Fifteen minutes later, however, the 9th Company of the same regiment succeeded in breaking through in its sector. The English launched an immediate counterattack, which was supported by two Mark II's, but it was turned back. The German attack then bogged down.

Major Beil, the commander of the *II./Artillerie-Regiment 155*, went forward during the crisis situation and looked for ways for his guns to engage the enemy defensive main effort. Although taking extremely heavy fire himself, he succeeded in locating the enemy's defensive focal point. He had his artillery reorganize and reposition itself and then had them rain down fires on the enemy position.

At 0835 hours, *Stukas* attacked the depths of the enemy fortifications and several enemy batteries were taken out by the dive bombers. It looked as though the Germans might succeed, after all.

Rommel appeared in the front lines in the sector of the righthand platoon and personally directed its continued advance. In a duel of hand grenades and bitter hand-to-hand combat, the enemy surrendered. Got el Ualeb had fallen, and the way west was clear for the *DAK*.

At this point, the *DAK* had only 130 operational tanks and Bir Hacheim was still holding out.

During the night of 1/2 June, Rommel committed the *90. leichte-Afrika-Division* and the *Trieste* Division against the southern bulwark. He intended to be personally involved in the attack. "Boys," he informed the assembled soldiers of the *I./Schützen-Regiment 115*, who would lead the attack, "this is just a good walk for you."

But the "walk" turned out to carry a lot of sacrifice with it. Rommel had parliamentarians attempt to convince the strongpoint to surrender before the attack, but when they were ignored, he gave the order to move out.

The men of the two divisions attacked. Once again, however, it was in vain.

Rommel had *Stukas* come in. The *I./Stukageschwader 3* attacked with 22 aircraft and obliterated some of the 1,200 dugouts. British fighters scrambled from Gambut and El Adem to intercept the dive bombers, including 11 "Tomahawks" of the South African squadron. The latter claimed 10 victims, with Captain Botha getting credit for three and a shared credit with Commander Beresfoord for a fourth. The *Stuka* group, on the other hand, reported the loss of only four aircraft. The rest returned, albeit with severe battle damage.

Kampfgruppe Wolz was then formed. It consisted of the consolidated *Flak* batteries of *Flak-Regiment 135, Aufklärungs-Abteilung 3 (mot.),* and *Panzerjäger-Abteilung 33. Oberst* Wolz's forces were employed against Bir Hacheim from the west. Covered by the dust of a *ghibli,* they closely approached the strongpoints before the enemy opened up with everything he had. That attack—conducted on 4 June—also came to a halt.

The next day, Rommel appeared at Wolz's command post and ordered the battle group to move to Bir Scerrara, northeast of Bir Hacheim. When Wolz and his men arrived there that afternoon, Rommel gave him a different mission: "Strong enemy forces have attacked the *Ariete* Division east of Got el Ualeb. The enemy has been turned back. The *DAK* will conduct a counterattack. Wolz, you will move out from here, move along the right flank of the *15. Panzer-Division,* take the *Trigh Capuzzo* east of Bellefaa, and prevent the enemy from retreating."

Rommel moved out with *Kampfgruppe Wolz.* To the east of Bir Harmat, the battle group ran into the enemy at 1830 hours. Wolz had his forces advance in leaps and bounds. With the last light of day, the four *Flak* batteries fired into a concentration of enemy armor. The *15. Panzer-Division* was also involved in the engagement on the left.

The fighting continued that night and into the morning of 6 June. The remainder of the enemy force turned away, leaving behind 50 tanks on the battlefield. The enemy had been defeated, and Rommel had succeeded once again in isolating an enemy force and shattering it.

On 6 June, *Hauptmann* Briel's *Fla-Bataillon 606,* along with some attached elements, was brought forward to Bir Hacheim. He had a motorized infantry battalion in support, as well as elements of *Panzerjäger-Abteilung 605.* Briel attempted to take the strongpoint with those forces in a frontal attack on 7 June. He failed.

The attack during the morning of 8 June also failed. He received two batteries from *Oberst* Wolz, which provided automatic cannon fire. The 2-centimeter cannon, which had been brought forward during the night in a lane cleared by engineers, were fixed in position at daybreak and had to dig in. Rommel personally called off that attack. He then had the command engineer for the *DAK, Oberst* Hecker, form a battle group. When Hecker stated that the forces he had available were insufficient, Rommel attached *Oberst* Menton's *Sonderverband 288* to him. The special-purpose formation had originally been earmarked for employment in Iraq.

Oberst Hecker had two groups attack Bir Hacheim in the afternoon. The attack was held up by British fighter-bombers. Then, on top of everything else, it entered a minefield. Of the 11 tanks that were supporting the attack, 6 were knocked out.

By the time evening fell, Hecker's men had worked themselves to within 500 meters of the main enemy fortifications. The mountain troopers in Menton's group got to a broad ditch. They jumped in and overwhelmed the defenders.

Early on 9 June, *Stukas* had been requested. *Oberst* Menton went forward into the minefield to observe the attack. The *Stukas* never arrived, and Menton's vehicle was identified and placed under fire. When he attempted to get out quickly, his vehicle ran over a mine, in the process of which Menton was wounded. When Rommel went to his location, the experienced combat engineer from the First World War told him: "Give me a battalion of mechanized infantry, and I'll do it!"

Oberst Bayerlein convinced Rommel, who had already decided to give up the efforts to take Bir Hacheim, to try one more time, this time with *Oberstleutnant* Baade's *Schützen-Regiment 115*. The attack started on 10 June and, by that evening, the motorized riflemen had entered the enemy's defensive system.

That night, the men of Bir Hacheim attempted to break out. The breakout effort was met by *Kampfgruppe Briel,* which knew about the operation from a prisoner. Briel had all of his guns trained on the breakout point. After the war, he told the author of his experiences during that night:

> I had all available tracer ammunition loaded into the magazines and belts. When I fired a designated pyrotechnic, we opened fire. A special surprise there was the use of the first six *MG 42's* we had, which had been "organized"[5] from the Army High Command by a few of my men.
>
> At midnight, we heard the loud sounds of engines coming from Bir Hacheim. There was the sound of tracks rattling among them. When the enemy fired smoke rounds to hide himself, I elbowed my messenger, *Gefreiter* Batz: "Go on, fire the pyro!"
>
> The terrain was lit up by the green star cluster with the red tracer. All hell broke loose the same instant. The artificial smoke did not help the legionnaires of General König at all. For the first time, the *MG 42* barked out with its 25 rounds a second.
>
> There was bitter close-in fighting at other points on the siege ring with the legionnaires, who were attempting to break out. Only

---

5. Translator's Note: "Organized" was German military slang for obtaining equipment or materiel unofficially, much as the term "procured" is used in the U.S. Army.

half of them were able to get through and fight their way through to the lines of the English 7th Brigade.

The next morning, *Oberst* Baade's riflemen entered the fortress. There were a dozen medics there and some 500 wounded.

The fighting for Bir Hacheim was over. *Generaloberst* Rommel acted without hesitation. He turned the tide when he had almost met his end himself a few days previously. He issued his next orders: "Tobruk! Everyone on to Tobruk!"

ON TO TOBRUK

While the fighting around Bir Hacheim was raging, the enemy tried to deliver his own deadly blow there as early as 6 June. The 2nd and 22nd Armoured Brigades attacked the *Ariete* Division after a one-hour artillery preparation. The Indian 10th Brigade and the 201st Guards Brigade also joined the attack.

To deceive the Germans of their intentions, the British had also attacked the sector of the *21. Panzer-Division* to the north. In that sector, the 4th Armored Brigade and the 2nd Royal Tank Regiment were committed.

The Italians had to fall back under the enormous pressure. They finally came into range of the field army's artillery, which succeeded in stopping the British attack.

Panzer-Regiment 8 conducted an immediate counterattack in the direction of Bir el Tamar, where Rommel had also gone with *Kampfgruppe Wolz*. The next day, the *21. Panzer-Division* was afforded the opportunity to inflict heavy casualties on the enemy. The British pulled back to the east, and the German armored division immediately pursued. The *21. Panzer-Division* did not afford the enemy any chance to establish himself anywhere.

General Ritchie had planned on decimating *Panzer-Armee Afrika* in a series of battles of attrition and then eliminating it completely. His calculations misfired, despite good opportunities initially. According to the Official History:

> General Rommel had estimated with great exactness the forces necessary to defend their positions and hoped that the British would exhaust their strength, which is what actually happened. With the ability unique to him to rapidly size up a battle, he quickly recognized that the enemy's plan had not succeeded, and he showed his capabilities in exploiting that advantage immediately.[6]

---

6. Translator's Note: This quote was reverse-translated, as are all of the other passages that were originally English in this section.

Because the German forces were freed up after the fall of Bir Hacheim, Rommel had *Panzer-Armee Afrika* immediately head to the northeast. The next attack objective was El Adem with its operationally important airfield. The "Desert Fox" committed the *15. Panzer-Division*, the *Ariete* Armored Division, and the *Trieste* Division against the airfield.

At the same time, the *21. Panzer-Division* was ordered to conduct a feint north of the ridgeline at Sidra and fix the British forces at the Knightsbridge strongpoint. The core of the British defense was to be bypassed and encircled.

By the evening of 11 June, the area south of El Adem had been reached.

In that critical situation, the two senior British commanders were not of like mind. While General Norrie was combining the armored brigades under the command of the 1st Armoured Division in order to stop the Germans with strong forces, Rommel was already having the *15. Panzer-Division* assault the 2nd and 4th Armoured Brigades from the south. He had also instructed the *21. Panzer-Division* to hit the enemy in the rear.

El Adem and the *Trigh Capuzzo* were taken. The defeat of the British armored forces was just a hair's breadth away. Rommel wrote about this in his diary:

> On the morning of 12 June, I had gone to a ridgeline southeast of El Adem with my battle staff and observed the course of the fighting from there that had flamed up between the *90. leichte-Afrika-Division* and the Indians. A British bomber formation uninterruptedly attacked and made it very difficult for the division. When I attempted to get to the *15. Panzer-Division* in the course of the morning, our vehicle was heavily engaged from the north *and* the south and held up for several hours. Because of that, I did not reach the *15. Panzer-Division* until the afternoon, which I then accompanied on its attack west. While doing that we were hit with bombs from *Stukas* in the evening.
>
> Once again, Bayerlein, the driver, and I escaped in one piece.

In the taking of El Adem by the *90. leichte-Afrika-Division*, the Indian 29th Brigade suffered heavy losses.

On the afternoon of that day that was so decisive in the fighting for Tobruk, General Ritchie radioed Cairo:

> We have no effective armored forces to counter Rommel's advance to the coast. If the Germans get to the sea, then our two most powerful divisions in the Gazala position, the South African 1st and the British 50th, will be cut off and lost.

Auchinleck immediately flew from Cairo to the headquarters of the 8th Army at Gambut. He ordered General Ritchie to continue the fighting in the Gazala–El Adem area until Rommel had "run out of gas." Prior to departing back to Cairo, he cabled London: "Atmosphere good here. The situation is being judged in a calm and decisive manner. The morale of the forces is good. Enemy intentions apparently have not gone according to plan."

The Prime Minister responded:

> I commend you decision to fight. Your success depends not only on
> your weapons but also on your willpower. God bless all of you.
> Winston Churchill

On 13 June, the fighting along the Gazala Line came to a close. The 201st Guards Brigade had to pull back from Knightsbridge, the core of the British defensive line. The tank elements that had been attached to the brigade suffered additional heavy losses during the withdrawal. Rommel and *Panzer-Armee Afrika* were the lords of the battlefield. Only one thing remained: Tobruk!

FROM THE RAMPARTS AND INTO THE FORTRESS

When General Ritchie announced the codeword "Freeborn" on 14 June, the South African 1st Infantry and the British 50th Infantry Divisions left their positions and headed towards Tobruk.

The *15. Panzer-Division* and the *21. Panzer-Division* moved out that morning to attack north. They wanted to clear the approach route and gain attack positions for the assault on Tobruk. The *90. leichte-Afrika-Division* advanced due east, with the *Ariete* and *Trieste* Division covering its flanks. Rommel followed in his command vehicle. The advance crawled to a snail's pace when a *ghibli* blew in, but the lead elements of the *15. Panzer-Division* reached the sea early in the morning of 15 June.

The *21. Panzer-Division* was turned to the east, so as to support the *90. leichte-Afrika-Division* and to attack El Adem, Batruna, and El Hatian, which were still holding out. The tanks of *Panzer-Regiment 5* had to soften up the pockets of resistance at Batruna, before the grenadiers of the light division could assault the strongpoint. Eight hundred British soldiers were taken prisoner. The light division's advance bogged down outside of El Hatian. *Oberstleutnant* Panzenhagen had attempted in vain to take the town with his *Panzergrenadier-Regiment 361* in a *coup de main*. The town, which had been transformed into a weapons-packed fortress, held out on 16 June. It was not until the morning of 17 June that it fell.

The *21. Panzer-Division* moved out against El Duda and Belhamed starting on 16 June and took both strongpoints. On 17 June, Rommel committed the light division against the few remaining holdouts among the British strongpoints. He ordered the *Ariete* Armored Division and the *DAK* to attack Gambut. Gambut fell on 18 June and the entire area between it and Tobruk was clear of the enemy. In Gambut, 15 intact British aircraft were captured. It was important for Rommel's plan to take Tobruk that the British airfield around the greater area of Gambut had been abandoned. Consequently, there would be no fighters available to attack the *Stukas* that would be bombing Tobruk.

On 17 June, the last British armored formation that could be committed against Rommel—the 4th Armoured Brigade of General Messervy—was decisively beaten. The 90 operational tanks of the brigade had been decimated by *Panzer-Regiment 5* and *Panzer-Regiment 8.* That evening, the headquarters of the brigade was taken prisoner along with some elements of the Indian 20th Brigade.

By the morning of 19 June, Rommel was able to assemble his forces on the southeast corner of the Tobruk defensive ring. The *90. leichte-Afrika-Division* received orders to continue on to Bardia.

The light division sent off a large number of radio messages as it raced east through the desert in an effort to deceive the British that the Germans were moving with all of their forces to the east and leaving Tobruk behind. The deception measure apparently worked. That afternoon, the 8th Army sent a message to Cairo: "Alert! Rommel is advancing on the Egyptian frontier!"[7]

To continue the deception, the Italian XXI Corps (Motorized) launched a feint against Tobruk from the west. The *DAK* and the XX Corps (Motorized) were to conduct the main attack on Tobruk from the southeast.

It was 0500 hours on 29 June 1942 when Rommel stood on a slight rise northeast of El Adem with *Oberstleutnant* Mellenthin from his staff. They were waiting for the opening phase to start: the attack from the air that was due to start at 0520 hours.

At exactly the appointed time, 80 *Stukas* appeared. Their job was to eliminate or incapacitate the fortifications in the desired area of penetration. Following them were 100 bombers, which had been loaded to the gills with bombs. The wire obstacles were destroyed. Mines went up in the air and rendered harmless. Mellenthin later wrote about his perception of the air attack:

> A gray cloud of dust and smoke rose over the section of front that had been attacked. While our bombs detonated in the English defensive

7. Translator's Note: Reverse-translated.

works, the German and Italian artillery joined together to deliver a huge, concentrated barrage.

At 0530 hours, the *21. Panzer-Division* rolled out, led by its commander, *Generalmajor* von Bismarck, as well as the *15. Panzer-Division*, still under the acting command of *Oberst* Crasemann. *Oberst* Menny led his *Schützen-Brigade 15* next to the tanks, followed by the soldiers of *Oberstleutnant* Panzenhagen's *Panzergrenadier-Regiment 361*.

Panzer-Regiment 5, led by the one-armed *Oberst* Müller, who had been christened *Panzer-Müller* by his tankers, blasted a path through the enemy armor. *Panzer-Regiment 8* likewise gave its all. By the time the two regiments reached the crossroads at Sidi Mahmud, they had knocked out a total of 50 enemy tanks. By evening, Fort Gabr Gasem was reached. Half an hour later, the soldiers at Fort Pilastrino surrendered. The area leading down to the city was reached, and Panzenhagen's Foreign Legionnaires stormed ahead to the airfield, which was taken by *Hauptmann* Klärmann's 2nd Battalion. Klärmann decided to continue on to the harbor. As it turned night, his soldiers had the harbor firmly in hand and had taken a few thousand prisoners.

One of the small assault detachments that was formed, for which Rommel was famous, was the *1./Flak-Regiment 617* of *Hauptmann* Hißmann. Initially, it was the division reserve of the *21. Panzer-Division* and kept near the division command post. When the riflemen started to receive machine-gun fire from the flanks, Hißmann's men fired back with their 2-centimter *Flak*, quickly quieting the pockets of resistance. In the afternoon, Hißmann attacked the enemy artillery that was firing with everything it had from the hills east of the harbor. The batteries were silenced, and a Colonel and his entire staff were taken prisoner.

Afterwards, the battery rolled into the city. After the war, Hißmann told the author of an encounter he had with Rommel:

On the way, we ran into Rommel, who was up front with his troops again. I reported and dropped off the English colonel. As I went to get back in my vehicle, Rommel called out: "You have a flat, Hißmann!"

"I know, *Herr Generaloberst*, but Tobruk has priority!"

"Go . . . go!" Rommel called out, and I took off.

The fighting in the city proper started. When Hißmann rounded a corner while standing in the first prime mover of his battery, he ran right into a British tank workshop. A tank opened fire at 300 meters. Hißmann felt the first round impact right behind his feet, flames shot into the air. A machine-gun started to fire as well. After a quick firefight with the remaining elements, both the tank and the machine-gun were silenced. A number of operational British tanks fell into Hißmann's hands in the maintenance facility.

The next morning, Hißmann and his battalion physician, *Dr.* Sydow, were ordered by the division commander to go over to the enemy forces still holding out and ask them to surrender. The tactic worked, and further bloodshed was spared.

Early that same morning, Rommel drove into Tobruk with his battle staff. He wrote the following in his diary:

> At 0940 hours, about 6 kilometers west of Tobruk, I met General Klopper, the commander of the South African 2nd [Infantry] Division and commander of the fortress (ever since 14 May).

Within 24 hours, Tobruk had fallen. The Germans took 33,000 prisoners in all. The path to Egypt was open for the divisions of *Panzer-Armee Afrika*, if Rommel wanted it. And how he wanted it! In his order-of-the-day for 21 June, this desire was unequivocally expressed:

> Soldiers!
> The great battle in Marmarica has been crowned by the rapid assault on Tobruk. In all, 45,000 prisoners were taken; more than 1000 tanks and almost 400 guns captured or destroyed . . .
> Now it is imperative to completely destroy the enemy. We will not rest until we have defeated the last elements of the 8th Army. Over the next few days I will demand great things of you once again so that we can obtain our objective.

ADVANCE ON MARSA MATRUH

"It was a great moment for Rommel and no goddess of fate whispered to him that he would never again experience a greater victory."[8]

Those words from the British Official History serve as a good introduction to this section. Although there were a few minor successes, the desired objective of Alexandria or possibly even Cairo would never be obtained.

Rommel, who was promoted to *Generalfeldmarschall* after the fall of Tobruk, was unleashed. For him, everything hinged on exploiting the victory. In the British camp, General Auchinleck relieved General Ritchie and personally took over command of the 8th Army.

8. Translator's Note: Reverse-translated.

On 22 June, Rommel went to Bardia, where the lead elements were resting. He issued orders to the *90. leichte-Afrika-Division* to continue to advance east. The light division was to assume the lead, followed by the two German armored divisions and the motorized Italian corps.

By means of captured documents, Rommel had discovered that the enemy intended to defend at Marsa Matruh. He wanted to prevent that and ordered a ceaseless pursuit. But by 24 June, the formations were suffering from a lack of fuel. It was not until the British supply dump at Habata was reached that they could refuel. The supply lines had grown to 1,500 kilometers. By 25 June, the area around Marsa Matruh was reached. During that critical period, the 8th Army owed a debt of gratitude to the Royal Air Force, since it was the primary reason Rommel's forces were held back.

The attack was continued with the light division in the north, the *21. Panzer-Division* in the center, and the *15. Panzer-Division* in the south. Due to a lack of fuel, the vehicles of the Italian XX Corps were left stranded.

On the morning of 26 June, there was a large engagement against strong enemy armored forces 40 kilometers southwest of Marsa Matruh. In and around the town proper, the Indian 50th Infantry Division and elements of the Indian 5th Infantry Division and the British 50th Infantry Division had set up for the defense.

In fighting against the British tanks, the two German tank regiments accounted for 18 vehicles. Nevertheless, the New Zealand 2nd Infantry Division was able to fight its way through the blocking positions of the *90. leichte-Afrika-Division* and reach Marsa Matruh.

On 27 June, elements of the defending force at Marsa Matruh attempted to break out to the east. A portion of the breakout force was stopped thanks to the fires of the *Littorio* Division, which had just arrived, and *Kampfgruppe Kiehl.* Nevertheless, a large portion of the New Zealanders were able to get out, heading due south.

During the morning of 28 June, Rommel was at the site of the British breakout effort. He ordered the *90. leichte-Afrika-Division, Aufklärungs-Abteilung 580, Kampfgruppe Menton*, elements of the two Italian corps, and assorted other battle groups to attack Marsa Matruh.

Stukas opened the attack at 1700 hours. It was the soldiers of *Oberstleutnant* Panzenhagen who were the first to start rolling up the enemy's bunkers and trenches. *Kampfgruppe Briehl,* the reinforced *Aufklärungs-Abteilung 3 (mot.),* knocked out some tanks attempting to escape. In a final effort, the legionnaires of Panzenhagen took the main defensive position. By the morning of 29 June, the town was in the hands of the attackers.

Rommel then sent all of his motorized formations in the direction of Fuka. On 29 June, Rommel gave Georg Briehl, a big man and one of his most trusted battle group commanders, a special mission: "Advance on Alexandria, Briehl. Afterwards, we'll have a cup of coffee together in the Sheppard Hotel in Cairo."

Five minutes after receiving the order, Briehl and his men took off. They took the designated objective of Alam Hiwig, 5 kilometers west of Fuka. Then, at 1802 hours, they reached the final objective for the day, a spot 25 kilometers west of El Daba. Once Briehl submitted his report, he was given a supplemental order: "Continue to advance on El Daba!"

At 2210 hours, Briehl had the following message radioed: "El Daba taken. Continuing to advance. Possibly as far as Sidi Abd el Rahman."

In an eerie movement by night, past British airfields and rearguard camps, Briehl reached the town around midnight. Up to that point, *Kampfgruppe Briehl* had covered 120 kilometers during the one day.

The next day, Briehl received another message from Rommel: "Hold the advance. Move back and pass lines through the *90. leichte-Afrika-Division*, which is closing up. Await further orders."

During the afternoon of that day, Rommel had assembled all of the commanders and commanding generals of his field army and issued the orders all of them expected: "Advance as quickly as possible through El Fajade to Cairo!"

THE FIGHTING FOR EL ALAMEIN

The divisions of the *DAK* rolled across difficult terrain in the middle of a sandstorm to the northeast. At 0230 hours on 1 July, Rommel left his command post at El Duba for the command post of the *DAK* to talk to Nehring. He then went on with his battle staff to Hill 31, where the new command post for the field army was to be established.

The enemy strongpoint at Deir el Abyad turned out not to be manned. But there were strong enemy forces in Deir el Shein. It was the freshly introduced Indian 18th Brigade that defended there. Despite its combat inexperience, it did a magnificent job of stopping the German advance until evening. It paid the price through its destruction, however. By doing so, it bought time for the British command to send antiaircraft and antitank guns to the remaining blocking positions.

Rommel participated in the attack of the light division He had personally brought forward *Kampfgruppe Kiehl*, which the division had requested. He later wrote about his experience, standing in the middle of the South African artillery fire with his Chief-of-Staff, *Oberst* Bayerlein:

British shells howled in from the north, east and south. Tracer rounds from the British antiaircraft guns buzzed through the formation. The attack bogged down in extremely heavy fire. We immediately dispersed concentrations of vehicles and took cover. Impact after impact resounded nearby. Bayerlein and I were fixed out there for two hours.

The fighting along the El Alamein front continued over the next few days. The attempt to break through to the coast on 2 July saw the two German armored divisions in a bitter struggle with some 100 enemy tanks and 10 batteries of artillery. General Auchinleck took personal command. The German attack did not make it through. It was repeated on 3 July. Once again, it bogged down in the face of massed artillery fires after some initial success.

On 3 July, the RAF flew 900 sorties against *Panzer-Armee Afrika*, four times as many as the *Luftwaffe* did. That evening, Rommel came to the conclusion that his forces needed a few days of rest so as to get back into fighting shape and make all of their weapons and equipment operational. His armored forces were in pitiful shape, reporting only 26 operational tanks. At the same time, the British 4th and 22nd Armoured Brigades could commit 100 between them. That evening, Rommel had situation reports submitted that stated that the divisions had trench strengths of only 1,000 to 1,500 men each.

The seemingly endless supply route made everything scarce: water as well as rations, ammunition as well as fuel. On top of all that, Rommel had to pull soldiers out of the rear-area services to serve up front. He later wrote:

During that time, I had to order every last German soldier out of encampments and rest camps and send him to the front, because the situation started to become extraordinarily critical.

By 8 July, a total of 50 tanks could be made operational within the *DAK*. Still, the personnel situation remained critical. Rommel: "In my opinion, the formations no longer deserved the designation of divisions."

Despite all that, Rommel remained optimistic. On 9 July, the *DAK* and the *Littorio* Armored Division assaulted the fortification at Quaret el Abd. When Rommel met Bismarck there, both of them agreed that it would be possible to continue far to the east from there, bringing about the fall of the El Alamein position that way.

But Rommel's confidence was not well founded. On the morning of 10 July, the British attacked the Italian positions at Tel el Eisa with the Australian 9th Infantry Division and rolled up their positions. Its assault groups then continued advancing, some passing near the command post of *Panzer-Armee Afrika* itself. The *Sabratha* Division was effectively destroyed. *Oberstleutnant* von Mellenthin quickly assembled a battle group consisting of soldiers from the headquarters and elements of *Infanterie-Regiment 382* of the *164. Leichte-Afrika-Division,* which had just been shipped over from Crete. At the last minute, he was able to stop the enemy advance.

The next day, however, elements of the *Trieste* Division were effectively destroyed. Tel el Eisa fell into enemy hands. Counterattacks fizzled out, and Rommel had to give up any offensive intentions in his northern sector.

Between 14 and 17 July, Auchinleck attempted to roll up the German positions along Ruweisat Ridge. The attack of the New Zealand 2nd Infantry Division early in the morning of 15 July did not succeed. Rommel had reinforcements hurriedly sent to that sector. They allowed the New Zealand 4th and 5th Brigades to approach closely before opening fire. The New Zealand division lost 1,405 men.

On 17 July, an English attack was launched against the *Trento* and *Trieste* Divisions. The penetration was sealed off and cleaned up in an immediate counterattack.

During the evening of 21 July, the Indian 5th Infantry Division attacked in the Deir el Shein sector. The New Zealanders moved out at the same time against El Mreir. The Allied attack bogged down, and the 23rd Armoured Brigade lost 87 fighting vehicles. The 2nd Armoured Brigade, which raced to help its sister formation, lost 21 combat vehicles.

The next Allied attack took place on 22 July, with the Australians hitting Tel el Eisa. They did not succeed. The Valentine tanks were stopped; 23 were knocked out.

The last of the attacks, conducted at the end of July, did succeed. Auchinleck committed the South African and Australian divisions at Mitireiya, but the casualties were high: a total of 1,000 men were lost.

After that round of heavy fighting on both sides, a break ensued. Through his intelligence services, Rommel learned that the enemy was replenishing his forces more and more. It was only a question of time before the 8th Army would move out offensively again.

On the German side, the aforementioned *164. leichte-Afrika-Division* had been shipped over from Crete. *Fallschirm-Brigade Ramcke,*[9] which had been formed for the invasion of Malta, was sent to Africa instead. It was sent to positions in the Qattara Depression at the southern end of the El Alamein position.

General Gott was designated to take command of the 8th Army. When he flew over the lines for a visual tour on 7 August 1942, he was shot down. He

---

9. Translator's Note: Parachute Brigade "Ramcke."

was succeeded by General Bernard Law Montgomery. He brought with him a new commanding general for the XXX Corps, Lieutenant General Brian Horrocks.

Rommel found himself in an extraordinarily difficult situation. He was at the outer extremes of the capabilities of his supply system and was no longer able to gain the initiative. Rommel decided to solve the dilemma in a typical manner for him: by attacking the southern part of the British positions, breaking through there, and then continuing on to Cairo and the Suez Canal. Of the several courses of action he was presented with, that was the most difficult one.

The easiest course of action would have been to simply retreat, a prospect he immediately dismissed. On the other hand, he knew that the Americans were supporting the British with enormous quantities of armaments, particularly tanks. The latest batch of tanks and guns had arrived in Egypt on 21 July. In addition, forty A 20 attack bombers, which had been earmarked for the Soviet Union, were diverted to the desert and it appeared the American war aid would take no end.

The German position continued to worsen. Among the German divisions of *Panzer-Armee Afrika*, there was a shortfall of 16,000 men. From 1 to 20 August, the field army consumed approximately twice as much as could be shipped over. There was a shortfall of 200 tanks, not to mention 175 reconnaissance-type vehicles and another 1,500 vehicles of all types.

Rommel did succeed in accomplishing one thing: he was relieved of the responsibility of reporting to General Bastico. He no longer needed to obtain nominal approval for his operations from the Italians. The only concession was the formation of an Italian liaison staff under General di Prun, which was responsible for addressing the administrative needs of the Italian forces under Rommel's command. In addition, the Italians sent one other division to the field, the *Folgore* Airborne Division, which, like *Fallschirm-Brigade Ramcke*, had been earmarked for the ill-fated attack on Malta.

Rommel believed he needed to attack if he were to have any chance at all of eliminating the enemy before he assumed overwhelming numerical superiority. He saw the end of August, with its nights of a full moon, as the best time. His attack plan was similar to the one he had had in May, when he marched around Bir Hacheim. The northern sector would remain static, while a feint would be launched against Ruweisat Ridge in the center. The *DAK* would then proceed to move to force a breakthrough along the right wing in the south. To that end, he had his old stand-bys, the *15.* and *21 Panzer-Division*, as well as mobile forces of the *90. leichte-Afrika-Division*.

In order to execute the plan, the *DAK* had to move at night through 50 kilometers of unfamiliar and heavily mined terrain!

The long-range objectives were ambitious: Bismarck's *21. Panzer-Division* was to advance on Alexandria and go around the city; the *15. Panzer-Division* and the *90. leichte-Afrika-Division* were to advance directly on Cairo. The Italian XX Corps (Motorized) would then be brought forward to relieve the German forces. Van Vaerst's *15. Panzer-Division* was to then advance on the Suez Canal, with the Italian forces securing the Nile Valley.

Rommel's plan called for advancing through Alam el Halfa. General Auchinleck had practically read Rommel's mind, however. Montgomery had the fortifications around Alam el Halfa vastly improved, to include protecting it from the rear. Two brigades of the 44th Infantry Division were brought into position. The 22nd Armoured Brigade was added to the mix, with its tanks dug in along the western slope of the ridge.

To the north, the 23rd Armoured Brigade was positioned as a mobile reserve. The 8th Armoured Brigade was established along the eastern side of the triangular fortress. The trap was also set to the south, where the 7th Armoured Division was waiting in the event Rommel attacked. The British were well prepared.

THE BEGINNING OF THE END

The soldiers of *Panzer-Armee Afrika* heard Rommel's order-of-the-day read to them on 30 August:

> Soldiers!
> Today the field army, reinforced by new divisions, moves out again to finally destroy the enemy
>   I expect that every soldier of my field army gives it his all during these decisive days.
> Rommel

The divisions of the *DAK* rolled out at 2000 hours. At the time it moved out, the *15. Panzer-Division* had 70 operational combat vehicles, the *21. Panzer-Division* 120.

Initially, the advance moved rapidly. Then, around midnight, the formations ran into a deeply echeloned minefield. The obstacle was covered by artillery, tanks, and infantry, and the British opened fire. The first few mines went up. Nehring rolled over a mine in his command vehicle, and he was wounded. *Oberst* Bayerlein escaped death because a radio set had intercepted the shrapnel where he was sitting. *Generalmajor* von Bismarck was killed at the head of his forces. The RAF flew sorties and started bombing the stalled elements of the *DAK*. At first light, fighter-bombers appeared.

Oberst Bayerlein assumed temporary command of the *DAK*, until van Vaerst could arrive. Van Vaerst, in turned, handed over the reins of his division to *Oberst* Crasemann, who had been in that position before.

All of 31 August was taken up with fighting from the middle of those minefields. Rommel's intent—to advance 50 kilometers the first night—was rendered null.

The "big solution" that Rommel had envisioned was most certainly out of the question. *Panzer-Armee Afrika* had to swing north earlier than planned and, as a result, ran into Alam el Halfa.

The attack against the ridge started in the middle of a *Ghibli* at 1300 hours. Progress was initially good, but the Italian divisions bogged down.

The attack was continued on 1 September by the *15. Panzer-Division*. Hans Kümmel, who had been promoted to *Major* and given official command of the *I./Panzer-Regiment 8*, was able to push the enemy back and advance to just in front of Hill 132. Then he had to stop due to a lack of fuel. It was then the turn of *Panzer-Regiment 5* of the *21. Panzer-Division*, but its attack was halted in the face of the strong British defensive positions.

That evening, Rommel had to call off his attack on Alam el Halfa. The divisions pulled back slowly to their jumping-off positions. Montgomery, the stony calculator, did not pursue Rommel. He stayed where he was.

The promised fuel for *Panzer-Armee Afrika* did not arrive. Of the 5,000 tons, half of it had been sunk on ships and 1,500 were still in Italy. Only 1,000 tons were inbound.

The Germans pulled back on 3 September and established defensive positions at Ron Shiag on the coast and running south through Tel el Eisa and Deir el Shein to the west of Deir el Munassib and then on to the Qattara depression. The six-day gamble had cost the Germans 2,910 men, 49 tanks, 55 field pieces and antitank guns, and 395 vehicles of all types.

Alam el Halfa was the turning point in the desert war. Without possessing air superiority or even parity, Rommel had attempted to conduct an armored battle and lost. He later wrote:

Anyone, even those with the most modern of means, who attempts to fight against a foe who has complete air superiority, is fighting like a bushman against modern European forces—with the same chances and under the same conditions

The fronts grew static and Rommel, who had been in Africa for 18 months without interruption, took the opportunity to fly to Germany to have a throat infection treated that threatened to become chronic. He felt comfortable in doing that since the enemy would not be able to attack before November, according to intelligence reports.

Rommel departed on 22 September, with a stop at the Adriatic town of Forli to visit Mussolini. He then went on to Rastenburg, where he reported to Hitler on 29 September. It was then that he started his cure in Vienna.

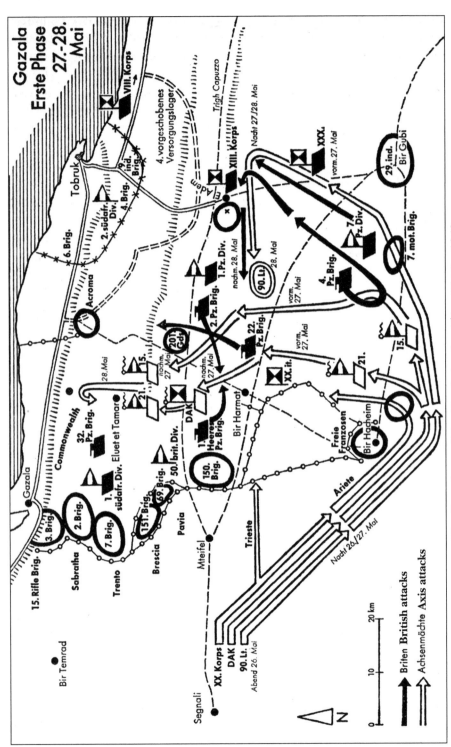

The first phase of the Gazala battles, 27 to 28 May 1942.

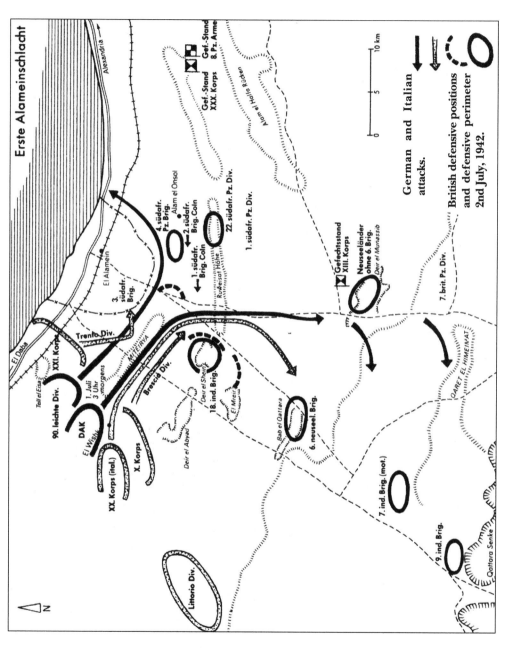

The first battle of El Alamein, 1 to 22 July 1942.

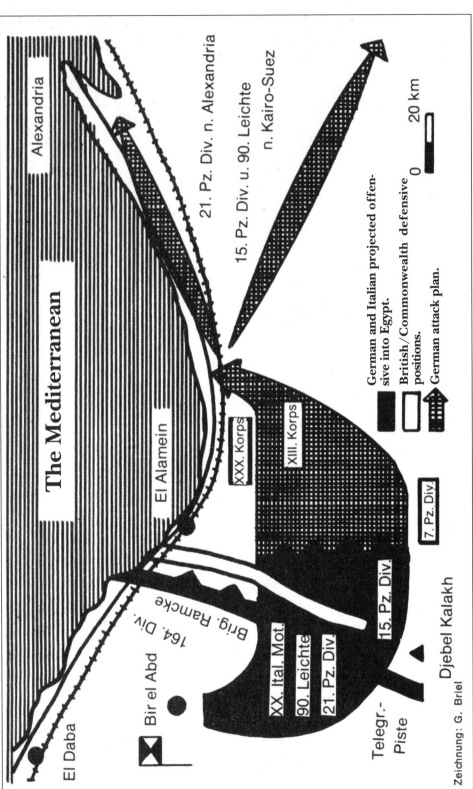

The German/Italian projected offensive into Egypt, with the objective of capturing Alexandria and seizing the Suez Canal.

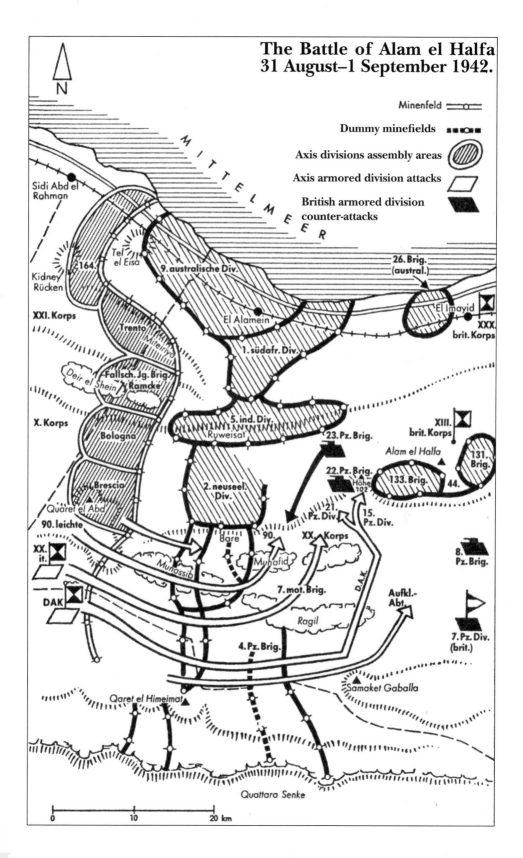

The Battle of Alam el Halfa
31 August–1 September 1942.

N

Minenfeld	▭▭○▭
Dummy minefields	▰▰▰◻▰▰
Axis divisions assembly areas	⬭
Axis armored division attacks	▱
British armored division counter-attacks	◆

MITTELMEER

Sidi Abd el Rahman

Tel el Eisa

164.

Kidney Rücken

9. australische Div.

26. Brig. (austral.)

El Imayid

XXX. brit. Korps

XXI. Korps

Trento Miteiriya

El Alamein

1. südafr. Div.

Deir el Shein

Fallsch. Jg. Brig. Ramcke

X. Korps

Bologna

5. ind. Div.
Ruweisat

23. Pz. Brig.

XIII. brit. Korps

Alam el Halfa

131. Brig.

22. Pz. Brig.
Höhe 102

133. Brig.

44.

Brescia

Quaret el Abd

2. neuseel. Div.

21. Pz. Div.

15. Pz. Div.

XX. Korps

90. leichte

Bare

90.

Munassib

Muhafid

D.A.K.

8. Pz. Brig.

XX. it.

DAK

7. mot. Brig.

Ragil

Aufkl.-Abt.

7. Pz. Div. (brit.)

4. Pz. Brig.

Samaket Gaballa

Qaret el Himeimat

Quattara Senke

| 0 | 10 | 20 km |

Carro Veloce 35 tankettes of the Italian *Ariete* armored division.

Award ceremony for the Sollum battle, from left: *Leutnant* Adam, *Lieutnant* Weiss, *Leutnant* Liestmann, and *Feldwebel* Pirath of *II./Panzer-Regiment 8*.
All four soldiers were killed in action on 23 November 1941 at Sidi Rezegh in combat with the British 7th Armoured Division.

Theodor Schwabach of *I./ Flak-Regiment 33 (mot.)*, after the award of the Knight's Cross to the Iron Cross.

Road sign on the *Via Balbia*, the main east/west highway in North Africa.

Rommel (center) in conference with German and Italian staff officers near Tobruk, June 1942.

Rommel (left) and *Generalmajor* von Bismark survey the battlefield from a command vehicle.

Christmas celebrations in the desert, a very different environment than the European winter. Small touches like this were very important for troop morale.

Rommel with his headquarters staff in the field.

"For you the war is over": prisoners from the Indian Division.

A prisoner-of-war collection site at Mechili. Some of the soldiers do not look too unhappy to be captured. Both sides treated their prisoners well.

A birthday party on 20 March 1942 for *General* Crüwell at Umm Er Rezem. From left: *Oberst* Menny, *Oberst* Bruer, an intelligence officer of the *DAK*, *Generalmajor* von Bismark, *Hauptmann* Johannes Kümmel, *Oberst* Gerhard Müller, *Oberstleutnant* Pfeiffer, and *Oberst* Herbert Ewerth.

Generaloberst Rommel in conversation with *Oberst* Müller at Umm Er Rzem.

These two photo-
graphs show Rommel
visiting a motorized
heavy infantry-gun
company. Rommel
was almost always in
the front lines.

Rommel in conference with
General Bastico, commander
of the Italian forces.

Rommel as a *Generalfeldmarschall.*
In this formal portrait, he is holding the elaborate Field Marshal's
baton.

On 21 June 1942, the day Tobruk finally fell, Rommel was promoted to *Generalfeldmarschall*.

CHAPTER 9

Eagles over the Desert

THE WINTER FIGHTING

At the start of the fighting in November 1941, the pinnacle of which was the major tank engagement at Sidi Rezegh on *Totensonntag*, *General* Fröhlich, the *Luftwaffe* commander in Africa, had a number of difficulties at his headquarters in Derna. During the fall, the enemy had considerably reinforced his air forces and enjoyed air superiority over the Axis forces. During the day, it was unusual for German or Italian air power to project much beyond the immediate confines of the front lines. Only aerial reconnaissance was continued over enemy territory on a longer-ranger basis.

After the war, Fröhlich provided the author with a firsthand account of those times:

> With the turbulent state of affairs at the time, special attention had to be paid to reconnaissance of the battlefield. That mission fell to the destroyers. Flying at low altitude and employed by squadron, they were charged with finding the enemy in his assembly areas or his approach marches and engaging him. A particular goal of mine was to have destroyers over the areas of fighting in as short a period as possible and at equally short intervals.
>
> Based on the targeting of the destroyers, the *Stuka* formations were employed. Fighters flew escort over the battlefield and conducted combat reconnaissance at the same time. The group of *Ju 88's* on hand was also used in a close-support role.
>
> In the middle of November, there was some severe weather, which lasted two days. After the sand cover on the ground was saturated, the basin-like areas around the *wadis* were changed into large water reservoirs, which attempted to empty themselves into the lowest point of the *wadis*. As a result, great waves of water came crashing through the *wadis* and pushed everything out of their path. The tent encampments of the *Luftwaffe* in Derna were flooded within a few minutes. A few soldiers drowned in the process.
>
> These catastrophic weather conditions had also taken their toll on the airfield at Derna. A portion of the taxiing area was under

water. Apart from that disastrous storm, however, there was constant good flying weather during that period of fighting.

Three times during the withdrawal in December, Fröhlich's men had to take off right in front of the enemy, some of whom had also gone past his airfields.

During the withdrawals, *Oberfeldwebel* Otto Schulz was one of the most successful fighter pilots. He shot down two aircraft on 30 November. One of them was the famous British pilot, Neville Duke, who was able to survive unwounded after a belly landing near Tobruk. He was up and flying again on 4 December, when 21 Hurricanes from the South African Air Force 1st Squadron and the 274th Squadron encountered a large number of *Stukas* and their German and Italian cover. In the ensuing aerial combat, Duke shot down a MC 200 and a Ju 87. In all, some seven Ju 87's, three Bf 109's, two G 50's and a MC 200 were shot down by the Allied pilots that day.

One of the most important destroyer pilots of the time was *Major* Kaschka, the commander of the *III./Zerstörergeschwader 26*. He particularly distinguished himself during the fighting at Sidi Rezegh. During his last sorties there, he took out a column of British trucks and their two armored car escorts. Based on the latest research, he was shot down by Sergeant Dodds around 1400 hours on 4 December. *Oberleutnant* Wehmeyer immediately landed next to the crash site, but *Major* Kaschka was near death; his radio operator, *Unteroffizier* Mühlhäuser, was already dead.

On the next day, 5 December, there was another so-called "*Stuka* party." Twenty-five Tomahawks from the 112th and 250th Squadrons encountered around 40 *Stukas* south of El Adem. They had 30 fighter escorts. While the 112th Squadron involved the fighters in a wild dogfight, the 250th Squadron took on the *Stukas* and shot down 15 of them. Flight Lieutenant Caldwell had five of them to his credit alone. Duke, however, was shot down again, escaping injury but forced to make a crash landing. The German fighters under *Hauptmann* Redlich shot down five of the Tomahawks.

On 6 December, *Oberfeldwebel* Schulz and *Leutnant* Marseille each scored two victories. In the middle of December, Hans Stahlschmidt shot down three Boston medium bombers. He was then grounded to become the group's adjutant. It was not until the new year that he climbed into a cockpit again.

On 13 December, *Oberfeldwebel* Albert Espenlaub had to make an emergency landing in the desert after an aerial duel. He was taken prisoner and killed when attempting to escape. He had a total of 14 aerial victories on Africa.

Schulz continued making a name for himself. He scored a "kill" on 15 December, three on 20 December, and several more in January.

The fighter pilots of the *I./Jagdgeschwader 27*, called "Neumann's colorful crowd," celebrated New Year's in Agedabia. Morale was miserable that night until *Leutnant* Stahlschmidt brought a bottle of cognac into the tent. It was a present to the 3rd Squadron from its commander. The mood suddenly changed.

The withdrawal continued. By the middle of January, the area around El Agheila had been reached. At the time, all of *Jagdgeschwader 53*, a *Ju 88* group, a destroyer group, and three *Stuka* groups were based on the airfields around that town and the *Arco dei Fileni*.

After the establishment of the headquarters of the Commander-in-Chief South under *Generalfeldmarschall* Kesselring, Air Command "Africa" no longer reported to the *X. Flieger-Korps. Generalmajor* Fröhlich reported directly to Kesselring's headquarters from then on. In January, Fröhlich was promoted to *Generalleutnant.*

After several victories on 13 January 1942, *Oberfeldwebel* Schulz was reported as missing south of Agedabia. The next day, however, he returned to his base on foot. The man seemed to have incredible luck!

In the middle of November, the RAF had 97 operational fighters and 28 bombers. By 17 December, 25 fighters and 28 bombers had been repaired and made operational, bringing the total number of aircraft to 122 fighters and 56 bombers. The German fighter formations, including the machines of the fighter-bomber elements and the *7./Zerstörergeschwader 26*, had a total of 83 aircraft, of which 26 were operational on 15 January 1942.

LONG-RANGE MISSION AGAINST FORT LAMY

During 1940 and 1941, the British special forces had been causing havoc behind Axis lines by raiding airfields and carrying out vital reconnaissance missions, which helped the British commanders to both plan their defenses and attack Axis supply lines. A special air unit—*Sonderkommando Blaich*—was set up under *Hauptmann* Theo Blaich, who had been a wealthy plantation owner and adventurer in Africa before the war, to counter the British Long-Range Desert Group and Special Air Service in the desert. The small unit consisted of a *Bf 108* and an *He 111.*

The Free French held the outpost of Fort Lamy in Chad, some 2,500 kilometers from the southernmost bases of the *Luftwaffe* in Africa. The fort was of major strategic importance to the Allies, as it was the main supply point inland from the African west coast ports and oilfields. It was also a vital supply depot for the Allied special forces. In light of Rommel's planned offensive in January, it was decided to bomb the fort and attempt to interrupt the operations of the LRDG and the SAS.

On 21 January, the small force took of for a flight into the unknown. The crew on board the *He 111* consisted of Blaich, *Leutnant* Bohnsack, *Feldwebel* Geißler, *Unteroffizier* Wichmann, and *Leutnant* Dettmann, a war correspondent. The bomber's first stop was for fuel at the tiny Italian air strip at the Hun Oasis. Blaich was greeted there by Major *Conte* Vimercati-Sanseverino, who had flown a Savoia there on 20 January. The Italian major had brought fuel with him for the return trip to the north for the German aircraft. He also joined the crew on the *He 111* for its continued flight south.

The small force started out again that same afternoon. Soon, Blaich had the crew assume combat stations. Fort Lamy appeared on the horizon with its airfield and gigantic fuel depot for the British forces in Africa.

Sixteen 50-kilogram bombs left the racks and tumbled earthward. The aircraft turned to observe and watched them hammer into the bays and storage tanks. Gigantic clouds of smoke raced skyward. All of the stored fuel went up in the air, some 400,000 liters of aviation fuel, as well as all of the various oils and lubricants. Ten aircraft were also destroyed on the ground. The one bomber had achieved a remarkable success; Fort Lamy was incapacitated for a number of weeks.

The *He 111* and *Bf 108* turned north, followed by antiaircraft fire from the completely surprised defenders, who had only then started to recover. Four hours went by; the sun sank. *Campo Uno*, the airfield in the oasis, was nowhere to be seen. The pilot informed Blaich that they needed to land.

The aircraft set down safely in the desert and the radio operator, *Unteroffizier* Wichmann, immediately began sending out an SOS from the presumed location, about 120 kilometers south of Agedabia. The attempts to reach Air Command "Africa" did not succeed at first. But Wichmann persevered and finally got contact 48 hours later.

Generalleutnant Fröhlich prepared to have a rescue operation launched immediately, but a sandstorm prevented the crews from taking off. The *ghibli* was raging at the location of *Sonderkommando Blaich* as well. Each of the six men was rationed at a quarter of a liter of water twice a day. On Sunday, 25 January, Blaich had an extra quarter liter issued as a "Sunday surprise." But Monday passed as well, without a single aircraft being sighted. On Tuesday, 27 January, the last drop of water had been issued. Exactly three minutes later, *Leutnant* Bohnsack spotted an aircraft.

"Fire pyro . . . quick . . . quick!" he called out.

The flares rose skyward. The aircraft turned towards them and landed. It was an Italian S 1, a short-range reconnaissance aircraft, that had ventured in their direction. The radio operator, Skorzone, jumped out of the aircraft and ran over to the men with two full two-liter canteens.

"We'll come back tomorrow and bring you fuel," he said. "*Campo Uno* is only a half hour by air from here."

"I always imagined angels as bigger and with wings on their shoulders," Wichmann joked. "Now I know what a real angel looks like!" All of the men felt laughter well up in them, as the watched the small aircraft take off so as to reach the camp before nightfall.

The next morning, another aircraft appeared over them It was a *Ju 52*, flown by *Oberleutnant* Becker of the desert rescue services. He had taken off on his own at midnight in order to look for the men. Not only had he found them, he was able to land safely and give them the three barrels of fuel he had on board so they could refuel the aircraft and return to their home base.

The bombing raid, which had been such a terrific success but appeared to be headed for a tragic ending, was over.

DUELS UNDER A HOT SUN

January 1942 passed by. Assisting their comrades in the *Luftwaffe* were the pilots, air crews, and ground personnel of the *Regia Aeronautica*. They were committed into the aerial fighting over the desert from bases at the *Arco dei Fileni*, Tamet, Sorman, and Castelbenito.

On 8 February, *Leutnant* Marseille was credited with 4 "kills," bringing his tally up to 40 and making him the most successful German ace in Africa. *Oberfeldwebel* Schulz was not far behind with 37 "kills." On 12 February, he scored another and, on the next day, two more.

The 15th of February turned out to be a memorable day for Schulz. At 1700 hours, 8 Kittyhawks of the 94th Squadron and 12 of the 112th Squadron attacked the airfield at Martuba.

As they swept over the field, Schulz ran to his machine, which was being serviced. He climbed in and, 30 seconds later, started rolling down the airfield. Within 10 minutes, he shot down five Kittyhawks. Exactly 20 minutes later, Schulz retuned to the airfield, waggling his wings five times.

Generalfeldmarschall Kesselring appeared at the airfield a few days later and presented Schulz with the Knight's Cross to the Iron Cross.

On 22 February, the *Luftwaffe* was employed far to the east. Its objectives were Sidi Barrani and Marsa Matruh. In order to get there and return safely, the aircraft were fitted with spare fuel tanks. Stahlschmidt was brought down by a Kittyhawk that day when he was attacked from below. He succeeded in bringing the *Bf 109* down for a rough landing in the sand in a smoke-filled cockpit. He walked away with singed eyebrows.

Three days later, he took off again. He flew escort for a *Bf 109* reconnaissance aircraft, along with *Feldwebel* Käppler. They reached the air space over Bir Hacheim. The high wall of dust kicked up from a *ghibli* blocked their ability to see. When they lost sight of the reconnaissance aircraft, they decided to fly to Bir el Gobi. Suddenly, both of them saw a concentration of trucks below them. Additional vehicles were approaching from Gobi.

"Let's attack, Käppler!" Stahlschmidt radioed.

They dove and strafed the column from low level. Suddenly, Stahlschmidt heard a loud clacking noise in the cockpit. The smell of something burning filled the cabin and oil started to splash on the windshield. The engine, although being flown at normal RPM's, suddenly raced to full throttle. Stahlschmidt flew around the vehicles and informed Käppler that he had engine problems.

Pulling back on the stick and opening his canopy Stahlschmidt was just clearing the trucks. He kept his right hand on the stick and used his left arm to shield himself from the hot oil that was spurting into the cockpit. The machine lost altitude and cut straight through a truck, coming to an abrupt stop a short distance away. Stahlschmidt jumped out and ran from the machine. Soldiers in green uniforms approached him.

"*Italiani?*" he asked.

But they were Poles. One of them hit him in the back with his rifle butt. The *Leutnant* fell to the ground and was then hit with sticks. One of the Poles ripped his awards from his flight jacket. Then he was shoved into a foxhole. A short while later, he was picked up by a Polish officer and taken in the direction of Gazala.

The following night, he succeeded in escaping. For 24 hours, he crisscrossed through the desert until he encountered a German outpost the next night. In all, he covered nearly 60 kilometers by foot. His comrades jubilantly greeted him, since they had given him up for dead or captured.

✠

On 24 February, Marseille also received the Knight's Cross to the Iron Cross. He wrote to his parents: "In a hurry: Received the Knight's Cross yesterday; am very proud. Love, Yours, Jochen."

In April, he was promoted to *Oberleutnant*, after having scored his 60th victory. After his 100th victory, he went on leave, a leave he was ordered to take.

Stahlschmidt became the commander of the 2nd Squadron. July became his single best month, when he was credited with 25 "kills."

But more and more of the German pilots failed to return from their sorties. That was thanks to the Desert Air Force, which was organized into three fighter wings in March. The 239th Wing had four squadrons of Kittyhawks; the 243rd with four squadrons of Hurricanes; and the 233rd Wing with two

South African squadrons and two English squadrons, which were outfitted with Kittyhawks and Tomahawks.

In the raid on Martuba, a British commando group attacked the airfield, destroying a number of machines. The commando party was wiped out after six hours of fighting.

The South African Air Force 2nd Squadron, which had participated actively in the air war over the desert. Received a shock on 25 April, when it was jumped by *Bf 109's*. Aircraft from the South African 4th Squadron joined the fray, but the two squadrons lost a total of 10 aircraft, of which two made belly landings.

On 30 April, the first Spitfires arrived in Africa and were assigned to the 145th Squadron, considerably enhancing the capabilities of the British fighter force.

One of the big successes of the British aviators during that time was the destruction of 15 *Ju 52's* and 2 *Bf 110's* on 12 May. Wing Commander Mayers was in charge of the formation that intercepted the transports coming in from Crete.

A *Ju 87* that was forced to make an emergency landing 30 kilometers south of Tmimi on 4 June was singled out for special protection by the escorting eight German fighters from the *II./Jagdgeschwader 27*. They circled above the stranded aircraft until a Fieseler *Storch* could land and pick up the crew, one of whom was the Commander-in-Chief South, *Generalfeldmarschall* Kesselring!

UP TO THE RETREAT

Not only did Rommel receive additional air assets for his upcoming offensive in May, a new Air Commander Africa was appointed, *Generalleutnant* Hoffmann von Waldau. In the first half of May, an additional 40 *Ju 87's*, 30 *Bf 109's*, and 15 *Bf 110's* arrived in Africa from Sicily. That raised the total strength of the *Luftwaffe* in Africa to 260 machines.

The *Regia Aeronautica* was also reinforced with a total of two groups and four squadrons after the new aircraft arrived.

By July, the area of fighting had moved east to the areas above El Alamein and Marsa Matruh.

August started with two victories by *Leutnant* Stahlschmidt. *Oberfeldwebel* Sawallisch, *Oberfeldwebel* Bendert, *Oberfeldwebel* Stiegler and *Leutnant* Remmer all enjoyed great success that month. On 12 August, the three noncommissioned officers all scrambled to intercept four groups of four fighter-bombers, escorted by 15 Tomahawks, between Alam el Kadim and Alam el Halfa. Of the 31 enemy aircraft, they shot down 12. Bendert accounted for five: two Hurricanes and two Tomahawks.

On 23 August, Marseille returned from his mandated leave. The wing was based at the Torbya airfield between Marsa Matruh and El Alamein. He rejoined his comrades and helped Stahlschmidt celebrate his 39th and 40th victories on 28 August.

On 1 September, there was a series of dramatic dogfights among the eagles over the desert. *Oberleutnant* Marseille shot down eight aircraft between 1155 and 1205 hours. That evening, he shot down another five between 1847 and 1853 hours.

✠

On 7 September, Stahlschmidt headed out for a sortie over the front to the south of El Alamein. He had 59 victories to his credit and more than 400 combat sorties. A short while after take off, an officer from Stahlschmidt's squadron called Marseille. Marseille was speechless; then he told his comrades he was heading out to the airfield, since Stahlschmidt was missing.

Marseille looked up the other pilots who had been in that sortie. One thought he saw Stahlschmidt's aircraft crash; another believed he saw a belly landing; a third had yet another version and thought he had seen a parachute.

Marseille asked his wing commander for permission to start a search and rescue flight. *Major* Neumann agreed to more than that: "The 1st and 2nd Squadrons will head out!"

But the search proved fruitless. Marseille and the others could find nothing. Stahlschmidt remained missing.

✠

The first *Stuka* sortie was launched west of El Alamein on 15 September. Fifteen *Bf 109's* of the *III./Jagdgeschwader 27* provided the escort. The German fighters became engaged in a savage dogfight with 20 Tomahawks and 8 Spitfires. One German fighter was shot down. *Leutnant* Schroer shot down three aircraft from 1240 to 1255 hours; *Oberleutnant* Althoff claimed a fourth.

That afternoon, the *Stukas* headed out again for another sortie against the British defensive lines west of El Alamein. On that mission, all 43 operational aircraft of the wing were flying escort. Dramatic dogfights ensued, in which Marseille claimed seven victories. *Unteroffizier* Krainik scored four "kills" and *Leutnant* Schroer another three. In all, 20 of the Tomahawks, Kittyhawks, and Spitfires were shot down. The Germans lost three fighters.

Marseille had claimed his 151st victory by the end of the day and had become one of the top three aces of the *Luftwaffe*. He was promoted to *Hauptmann*. At 22, he was the youngest officer of that rank in the *Luftwaffe*.

☩

During this time period, the *Stukas* were launching sorties with practically no interruption, in order to support the forces on the ground, who were getting ready for another exchange of blows. The "aerial artillery" attempted to shatter enemy positions at decisive areas. They were always escorted by either *Bf 109's* or *MC 202's*.

The 30th of September turned out to be a black day for the fighter pilots. After Beaufighters of the 272nd Squadron had shot down two *He 111's* and a *Ju 88* that morning, *Hauptmann* Marseille and eight other aircraft set out to provide escort for the *Stukas* flying sorties over El Alamein. Once the *Stukas* were done, the aircraft were released to hunt Allied aircraft. Following Marseille and his pilots were another 15 aircraft from the *III./Jagdgeschwader 27* and 10 from the *III./Jagdgeschwader 53*.

Marseille flew a brand-new *Bf 109 G2* for the first time that day. His squadron did not make any enemy contact. As they flew back, Marseille's aircraft developed an engine-oil fire. Heavy smoke developed, which blanketed the cockpit.

Marseille continued towards the German lines, which he also reached. He jettisoned the canopy and set the aircraft on its back in order to facilitate punching out. The aircraft immediately went into a steep back glide. After 200 meters, he left the aircraft, but his body struck the tail assembly. He was knocked unconscious, falling to the ground and striking it horizontally. He was killed instantly.

September thus saw the loss of four of the most successful pilots of the group. In addition to Marseille and Stahlschmidt, Steinhausen and Hoffmann were also killed.

The aerial war in October was primarily marked by *Stuka* and fighter sorties again. The destroyers were used for reconnaissance and strafing attacks against truck convoys behind the lines.

On 8 and 9 October, when the torrential downpour stranded the German aircraft on the ground at the El Duba and Fuka airfields, the Desert Air Force flew several attacks to catch the hapless Germans. The RAF flew more than 500 sorties on 9 October alone. The Germans were only able to respond with 102. When British fighters swarmed to strafe the airfield at El Duba, 19 *Bf 109's* scrambled at Fuka. There were some 45 German aircraft involved in the ensuing dogfights, including those already in the air. They shot down 12 enemy aircraft to a loss of only 3 of their own.

The British bomber formations joined the fighting early in the morning. An initial raid was launched on the German airfields with 18 aircraft; 30 minutes later, another 30 appeared on the horizon. At 1700 hours, 50 bombers appeared over El Duba, escorted by Spitfires. In both high- and low-level raids, the Desert Air Force was attempting to force a decision. In the British history books, this day was recorded as "Daba Prang—Death Blow on Daba." The British believed they destroyed at least 15 aircraft on the ground, along with another 10 in the air. Air Command Africa reported the loss of 10 aircraft on the ground, with another 20 damaged.

Italian fighters that joined the fray that day shot down 10 British fighters. The Germans claimed 16 victories.

✠

A British air offensive was launched on 19 October as a precursor to the ground offensive Over the next three days, the Desert Air Force attempted to paralyze the German airfields so as to protect their ground forces from German aerial attack.

At noon on 20 October, 25 Baltimore bombers attacked, escorted by 30 Kittyhawks of the Australian 3rd Squadron and the British 112th and 250th Squadrons. In the dogfights that followed, both sides lost 11 aircraft each. Thanks to thick cloud cover on 21 October, aerial activity was reduced. When it cleared on 22 October, however, German airfields were attacked three times.

The British air offensive continued on 23 October. German reconnaissance aircraft were unable to get through, with the result that British assault forces were able to move forward that night and remain undiscovered. That evening, the Desert Air Force reported an end strength of 605 fighters, 254 light and medium bombers, and 61 heavy bombers.

The Germans, for their part, had 347 fighters, 72 *Stukas,* and 171 medium bombers. Of those numbers, more than half were Italian aircraft. Although those were on-hand strengths, only about two-thirds of those numbers were operational.

A *Bf 110C*, in high-contrast splinter camouflage, on a reconnaisance mission in Spring 1942.

The crowded airfield at Derna. The aircraft are primarily *Bf 110's* and *Ju 52's*.

Detaching the film canister from the *Rb 50/30* camera of a *Bf 110*C-5 reconnaissance aircraft.

Hans-Joachim Marseille, the "Star of Africa." The top-scoring pilot on either side in Africa with 151 victories.

Hans-Arnold Stahlschmidt of *I/JG 27* posed next to the rudder of his *Bf 109*, marked with 48 victories (total 59). Killed in action on 7 September 1942.

A *Ju 87R Stuka* with its wing-mounted long-range fuel tanks. The camouflage scheme is sand-yellow with a hard-edged dark green mottle.

CHAPTER 10

From El Alamein to the Mareth Position

THE BATTLE OF EL ALAMEIN

The German-Italian forces had set up defensive positions outside of El Alamein from a distance of 60 kilometers. The five Italian infantry divisions and the *164. Leichte-Afrika-Division* were in the front lines. Behind them were three motorized/mechanized German divisions and two Italian armored divisions functioning as a ready reserve: the *90. leichte-Afrika-Division* west of El Daba on the coastal road, the *15. Panzer-Division* and the *Littorio* Armored Division south of Sidi Abd el Rahman, and the *21. Panzer-Division* and the *Ariete* Armored Division in the southern portion of the front.

The senior engineer for the field army, *Oberst* Hecker, emplaced a witch's brew of mines in front of the German lines and between the various strongpoints. The Axis forces were conditionally ready for the enemy's next move. The fact that it would come as early as 24 October came as a surprise to the Germans, however.

✠

At 2140 hours on 23 October 1942, some 1,000 British artillery pieces opened fire in a preparatory barrage along 10 kilometers of frontage. It was an artillery preparation the likes of which had not heretofore been seen or experienced in the desert. The guns fired for exactly 20 minutes on that small stretch of front. The fires then shifted to the rear and the British assault groups moved out through the lanes and gaps in the minefields. The 1st and 10th Armoured Divisions attempted to cut a path through the German front. In the south, the 7th Armoured Division attacked at Himeimat. The British offensive had started!

The Australian 9th Infantry and the Scottish 51st Highland Divisions attacked in their sectors and started 10 days of fighting after their operations had commenced with a barrage fire lasting five hours.

191

The enemy's artillery fires succeeded in destroying almost all of the German land lines. An hour after midnight, British infantry broke through the frontage held by the Italian 62nd Infantry Regiment. Two battalions of the recently introduced *164. leichte-Afrika-Division* were likewise lost in the initial maelstrom along the front.

When it turned light, Rommel's temporary replacement while he was on leave for a health cure in Germany, *General der Kavallerie* Stumme, headed to the front.

"Take an escort and a radio vehicles with you!" *Oberst* Westphal recommended. Westphal was likewise a temporary stand-in as the field army's chief-of-staff, who was representing *Oberst* Bayerlein, who was on leave.

But Stumme did not take the additional vehicles. He went to the command post of the *164. leichte-Afrika-Division* with *Oberst* Büchting, the field army's senior signals officer. When the men reached Hill 28, they were engaged by enemy antitank guns and machine guns. Büchting was shot in the head and killed. Stumme suffered a heart attack and died. Assuming acting command of *Panzer-Armee Afrika* until Rommel could return was *Generalleutnant Ritter von Thoma*, who had been the acting commander of the *DAK*.

Oberst Westphal had already sent a situation report to the Army High Command. A few hours later, a radio message was received from the *Führer* Headquarters asking exactly what was going on. Westphal responded: "The long-expected British offensive. Return of *Generalfeldmarschall* Rommel necessary."

Rommel was called at his sick leave location immediately by *Generalfeldmarschall* Kesselring. Hitler called twice, the second time asking Rommel to fly immediately to Africa. Rommel was well prepared for the eventuality. He knew what he could expect there and noted the following in his diary: "I knew that I would earn no more laurels in Africa since I had discovered from my officers that not even the minimal amount of requested supplies had been delivered. I had no idea, however, as would soon be seen, *how* bad the situation in Africa was with regard to supplies."

When Rommel arrived in Rome on 25 October, *General* Rintelen briefed him on the situation. He flew on immediately and met with *Oberst* Westphal a short while later, who briefed him again.

✠

On 24 October, the forces of the British 8th Army had attacked constantly in the southern sector, where the *15. Panzer-Division* of *Generalleutnant* von Vaerst was positioned as the reaction force. When the British forces broke through the Italian sector of the front, the guns of the *1./Panzer-Artillerie-Regiment 33* opened fire. *Oberleutnant* Orth, the battery commander, personally sighted his guns and directed the fires. The first few enemy tanks were hit and set alight. When the enemy attack started to bog down, *Hauptmann* Stiefelmayer's *I./ Panzer-Regiment 8* launched an immediate counterattack. The German tanks, moving by leaps and bounds, succeeded in driving the enemy back into one of the deeply echeloned minefields.

Within a short period, 35 enemy tanks were on fire or immobilized by mines. The breakthrough effort in that sector of the front had failed.

General Montgomery shifted his offensive main effort north, after the *15. Panzer-Division* turned back a second British armored attack on 25 October and he suffered another 30 tanks lost. But *Panzer-Regiment 8* lost 88 tanks during the two days of fighting. One more British attack might have sufficed to wipe out the remaining 31 operational tanks of the regiment.

Rommel concentrated all of his mobile forces, with the exception of the *21. Panzer-Division*, in the north on 26 October. He wanted to counter the offensive with a hard counterattack of his own. When Rommel discovered through radio intercepts that Montgomery was moving all of his major forces north, Rommel also had the *21. Panzer-Division* move north as well. He had half of the artillery shift to the north as well.

As a result of his lightning-fast reflexes, he was able to close a gap in the north. Early in the morning of 28 October, the *21. Panzer-Division* , which had just arrived, attacked through the *15. Panzer-Division*, which was holding out in that sector. The division commander, *Generalmajor* von Randow, led from the front along with his operations officer, *Major i.G.* von Heuduck. The tanks of *Panzer-Regiment 5*, under the acting command of *Oberstleutnant* Mildebrath, followed behind. *Oberst* Teege then brought up the rear of the attack force with what remained of his *Panzer-Regiment 8*.

Despite the enemy's heavy antitank gun and artillery fire, the attack succeeded on a local level. A number of enemy tanks were knocked out in individual engagements, but the newly introduced American M4 "Sherman" was superior to the German tanks then being employed.

Over the next few days, all of the Axis forces became involved in the defensive fighting. The counterattack launched by the *90. leichte-Afrika-Division* against Hill 28, which had been lost, did not succeed. The enemy had reinforced his gains there with antitank guns, artillery, and tanks. The *15. Panzer-Division*, the *21. Panzer-Division*, and the *Ariete* Armored Division attacked the British positions between Minefields L and J. They were then inserted into the line where the infantry had suffered heavy losses. *Grenadier-Regiment 125* of the *164. leichte Afrika-Division* was practically wiped out. Its remnants were able to finally pull back after a relief attack by the *90. leichte-Afrika-Division*.

On 29 October, the British regrouped. The head of the British intelligence had provided Montgomery with reports concerning the shifting of the German armored forces to the north. Montgomery decided to launch a feint in the north. He then set the New Zealand 2nd Infantry Division on a hook to the southwest on the *Tel el Aqqaqir*, where the *Littorio* Division was holding. The Scottish 51st Highland Division attacked the *Trieste* Division further to the south. The *Tel el Eisa* was bypassed just to its south by the Australian 9th Infantry Division.

To the south of the Scottish 51st Highland Division and adjoining it offset to the east was the South African 1st Infantry Division. Facing the *Deir el Shein* and opposing the Italian *Bologna* and *Brescia* Divisions, which were positioned to the north and south of it, was the Indian 4th Infantry Division. The British 50th Infantry Division had moved up to the southernmost portion of the front, minus its 151st Brigade, which had been detached in support of the New Zealand forces.

The 30 October passed with small skirmishes and engagements. The Fuka position was reconnoitered by German staff officers to determine its potential for defense.

During the night of 30/31 October, the *21. Panzer-Division* was pulled out of the front lines by Rommel. The field marshal wanted to have at least one armored division in reserve as a ready reaction force with the ability to seal off and clean up penetrations. It was replaced in the front lines by the *Trieste* Division.

While those movements were taking place, the positions of *Grenadier-Regiment 125* in the northern sector were placed under heavy artillery fire. Just to the southeast of it, the Australian 9th Infantry Division attacked and hit the German regiment in the right flank. At the same time, strong armored forces advanced north of Hill 28 to the north and reached the coastal road. The British forces then encountered *Oberstleutnant* Panzenhagen's *Panzergrenadier-Regiment 361* there.

Panzenhagen's men were able to hold up the enemy's advance and destroy a number of enemy tanks that had penetrated. By doing so, Panzenhagen's regiment created the opportunity for Rommel to commit *Aufklärungs-Abteilung 33 (mot.)*, which he personally led, in an immediate counterattack. The reconnaissance battalion was followed by the main body of the *21. Panzer-Division*, which succeeded in throwing back the enemy.

Rommel then went to Sidi Abd el Rahman. He set up his command post east of the mosque. At 1000 hours, he gave *Ritter* von Thoma orders to conduct a counterattack with the *21. Panzer-Division* and elements of the *90. leichte-Afrika-Division*, which had been pulled out of the front. Rommel announced that the counterattack would be preceded by both a *Stuka* attack and a massed artillery preparation.

The attack moved out at 1200 hours. Despite the heavy enemy artillery fire and the bombing runs by the Desert Air Forces, it was possible to re-establish contact with *Grenadier-Regiment 125* after intense fighting with enemy infantry and tanks. The two encircled battalions were relieved, and the enemy was pushed back to the south and across the railway line.

Rommel stood on Hill 16 early on the morning of 1 November with *Ritter* von Thoma, *Generalmajor Graf* von Sponeck (commander of the *90. leichte-Afrika-Division*) and *Oberst* Bayerlein (chief-of-staff of the field army) and counted 47 knocked-out enemy tanks in the vicinity of the railway station. There was a Red Cross flag waving at the train station, and the German artillery had ceased firing to allow the evacuation of the wounded.

The enemy still had around 800 armored vehicles at his disposal, which he was assembling for the intended decisive blow of Operation "Supercharge." Opposing that armored armada were some 90 German and 140 Italian armored vehicles.

In a complete misreading of the situation, the Italian military's chief-of-staff, Count Cavallero, had wired the congratulations of the *Duce* to the forces in the field on the successful conclusion to the defensive fighting.

The English attack associated with "Supercharge" was launched during the night of 1/2 November. The artillery preparation lasted three hours. That was followed by night bomber attacks with all available machines. The divisions then moved out.

The British armored forces advanced past both sides of Hill 28 in the sector of *Grenadier-Regiment 200*. They were able to advance far to the west before the reserves—the *90. leichte-Afrika-Division*—were committed. They were able to bring the Allied assault to a stop. That morning, the German's two armored divisions were committed to a counterattack. They were able to knock out a number of enemy tanks, but the success was bought dearly. Eventually, the point of penetration was narrowed to four kilometers, but the enemy had already funneled no fewer than 15 artillery regiments through the point of penetration.

The evening of that bloody 2 November saw the British bring up their second wave, consisting of another 400 tanks. Opposing them were 35 operational tanks of the *DAK*.

Rommel came to the realization that he needed to withdraw. *Panzer-Armee Afrika* had been badly battered and every day of resistance could bring about its complete destruction. On the morning of 3 November, the necessary orders were issued. These were countermanded by Hitler, who demanded the field army continue the struggle to the bitter end: "Victory or death!"

Rommel hesitated somewhat. When *Feldmarschall* Kesselring showed up at Rommel's headquarters on 4 November, he was thoroughly briefed. After intense discussions, he agreed with Rommel and the operations officer of the field army, Westphal, that Hitler's "hold" order could not be executed. Rommel and Kesselring reported that to the German Armed Force High Command. Following that, Rommel went to the headquarters of the *DAK* and ordered a withdrawal of the German and Italian forces to the Fuka Line.

The withdrawal started. In the middle of the withdrawal movements, the *Ariete* Division sent a final radio transmission: "Enemy tanks had broken through south of the '*Ariete*'. The division is surrounded. It is approximately five kilometers northwest of Bir el Abd. The tanks of the '*Ariete*' will fight to the end."

During the evening of 4 November, the main bodies of the divisions of the Italian XX Corps were effectively destroyed. By doing that, the British had succeeded in creating a 20-kilometer path through the Axis defensive positions.

The withdrawal continued during the night of 4/5 November along a broad front towards Fuka, some 100 kilometers distant. It was a race against British tanks and night bombers. Early on the morning of 5 November, the headquarters of the field army reached the wire obstacles at the Fuka airfield. During the day, the main body of the *DAK* arrived, as did the *90. leichte-Afrika-Division* and the remaining elements of the XX Corps (Motorized).

The rearguards of the *DAK* were involved in a desperate struggle against 200 British tanks that were in hot pursuit, which were followed by an additional 200 armored personnel carriers.

The Fuka position could be held for a day. That allowed a number of other formations, most of which were not motorized, to escape British captivity. That included Ramcke's brigade, which had been stranded at the southern end of the Qattara Depression without motor transport.

Generalmajor Ramcke had received orders as early as 2 November to disengage from the enemy and pull back to new positions between Duweir el Tarfa and the minefield at Deir el Quatani. The paratroopers covered the 30 kilometers by foot. That evening, new orders arrived having the paratroopers regroup, disengage from the enemy, and occupy new positions west of Fuka. That was to signal the start of an odyssey that was never to be forgotten by the participants.

The movement called for crossing 100 kilometers of desert—as the crow flies—all largely without vehicles or recognizable trails, always subject to attack from the air by the Desert Air Force. It seemed the brigade was doomed from the start.

When Ramcke's men moved out, the enemy attacked, hoping to wipe out the force in a movement to contact. The antitank battalion, which was functioning as a rearguard, knocked out a number of British tanks and gave the paratroopers a small bit of breathing room.

Generalmajor Ramcke moved ahead in his command vehicle to reconnoiter. With him were his operations officer, *Major* Kroh, *Major* Fenski, and *Oberleutnant* Wetter. When they hit a high plateau, they encountered a British tank regiment. Ramcke had his men move further south. The next day they were spotted by British reconnaissance aircraft. An hour later, Allied tanks attacked. They were successfully engaged and driven back by the antitank guns, however. The force was constantly attacked throughout the day by British armor. It always managed to extricate itself, leaving behind a trail of burning hulks.

During the night of 5/6 December, the brigade encountered a column of British trucks at rest. Ramcke ordered the formation of small assault detachments that then snuck up and surprised the bewildered and largely sleeping enemy forces. At a pre-arranged pyrotechnical signal, the detachments rushed the trucks. With little fire being exchanged, the hapless British were simply left behind in the desert. Not only did the men of the brigade then have trucks, they also found their new vehicles to be full of fuel, ammunition, and rations.

During the morning of 7 November, the long withdrawal movement was crowned with success. The men were received by a reconnaissance battalion and passed through the hastily established German lines. Ramcke reported in to a surprised Rommel in the middle of an orders conference with the words: "He's still alive!"

By then, Rommel had started to take stock of the situation. Of the three Italian corps, only the X Corps had succeeded in escaping relatively intact. It was continuing to retreat south of Fuka. The remaining two corps—the XX Corp (Motorized) and the XXI Corps—had either been wiped out or taken prisoner during the retreat.

The divisions of the *DAK* and the *90. leichte-Afrika-Division* had all been reduced to the size of powerful *Kampfgruppen*. Some of the mechanized infantry regiments and other formations had emerged relatively unscathed, including Panzenhagen's men and elements of the *164. leichte Afrika-Division*.

On 7 November, the *15. Panzer-Division* and the *90. leichte-Afrika-Division* moved into the defensive sectors designated for them southwest of Fuka. The *21. Panzer-Division* remained southwest of Quasaba, since it had run out of fuel. It established all-round defensive positions there.

Sixty enemy tanks attacked those defensive positions of the *21. Panzer-Division* to administer the *coup de grace*. Giving their all, the Germans stopped the enemy. When the engagement was still undecided, *Hauptmann* Voß, who had only recently been one of Rommel's liaison officers but who had been given command of *Aufklärungs-Abteilung 580*, hit the enemy in the rear with his battalion, which was rolling back from Fuka as a rearguard. The enemy was dealt a crippling blow, with most of his tanks being left behind as battlefield wrecks.

Of most assistance to the field army, however, was the fact that it started to rain on 6 November. The rain lasted 48 hours. Of course, the heavy rainfalls were also a hindrance for the Germans, but they were withdrawing. The British decided the weather was too much of an obstacle and stayed where they were.

The fuel situation for the Germans was catastrophic. Although 5,000 tons of fuel had arrived in Bengasi on 4 November, none of it reached the front. *Panzer-Armee Afrika* muddled its way westward with difficulty. Its lead elements started to reach Halfaya Pass and Sollum. On the afternoon of 7 November, the *21. Panzer-Division* had to blow up its remaining operational tanks. At that point, *Panzer-Armee Afrika* had four operational tanks left.

When the British forces succeeded in shooting past Marsa Matruh to the south, the Axis forces were forced back to Sidi Barrani. The *90. leichte-Afrika-Division*, fighting with the courage of desperation, served as the field army's rearguard.

During the afternoon, the signals center of the field army received message traffic of an event that sent shivers up and down the spines of the senior command: the Allies had landed in West Africa at three locations. At the command post of the *DAK*, Rommel said to Bayerlein: "The campaign has been lost, Bayerlein. Africa is lost. If they don't see that in time in Berlin and Rome and take measures to save my soldiers, then one of the bravest armies will go into captivity. But who will then defend Italy against the invasion that threatens to follow?"

Rommel requested that Marshal Cavallero and *Generalfeldmarschall* Kesselring come to Africa after the full extent of the Western Allies' landings at Casablanca, Oran and Algiers were known. He wanted to personally report to them what had happened and also wanted to hear what they had to say with regard as to how Tunisia would be defended and his own field army, which he intended to pull back to Marsa Matruh, could be supplied. He later wrote in his diary: "Neither Cavallero nor Kesselring came to Africa. I therefore decided to send *Hauptmann* Bernd the next day to the *Führer* Headquarters to brief high command on our situation."

While the invasion was rolling and the 105,000 soldiers who had been landed approached Tunis—with the German response limited to the employment of companies to prevent the worst from happening and hold open the rear area for *Panzer-Armee Afrika*—British tanks from the 8th Army were slamming into German columns.

Marsa el Brega was reached, followed by the main body in El Agheila on 23 November. It had been intended to hold the latter, but it proved impossible and the withdrawal continued. Rommel then made a recommendation for defense. He briefed Bastico, Cavallero, and Kesselring on different occasions on establishing a position along the Gabes Defile, which ran from the sea to the southern salt lakes. He considered that a good blocking position with secure flanks. The frontage was not extensive and could be held with the few forces he had at his disposal.

He believed Montgomery would start to have supply problems of his own as his lines of communication lengthened. It might be possible, despite the desperate situation, to bring some reinforcements to Rommel's forces. When the British to the east were held up, Rommel could then turn west and attack Eisenhower's forces in Tunisia while they were still relatively weak. Once that was accomplished, Rommel then intended to return his attention to Montgomery and throw him back.

According to the British historian Ronald Lewin: "Given the circumstances, that would have been the best operations solution for Rommel, if its execution had been permitted to him."[1]

Starting on 22 November, Rommel was placed under the command of General Bastico again. Rommel realized that he would be unable to achieve much dealing with the Italian command in Africa. Since his urgent telegrams to Germany also seemed to be falling on deaf ears, he decided to fly to Germany himself to draw attention to the situation in Africa.

He arrived at the *Führer* Headquarters in Rastenburg on 28 November. When Hitler received Rommel, the latter presented a stark picture of the situation. But Hitler was in no mood to hear facts. He made the accusation to Rommel that his soldiers had thrown their weapons away and had cowardly fled the enemy. Rommel was appalled. He wrote in his diary: "It was clear to me that Hitler did not want to see the true nature of events and reacted emotionally against that which his reason had to say to him."

The withdrawal continued on to Tripoli.

---

1. Translator's Note: Reverse-translated.

CHAPTER 11

Operation "Torch":
The Landings in Northwest Africa

As early as 24 July 1942, the Western Allies had decided to occupy Northwest Africa. Tunisia was to be occupied as part of Operation "Torch". It was hoped that such a move would bring decisive relief to Malta. Three beachheads were established: Casablanca, Oran, and Algiers.

The forces landing in Casablanca were under the command of General Patton and consisted of an armored division, an infantry division and, one of the combat commands of the U.S. 2nd Armored Division. In all, he fielded a force of some 35,000 men.

The center beachhead at Oran was under Major General Fredendall, who had a total strength of 39,000 soldiers under his command.

The Eastern Task Force of Major General C. W. Ryder was tasked with occupying Algiers with a force of 33,000 men. Immediately after the taking of Algiers, overall command of the Eastern Task Force was to pass to General Anderson, a British General and the commander-in-chief of the British 1st Army, which was to advance as rapidly as possible to Tunis and take the city.

The surface shipment of the British forces started during the first few weeks of October from England to Gibraltar. By 1 November, there had been an additional four major convoys. The combat vessels—some 160 ships of all types—shipped out from Scapa Flow at the end of October. The U.S. combat vessels and the troop transporters lifted anchor from the U.S. between 23 and 28 October.

General Eisenhower and his staff left England from Gibraltar on 5 November in five B-17's.

On the evening of 6 November, the first convoys reached the waters of the coastline of Northwest Africa. The southernmost group put ashore at 0400 hours on 8 November at Safi. Despite some French resistance, all vessels landed safely, although some pockets of resistance held out until the following evening.

The landing operations in Algiers went without a hitch, because the French general in the sector, Mast, had been co-opted by the U.S. ambassador,

Murphy, in advance. The overall French military commander in Algiers, General Juin, also sympathized with the Allies.

The French forces in Oran also put up resistance in places, with fighting continuing—some of it quite bitter—until 10 November.

The landings, which have only been presented in a summarized form here, had the telephone lines running hot in Germany. Hitler immediately had himself connected with the Commander-in-Chief South, *Generalfeldmarschall* Kesselring, and implored him to send everything he had in the way of ground forces to Tunis.

At the time, the only forces immediately available were two battalions from *Fallschirmjäger-Regiment 5* and Kesselring's personal headquarters escort battalion.

U-Boote were ordered to pounce on the convoys at the western entrance to the Mediterranean as well as within the sea itself. They were able to achieve some notable successes, but they were unable to change the tide.

On 9 November, Hitler gave Kesselring a free hand with regards to operations in Tunisia. The German Armed Forces Operational Staff received permission from Marshal Pétain to land German forces in Tunisia.

It was not until 11 November, however, that the first paratroopers of *Oberstleutnant* Koch's regiment, the guard battalion, and some *Luftwaffe* elements—primarily fighters and *Stukas*—landed in Tunis.

One thing was certain to Kesselring: he had to commit strong German forces as quickly as possible against the Allied forces that had landed and were then advancing like an armored avalanche to the east. If that were not done and the 100,000-man-strong Allied force occupied the port of Tunis in the rear of *Panzer-Armee Afrika*, then the latter would surely be lost. Those circumstances dictated the German's operational planning: "Delay the Allied landings. Secure Tunis; push friendly forces west and south to establish a strong bridgehead in Tunisia."

General der Panzertruppen Nehring, who had recovered from wounds suffered on 31 August, was entrusted with the formation of the *XC. Armee-Korps* in Tunisia. He immediately took up the task with his operations officer, *Major i.G.* Moll. Initially, they only had meager forces: *Kompanie Sauer* (an airborne company), Field Battalion "Tunis," and the first arriving elements of *Fallschirmjäger-Regiment 5*. By 15 November, the main body of the latter regiment had arrived in theater. *Kampfgruppen Schirmer* and *Sauer* took up screening positions to the south and west of Tunis. The *III./FJR 5* of *Hauptmann* Knoche reported to the western defensive elements.

On the evening of 15 November, Nehring had the following forces at his disposal:

Fallschirmjäger-Regiment 5 (*Oberstleutnant* Koch)

Korps-Fallschirm-Pionier-Bataillon (*Major* Witzig)

One cadre battalion

One battery of 8.8-centimeter *Flak* with four guns

One armored car company under *Oberleutnant* Kahle

Two battalions of Italian marine infantry (under an Italian admiral, situated near Bizerta)

Two battalions from the *Superga* Division (in the vicinity of Pont du Fahs)

Kesselring had given Nehring the following mission: "Immediately advance to the Tunisian-Algerian frontier. Take the western slopes of the country to establish good options for defense and establish a deep bridgehead."

In the meantime, the British 78th Infantry Division had advanced on Bizerta and passed Abiod and the mountain of the same name, where it encountered *Major* Witzig's airborne combat engineers. Witzig and his men held up the British for 48 hours. The heavy weapons from the *Superga* Division supported the paratroopers, and the *Luftwaffe* supplied much needed held from the air.

At the same time, British paratroopers—the 1st Battalion of the 1st Airborne Brigade of Lieutenant Colonel Hill—jumped in. They landed on 15 November at Souk el Arba and attacked Qued Zarga. Supported by Task Force Blade, which was a British battle group of 25 armored vehicles under Lieutenant Colonel Hull, they took the village, which is located halfway between Béja and Medjez el Bab.

Witzig's men were forced back from their positions on the *Djebel Abiod* and moved into the area around Jefna. They occupied excellent defensive positions in the so-called Jefna Tunnel.

Major General Eveligh's 78th Infantry Division was pivoted south and into the area around Medjez el Bab. He was directed to take the village, which is considered the gate to Tunis.

Since that village was turning into a pivotal fight in the battle for Tunisia, Nehring rushed *Hauptmann* Knoche's *III./FJR 5* there on 19 November to attack.

In the meantime, elements from *FJR 5* were also employed in the southern part of Tunisia to take important villages by surprise. In one case, *Leutnant* Kempa was sent to take Gabes, but the French decided to put up a fight, and he was greeted with a hail of bullets. It was not until additional forces could be air-landed that Gabes could be wrested from the French on the morning of 18 November, who suddenly turned tail.

When U.S. tanks showed up outside of Gabes 48 hours later, they were turned back by the paratroopers and two battalions of the "Brigade L" of General Imperiali. The Italian force had arrived as reinforcements in the meantime.

In the Medjez el Bab area, *Hauptmann* Knoche's men prepared for the Allied onslaught. In addition to French forces, there was a regiment from the 78th Infantry Division positioned along both sides of the Medjerda River and the town of the same name. The infantry regiment was supported by both tanks and armored cars.

On the morning of 19 November, two *Bf 109's* flew over Medjerda and drew fire from British antiaircraft weaponry. The promised *Stukas*—12 of them—arrived two hours later. They primarily engaged the identified French positions on the near side of the river.

Knoche's paratroopers then moved out, taking the eastern side of Medjerda and getting as far as the bridge. They were stopped there by the incessant artillery fire coming from the 78th Infantry Division. The bridge itself was covered by extremely heavy machine-gun fire that allowed nothing across.

An assault detachment under *Oberleutnant* Bundt went down river, crossed, and then entered the western portion of the town. In a desperate fight, the assault detachment was practically wiped out. *Oberleutnant* Bundt was killed by a round through his mouth. Four survivors crawled back to the river, swam across, and informed *Hauptmann* Knoche of what had happened.

In the afternoon, Italian reinforcements arrived. Accompanying them was the German regimental commander, *Oberstleutnant* Koch. He had brought demolitions with him on a truck from Tunis. He had an idea. He wanted to replicate what he had done in May 1940 when he had sent one of the key fortifications at Eben Emael flying into the air.

He had 10 assault detachments formed. These assembled and moved out at midnight with submachine guns, shaped charges, and other demolitions. They waded through the river at positions that had been scouted previously, reached their targets, and then set of the demolitions at the same time. It was 0107 hours when 10 different charges went off in different parts of the town. At the same time, the German forces on the east bank opened fire and the assault detachments contributed to the confusion by firing with their small arms as well. Supply dumps, guard posts, and billeting areas flew into the air. As it turned light, the enemy fled from the town.

Hauptmann Schirmer was sent forward to relieve *Hauptmann* Knoche, who had gone without sleep for 96 hours. The paratroopers then followed the retreating enemy as far as Oued Zarga, whereupon he was ordered back to Medjez el Bab.

In the meantime, the towns of Sousse and Sfax had also been taken in *coup de main* actions, in addition to Gabes. Additional forces were flown in in an effort to keep the road to Tripoli open.

During the night of 20/21 November, the first elements of *Generalleutnant* Fischer's *10. Panzer-Division* started arriving in Tunis from France, where it had been undergoing reconstitution. They were sent forward to the area around Tebourba and Djedeida. Upon their arrival, the paratroopers were sent forward into the area around Medjez el Bab and El Aroussa. When the first U.S. tanks arrived there on the afternoon of 21 November, they were held back by *Kampfgruppe Knoche*, which was supported by the heavy weapons of the *14./Infanterie-Regiment 104* and a *Flak* detachment. Some of the enemy tanks were abandoned, burning, on the open plains.

When Kesselring arrived in Tunis on 19 November, Nehring was able to report the arrival of additional formations. But Nehring pulled no punches in stressing that a front of some 500 kilometers needed powerful combat formations with heavy weapons and tanks.

In the meantime, all of the *Superga* Division had been transported to Africa in record time. It established defensive positions in the Mateur area, receiving its final elements, which landed at Bizerta, on 19 November. The division commander, Lorenzelli, landed at the airfield at La Marsa, established battle groups, and sent the main body of his division advancing in the direction of Sidi bu Acid and Sidi Belkai. The division took those transportation nodal points, thus further blocking access by the Western Allies into Tunisia.

THE ALLIED ADVANCE

General Eisenhower arrived in Algeria on 23 November. Generals Clark and Oliver were involved in discussions when he arrived. They were deciding who would conduct the advance with Brigadier Robinett's Combat Command B.

Eisenhower approved the offensive preparations, and during the next 48 hours, elements of the U.S. 1st Armored Division were rolling eastward in the direction of Tebourba. After an engagement with German paratroopers, the U.S. force turned off in the direction of Djedeida. An American patrol under a Lieutenant Hoker found a German airfield there that was lacking in defenses.

There were several 2-centimeter *Flak* at the edge of the airfield. They attempted to stop the U.S. attack, but paid the ultimate price in being wiped out. The German aircraft, including *Bf 109's* and *Ju 52's*, were blown apart by the American tanks. In all, some 14 *Bf 109's* and 24 *Ju 52's* were left on the airstrip as smoldering ruins.

When the tanks attempted to advance further in the direction of Tunis, they ran into two 8.8-centimeter *Flak* 15 kilometers outside of the city. The guns had personally been sent there by Nehring. Within two minutes the two guns knocked out six American tanks. The remaining tanks turned around and returned to Djedeida. It was thanks to those two guns that Tunis did not fall immediately to the Western Allies.

On the morning of 25 November, the British 78th Infantry Division attacked twice from Oued Zarga in the direction of Medjez el Bab. The attack was joined by elements of the U.S. 1st Armored Division and other armored elements.

Oberstleutnant Koch had to abandon the town after a fight. He pulled back to Massicault and had positions occupied there. In the fighting that followed on 27 and 28 November around Tebourba, the Allies lost a number of tanks.

The 1,000 men of the 2nd Battalion of the British 6th Airborne Division commanded by Major Frost jumped into Depienne early in the afternoon of 28 November. The jump started at 1230 hours and was not disrupted by any German forces, since there were none in the vicinity. After the battalion had assembled, it marched in the direction of Oudna, where there was a German airfield they were supposed to take by surprise. On the way there, however, Frost discovered that the airfield had been abandoned by the Germans.

Over the next two days, during which the battalion attempted to make its way back to its own lines, the British paratroopers were attacked several times by German paratroopers of *Fallschirmjäger-Regiment 5*. By 2 December, the British had lost 16 officers and 250 enlisted personnel. Captain Richard Spender later wrote: "The sun sank silently over Medjerda Valley, where so many of my comrades had shed blood needlessly."[1]

THE FIGHTING AT TEBOURBA

At the end of November, the situation was all but stabilized for the Germans in the Tunis Bridgehead. Although elements of the *10. Panzer-Division* had arrived and established themselves between Tunis and Bizerta, the situation was still catastrophic for the Germans when the force ratios are considered.

Nehring reorganized his forces on 30 November, by which *Oberst Freiherr* von Broich assumed command of the forces in the northern portion of the bridgehead. *Generalmajor* Fischer commanded the western defensive sector. Lorenzelli, the commander of the *Superga* Division, held the reins of command in the south. *Generalmajor* Neuffer's *20. Flak-Division* guarded the coast to the north of Tunis. He was also responsible for the fortress of Bizerta.

It became increasingly clear that the Western Allies intended to advance on Tunis from the Tebourba area, with a second advance headed for Bizerta from Mateur. Nehring wanted to beat the Allies to the punch and issued attack orders on 30 November: "The enemy in the Tebourba area is to be attacked and eliminated!"

---

1. Translator's Note: Reverse translation.

He employed *Fallschirmjäger-Regiment 5* against the enemy's rear. Nehring had ordered the airborne regiment to move out of its positions around Medjez el Bab and through El Batahan to do that. If the Germans succeeded in their planned maneuvers, the Allied forces around Tebourba would be encircled. Tebourba itself had not yet fallen to the Allies, being held by an airborne company and a platoon of engineers.

Generalleutnant Fischer assumed command of the area of operations. It was intended for him to attack from the north and the northeast with his *10. Panzer-Division*. Attached to the German armored division was also *schwere Panzer-Abteilung 501*, a *Tiger* battalion, which was employed in combat operations for the first time on North African soil. The *1./schwere Panzer-Abteilung 501* of *Hauptmann Baron* Nolde reported directly to the *10. Panzer-Division*. *Kampfgruppe Lueder*, named for the commander of the *Tiger* battalion, was directed to attack Tebourba directly. In addition to his *Tigers*, Lueder had two tank companies from *Panzer-Abteilung 190* and a motorcycle infantry company from the *10. Panzer-Division*, which was led by *Oberleutnant* Pschorr.

The fighting for Tebourba started on 27 November. It bogged down in the defensive fires of the enemy's antitank guns and handful of tanks. Eight German tanks went up in flames.

Kampfgruppe Lueder, which was then reinforced by a *Panzergrenadier* company under the command of *Hauptmann* Pomme, reorganized for another attack on the high ground north of Chouigui. The next attack started on the morning of 1 December, with the tanks of *Panzer-Regiment 7* of the *10. Panzer-Division* in the lead. Nehring had committed everything to this attack, with about 30 German soldiers remaining behind in Tunis.

The attack moved ahead rapidly. By first light on 2 December, the attack force had closed to within 1 kilometers of the town's center. The *Tigers* attacked from Djedeida and encountered three battalions of the U.S. 13th Armored.

With their 8.8-centimeter main guns, the *Tigers* made mincemeat of the U.S. armor. They then advanced into an olive tree grove, where the attack came to a standstill.

The attack was continued that day. The British 11th Brigade and Combat Command B were scattered. The *1./schwere Panzer-Abteilung 501* paid with the life of its commander, who was killed by a tank main gun round when he stepped outside of his *Tiger*. The round tore off both of *Hauptmann* Nolde's legs. *Hauptmann* Teddy Deichmann assumed command. His *Tiger* destroyed both of the enemy tanks that had taken the life of his comrade. Deichmann, however, met the same fate when he dismounted his *Tiger* a while later to reconnoiter. The only difference was that he was felled by a rifle round.

When the day drew to a close, the Allied forces had lost 34 tanks and 6 armored cars. Fischer then attempted to go around the enemy with his mobile elements. He had to advance via the northwest to the south in an effort to link up with the weak airborne forces still in the town.

What had happened to them?

FALLSCHIRMJÄGER-REGIMENT 5 ATTACKS

On 30 November, *Oberstleutnant* Koch had received his orders for the attack on Tebourba. He had elements of his paratroopers advance on both sides of the road to Medjez el Bab, turning in the direction of El Bathan during the night.

Near a farm in the vicinity of Fourna, the 2nd Platoon of the 10th Company received orders to leave behind its heavy weapons, head east, and establish contact with Arent's engineer platoon. Arent and his men had already taken the bridge four kilometers west of El Bathan that was so important for the enemy. Although it had succeeded in knocking out British supply vehicles on the bridge—effectively blocking it temporarily—the tiny element was still holding it all by itself. The bridge represented the lifeline to the British 11th Brigade and the U.S. 1st Armored Division around Tebourba.

At the same time, the main body of the regiment headed directly for El Bathan. The battalions advanced simultaneously. *Leutnant* Kauz, who led the forward elements of the 12th Company, got to the rear of the town by taking back roads. His advance was concealed by olive and cork trees. However, when the Americans identified the movements, they opened with artillery and mortar fire. Kauz soon received relief in the form of nine *Stukas* that roared overhead, escorted by two *Bf 109's*. They succeeded in hitting and destroying the supply dump the Americans had established near Tebourba.

Kauz had his men dismount and follow him. They continued their advance on foot until they reached the American headquarters. A U.S. tank suddenly blocked their retreat route from the rear. Three more followed. They stopped and fired at the German forces.

Tank gun main rounds started to rain down on the airborne soldiers. *Leutnant* Kauz and two other soldiers were killed almost instantly. The remaining men continued their assault, however, and attacked the building. The Americans inside surrendered.

British tanks—Churchills—then arrived. They were knocked out by hand-held improvised antitank devices. Both the Americans and British then started to pull out to the southwest.

By then, *Oberleutnant* Wöhler and the rest of the 12th Company had closed up. They reached the *Djebel Lanserine* and the *Bou Aoukaz*. There they were stopped by enemy defensive fires. An attempt to take the final enemy positions by storm on 1 December failed. It was not until 4 December that the forward high ground was taken by the parachute regiment, signaling the end of the fighting for Tebourba.

In three days and nights, the Western Allies had lost some 134 armored vehicles. More than 1,100 prisoners were taken by the Germans. In addition, 40 artillery pieces were captured intact, along with their ammunition. They were pressed into service by the Germans.

A map found in an American command tank confirmed that Nehring's assumptions about Allied intentions had been correct. The enemy had wanted to advance between Bizerta and Tunis, only to turn south later and take the airfield and the city from the rear.

The victory at Tebourba took a lot of pressure off the *XC. Armee-Corps* and freed it from the danger of immediate destruction. In the official U.S. history, it is written: "The Germans won the race for Tunis."[2]

THE *5. PANZER-ARMEE* IN TUNISIA

The request of the Commander-in-Chief South to the German Army High Command to create a field-army headquarters for Northwest Africa was granted. *Generaloberst* von Arnim arrived at the *Führer* Headquarters in Rastenburg on 3 December, where Hitler personally briefed him on the situation. In a conversation with *Generalfeldmarschall* Keitel that followed, the latter promised von Arnim three armored divisions and three motorized rifle divisions in short order.

On 6 December, when *Generalmajor* Gause and *Oberst* von Manteuffel arrived in Bizerta, they informed Nehring that they had brought an ultimatum from Hitler with them for Admiral Dérrien, the French commander in Tunisia, to lay down his arms, surrender his forts, and discharge his soldiers. If the French commander turned down that demand, Gause was authorized to use force to make it happen.

Nehring was surprised. Up to that point, the French in their coastal fortifications had done nothing against the German forces already there. But, he had to admit, they could turn against the Germans in a crisis situation, in which all of Tunisia and the German forces there would be lost.

Generalmajor Gause brought another bit of news. He informed Nehring that von Arnim would soon be taking over command in Tunisia and that he would be arriving in Tunis around 8 December.

In fact, von Arnim did arrive on 8 December. Nehring had continued his preparations for a continuation of the attack on 9 December. While that

---

2. Translator's Note: Reverse-translated.

attack was launched, Nehring announced to his forces that he was taking his leave of them as Commanding General of the *XC. Armee-Korps*. That same morning, the special operations against the French forces in Bizerta were conducted. Gause succeeded in convincing Dérrien that the spilling of any blood would be senseless. Dérrien and his forces were allowed to keep their weapons until 1700 hours and strike their flags with full military honors.

Events unfolded at other French bastions similarly. The French forces in Ferryville surrendered, as did their naval vessels at anchor outside Ferryville and Bizerta.

✠

The German attack on 9 December, spearheaded by the *10. Panzer-Division*, rolled out as planned and was successful. The enemy armored forces, which had advanced far forward, were thrown back. The situation in the bridgehead stabilized further. The German armored forces initially reached the area around Toum, southwest of Tebourba. By that evening, lead elements were three kilometers northeast of Medjez el Bab. The paratroopers of *Fallschirmjäger-Regiment 5* went forward and established defensive positions in the area north of the salt lake at Sebchet el Kouriza at a farm. It was later referred to as the "Christmas Farm." A German 5-centimeter and two Italian antitank guns were established along the road to Goubellat.

The *10. Panzer-Division* and the *Superga* Division moved to the left wing of the Axis positions in Tunisia, establishing themselves on a line running along Pont du Fahs–bottleneck north of the *Djebel Saidar*–bottleneck southwest of the *Djebel Garce* (15 kilometers west of Enfidaville)–southwest edge of the lake south of Enfidaville.

The various attacks by the Allies on 23 and 24 December were turned back by *Fallschirmjäger-Regiment 5.*

Kampfgruppe Bürker, named after *Oberstleutnant i.G.* Bürker, the operations officer of the *10. Panzer-Division*, successfully launched an attack against "Christmas Mountain" on 24 December in unbelievably tough fighting against the trench lines of the British 78th Infantry Division. The next morning— Christmas Day—General Evelegh committed his Guards Brigade against the hill, which the British referred to as "Longstop Hill," which then again changed hands.

At the same time, tanks of the British 6th Armoured Division advanced on Massicault on the right flank and took it. The Northants Infantry reached the Tebourba Plateau. It looked like the Allies would launch another raid against Tunis.

At the moment, the weather intervened in favor of the Germans. A winter rain started and, two hours later, all of the vehicles were stuck in the seemingly bottomless mud.

On 26 December, *Oberstleutnant* Bürker tried to take back "Christmas Hill." His battle group took the first three hilltops in quick succession. The remaining three hilltops had to be taken in hard hand-to-hand combat against the dug-in enemy, however. After the dramatic fighting, 500 English surrendered. The hills, which secured the Tunis Bridgehead to the west, were again in German hands.

✠

On the Allied side, 24 December had been earmarked for an attack. When General Eisenhower arrived at Souk el Khemis, the headquarters of the British V Corps, the Commanding General reported that the preparatory attacks were underway as well as a feint on Goubellat. He added that the rain was making things difficult, however.

Eisenhower, not quite convinced of Allfrey's optimistic report, headed for the front in the pouring rain. He quickly became convinced that no attack could be conducted in the mud porridge that he was trying to navigate through. He had the U.S. II Corps, which was still in the greater Oran area to move forward to the area around Tebessa. Major General Fredendall was to have the 1st Armored, the 1st Infantry, the 9th Infantry, and the 34th Infantry Divisions—all U.S. formations placed under his command. As soon as the U.S. corps had staged in the south, it was to advance in the direction of Sfax and Gabes in order to block the retreat route of *Panzer-Armee Afrika.*

On the German side, the bridgehead of Tunisia had been divided into four defensive sectors at the end of December: A (area around Mateur under *Gruppe* von *Broich*); B (area around Medjez el Bab under the *10. Panzer-Division*); C (area to the south of Tunis under the *Superga* Division); and D (area around Sfax and Gabes under General Imperiali's "Brigade L").

The *Luftwaffe* had destroyed the bridge over the Medjerda at Medjez el Bab. That held up the Allied supply columns considerably.

On 31 December 1942, the situation had stabilized for the Germans somewhat. The recently formed *5. Panzer-Armee* had 103 *Panzer III's* and *IV's* and 11 *Tigers* at its disposal. In addition, *Panzer-Abteilung 190* had another 53 tanks, and it was making its way to Kairouan. In the meantime, nearly the entire *334. Infanterie-Division* had been transported to Africa.

The heavy rainfalls in January barely allowed any troop movements, with the result that the front lines became solidified. It was only in the south in the sector of the *Superga* Division that there were any operations. The French

XIX Corps of General Koeltz with its three divisions and a brigade attacked from the area around Tebessa. Without anyone initially opposing it, the French corps was able to advance as far as the valley outlets to the east. But its offensive never really went anywhere.

On the German side, an attack was launched from the area around Pont du Fahs with the Codename "Courier I." The attack was launched in the middle of January towards the southwest and placed under the overall command of *Generalmajor* Weber, the commander of the *334. Infanterie-Division*. In addition to his division, Weber had elements of the *10. Panzer-Division, schwere Panzer-Abteilung 501*, two batteries of additional artillery, and *Pionier-Bataillon 49*. The main formation from the *334. Infanterie-Division* was *Gebirgsjäger-Regiment 756*.

A supporting attack was also launched to the south by *Infanterie-Regiment 47*, which also had Italian formations in support.

The attack started on the morning of 18 January. A French Foreign Legion Regiment at the *Djebel Solbia* was defeated. *Kampfgruppe Weber* then advanced against the *Djebel Mansour*, which could not be taken in the first assault. The French, who had been reinforced with tanks from the U.S. 1st Armored Division and additional artillery, slowed down the German advance. There was bitter fighting south of the *Djebel Chirich*, which the Germans were able to decide in their favor. *Djebel Mansour* was taken, but the British Guards, who were inserted into the line, retook the position.

The mountain troopers of the *334. Infanterie-Division* under *Oberst* Lang counterattacked and retook the hill. It was then held against several enemy attacks.

The German advance then continued in the direction of Pinchon. *Infanterie-Regiment 47* of *Oberst* Buhse attacked into the village and took it. The German forces were soon forced back, however, when the enemy attacked with superior forces. The German infantry pulled back to the high ground east of the village.

After 48 hours of bitter fighting, the main effort of Weber's forces reached Ousseltia. The French forces were scattered. More than 2,000 soldiers of the *Oran* and *Constantine* Divisions were taken prisoner.

What had happened to *Panzer-Armee Afrika* in the meantime?

CHAPTER 12

The Retreat of *Panzer-Armee Afrika*

TO THE MARETH POSITION

The withdrawing *Panzer-Armee Afrika* reached the Marsa el Brega position on 26 November, where it defended until 12 December. That was followed by defensive fighting in the arc around Sirte, then both sides of Buerat. The fighting continued from 16–30 January around the Tarhuna–Homs position, where the *90. leichte-Afrika-Division* bled itself white. That line needed to be held for as long as it took to evacuate Tripoli and remove anything of value. The evacuation of Tripoli was started on the night of 22/23 January and concluded on 28 January.

The intense attacks of the British 8th Army in the middle of January were unable to throw the Germans off the timetable for their deliberate withdrawal. An advance against the southern wing was turned back by the *15. Panzer-Division. Oberst i.G.* Irkens, who was the commander of *Panzer-Regiment 8*, inflicted heavy losses on the enemy, who left 30 knocked-out tanks behind on the battlefield.

Once Tripoli was evacuated, the last defense of Italian colonies in Africa was abandoned. What remained was the sheer survival of the Italian and German forces.

Irkens's tank regiment served as the rearguard for *Panzer-Armee Afrika*. It performed admirably south of Tripoli, as well as at Ben Gardane. A bitter tank engagement was conducted at Metameur.

Thanks to the self-sacrificing actions of his rearguards, Rommel was able to pull his battered field army back towards the Tunisian border. The seven battered Italian divisions of the field army were consolidated into three on 25 January. With the permission of both the German and Italian high commands, they were sent ahead of the German forces to Tunisia.

On 26 January, Rommel received a radio message from the *Comando Supremo*. He was informed that he would be relieved of his post due to his poor health as soon as his field army reached the Mareth position. The movement to that position was to be determined by Rommel, however.

The designated successor to Rommel was General Giovanni Messe, who had commanded Italian forces in the Russian Campaign. Colonel General Bastico returned to Italy on 31 January.

While all that was happening, Rommel had hatched a new plan. *Panzer-Armee Afrika* was to attack into the rear of the Western Allies from the Mareth position. Following that, he wanted to turn his forces back around, force Montgomery back, and then continue east.

The plan was rejected not only by the *Comando Supremo* but also the German Armed Forces High Command.

Discussions between Rommel and Messe, who arrived in Africa at the beginning of February, resulted in a compromise. The Mareth position would be held, primarily by Italian forces, which would then free up Rommel's field army to turn its attention to the problem in Tunisia.

In the meantime, the enemy had occupied Faid Pass. In order to combat that threat, *Generaloberst* von Arnim had the *10. Panzer-Division* pulled from its previous sector, which had been quiet, and move south to reorganize. Since the *21. Panzer-Division* had moved out of the Buerat position back to the Mareth position—making it the first German division of Rommel's field army to cross the frontier into Tunisia and placing it under the area of operations of the *5. Panzer-Armee*—it was also employed with the *10. Panzer-Division* against the Allied forces at the Faid Pass.

Both divisions moved out to attack on 30 January under the overall command of *Generalleutnant* Ziegler, von Arnim's deputy.

The fighting lasted 48 hours but, in the end, the Germans took the pass back. The U.S. forces employed there pulled back to Sidi Bou Zid.

A second attack group, consisting of the *Centauro* Armored Division and German elements provided from the two German armored divisions, attacked through Maknassy in the direction of Gafsa. That attack came as a complete surprise to the U.S. II Corps. The U.S. 1st Armored Division, which had established itself in the saddle of the Faid Pass, was ejected. Gafsa was evacuated.

On 5 February 1943, an incident occurred that deprived the *10. Panzer-Division* of its commander. *Generalleutnant* Fischer, who wanted to conduct a leader's reconnaissance in the sector of the *Superga* Division, ran over a mine in his command car shortly after departing forward of the Italian main line of resistance. The force of the explosion tore off both of his legs and an arm. He died a few minutes later, writing a letter to his wife. The liaison officer and the driver were killed instantly. The division's operations officer, *Oberstleutnant i.G.* Bürker could be retrieved from the vehicle, badly wounded. *Oberst Freiherr* von Broich assumed command of the division, with his operations officer being *Oberstleutnant i.G. Graf* von Stauffenberg, who later became famous for his involvement in the plot to kill Hitler in 1944.

It was anticipated that the Allies would attack in the south in an effort to reach the sea and separate the two field armies.

ROMMEL ON THE MOVE!

When the withdrawal of *Panzer-Armee Afrika* stopped at the Mareth position, it was the middle of February. The Italian XX and XXXI Corps, reinforced by *Oberst Freiherr* von Liebenstein's *164. leichte Afrika-Division*, held the positions initially. The "Sahara" Group of General Mannerini was positioned from the mountains at Matmata down to Toum-Tatahouine along the *Schott el Djerid*.

To the west of Sfax, Rommel positioned two battle groups. One was the 131st *Centauro* Armored Division, which he intended to use to advance on Gafsa with its armored elements. The second battle group was the combined force of the *10. Panzer-Division* and the *21. Panzer-Division*, both led by *Generalleutnant* Ziegler. Its attack objective was the Faid Pass. The latter force was actually under the command of the *5. Panzer-Armee*.

When the attack was launched on 14 February, the tanks kicked up a tremendous amount of dust, which affected the *21. Panzer-Division* the worst, since it had the longest stretch to cover through the open desert.

The *10. Panzer-Division* rolled up to the pass and opened fire on the U.S. tanks, which started to be identified. The Americans were caught by surprise, and their first vehicles burst into flames. The Germans were able to take the pass in the first charge and continue their advance. At the *Djebel Lessouda*, the division swung south, where it intended to link up with the *21. Panzer-Division*, which had already reported in by radio from the Sidi bu Zid area.

As the *10. Panzer-Division* headed south, it encountered concentrations of American armor from the U.S. 1st Armored Division. The tank commanders had to move south with their heads out of the hatches due to the thick swarms of sand and dust. As things started to turn critical for the *10. Panzer-Division*, the *21. Panzer-Division* showed up in the enemy's rear. Engaged from three sides, the main combat power of the U.S. II Corps was effectively eliminated by that evening. The U.S. forces pulled back, leaving 70 burning and smoldering wrecks on the battlefield.

Early on 15 February, *Kampfgruppe Ziegler* advanced along the aqueduct in the direction of Sbeitla. In its advance, it encountered Combat Commands A and C, with their tanks, artillery and antitank guns. The 2nd Battalion of the 1st Armored under Lieutenant Colonel Alger fought until it was effectively wiped out, with the commander being taken prisoner.

The U.S. forces lost an additional 95 tanks and armored cars on that day. More than 2,000 prisoners were taken.

When the report of what happened reached the White House, President Roosevelt turned to his advisors and asked: "Can't our boys fight?"[1]

On 16 February, the *10. Panzer-Division* swung north and rolled on Pichon, where there was a large French battle group. Before the town could

---

1. Translator's Note: Reverse-translated.

be reached, however, *Generalleutnant* Ziegler received orders to call off the attack. The *21. Panzer-Division*, which was headed for Kasserine Pass, was also stopped. Something had occurred that caused Rommel to receive overall command of not only *Panzer-Armee "Afrika,"* but also of the two divisions that had been attached to the *5. Panzer-Armee*. As the old hands in Africa said: "It's rommeling again!"

When the U.S. II Corps abandoned Gafsa, Rommel instructed *Oberst* Menton and his *Panzergrenadier-Regiment "Afrika"* to take it, which Menton promptly did. A reconnaissance-in-force was dispatched in the direction of Feriana and, by 17 February, elements of the *DAK* had entered the town.

Given that situation, Rommel's plan no longer appeared so "audacious, as was first thought" by the Army and Armed Forces High Commands. Rommel recommended advancing as far as Tebessa, appearing in the rear of the enemy, and cutting of his frontline forces from their supplies. After the airfield at Thelepte, just north of Feriana, had been taken by the *15. Panzer-Division*, Rommel was given back command over the two other armored divisions. He was given the green light to advance on Tebessa.

The *21. Panzer-Division* took Sbeitla in hard fighting and blocked the road. Rommel sent the *10. Panzer-Division* in the direction of the Kasserine Pass. That pass was the gate to the Tunisian mountain country. The attack there started on 19 February. At the same time, German and Italian forces advanced on Tozeur and took it. Patrols of both *Aufklärungs-Abteilung 3 (mot.)* and *Aufklärungs-Abteilung 33 (mot.)* went around the pass and rolled along the trail to the northwest in the direction of Tebessa, passing the *Djebel Dernaja* and the *Djebel Chettabis*.

After an artillery preparation on the evening of 19 February, the tanks of the *10. Panzer-Division* advanced. Other reconnaissance elements from *Aufklärungs-Abteilung 3 (mot.)* stormed the pass. After two hours of bitter close combat, they were forced back. It was then the turn of *Oberst* Menton and his "Africans." They, too, were forced back without obtaining their objective.

On the morning of 20 February, the *Bersaglieri* of the *Ariete* Division also joined the fight. Despite fighting bravely and taking a lot of casualties, they were also unable to force a decision against the stubborn defenders.

The Axis forces started to jam up in front of the pass. Had the Allies bombed, they would have reaped a rich harvest.

The Germans tried one more time. The rocket launchers of *Oberst* Andrae's *Werfer-Regiment 71* fired a preparation. Before the reverberations had faded from the last impact, the tanks of *Hauptmann* Stotten's *I./Panzer-Regiment 8* moved out. He was among the lead vehicles. The tanks thundered through the pass and engaged the enemy's tanks and antitank guns. They broke through!

General Anderson, the Commander-in-Chief of the British 1st Army, issued orders: "No one pulls back a foot, unless it's in the direction of the enemy!"[2]

Up to that point, the Axis attack had cost the Allies 169 tanks, 95 armored cars, 36 self-propelled guns, and 50 artillery pieces.

True to form, Rommel decided to exploit the situation. He employed the *10. Panzer-Division* that evening in the direction of Thala, while the *21. Panzer-Division* was directed to march around the foothills of the mountains. To support these movements, *Oberstleutnant* Buhse's *Infanterie-Regiment 47* was ordered to also advance through Pichon to the northwest and attack Kesserea.

Rommel's main effort took another pass during the fighting on 21 February. The only pass remaining to fulfill Rommel's plan was at the *Djebel el Hamra*. The *10. Panzer-Division* succeeded in taking Thala. The Allies began to worry. General Alexander, who had just assumed overall command in Tunisia, immediately headed in the direction of Thala with his battle staff. As he advanced, he brought along any forces that crossed his path and redirected others. In the end, he sent the 6th Armoured Division towards the German spearheads, as well as the British Guards forces.

The 6th Armoured Division engaged the *10. Panzer-Division* outside of Thala, with the latter division losing 10 tanks. Combat Command B of Major General Robinett also moved forward, where it engaged the exhausted forces of the *DAK*. The fighting raged back and forth on 22 February. As soon as it had turned light, the Allied air forces swooped down on the Axis forces. The attack of the *DAK* bogged down. Rommel, who raced forward with his operations officer, *Oberst* Bayerlein, was caught in an artillery barrage and had to escape to a nearby patch of woods.

The news from the Mareth position did not bode well for Rommel, either. Rommel's attack gamble had based itself partially on the assumption that Montgomery's 8th Army would need more time to launch its next offensive than it actually did. Rommel was taught a lesson. Rommel called off his attack; his forces had been too weak after all.

After a commanders' conference at Kasserine Pass, at which Kesselring was also present, after having flown over from Frascati, Rommel ordered his forces back to their jumping-off positions. In the course of the withdrawal, many stretches were heavily mined and all of the important facilities and bridges were blown up.

During the conference, Kesselring asked Rommel whether he would be healthy enough to assume command of *Heeresgruppe Afrika*—Army Group

---

2. Translator's Note: Reverse-translated.

"Africa"—so that command-and-control relationships could be firmly established between and among the two field armies.

The doctors had given Rommel only four weeks before he started another 8-week cure. Rommel accepted the invitation to command, at least temporarily. On 23 February, Kesselring ordered the new command-and-control relationships. *Heeresgruppe Afrika* was formed, even though it never had nearly the forces, equipment, and formations to make it even remotely close to approaching a true field-army group. Rommel was given command, with von Arnim designated as his deputy.

ROMMEL LEAVES AFRICA

The situation for *Heeresgruppe Afrika* had stabilized somewhat at the beginning of March. The length of the frontage was some 450 kilometers. In addition, there were 400 kilometers of coastline that also had to be guarded, since Allied landings were also possible there.

At the time, the Western Allies had the British 1st Army, with its three divisions and two special-purpose brigades, with an end strength of 50,000 men, 240 artillery pieces, 400 antitank guns, and 166 tanks. The U.S. II Corps had some 40,000 men with 200 artillery pieces, 200 antitank guns and 200 tanks. There was also a Free French corps that had 40,000 men, but little in the way of heavy weapons.

Those forces were arrayed against the *5. Panzer-Armee* in the north. To the south, around the Mareth position, was Mongomery's 8th Army, which was facing General Messe's Italian 1st Army. The British forces there consisted of 80,000 men, 400 guns, 550 antitank guns, and 900 tanks.

Heeresgruppe Afrika had an end strength of 80,000 German and 40,000 Italian soldiers in the front trenches. Rear-area services accounted for another 230,000 personnel, of which 150,000 were Italians. The amount of artillery and other heavy weapons on hand was less than 50% of authorized strength.

At the time, it was imperative for the Axis forces to hold the Mareth position and disrupt the Allied buildup for the spring offensive as much as possible. To achieve the latter goal, Rommel planned an attack from the Mareth Line in the direction of Medenine. To that end, he employed his three German armored divisions and the *164. leichte Afrika-Division*. The German forces earmarked for the attack occupied their staging areas by 5 March.

The attack was initiated with a powerful artillery preparation on 6 March. *Oberst* Irkens had been designated as the *Panzerführer Afrika* and, in his capacity as the senior armor officer in the theater, had command and control over both *Panzer-Regiment 8* and *Panzer-Regiment 5*. Together with *Oberst* Gerhardt's *Panzer-Regiment 7* of the *10. Panzer-Division*, they attempted to force a breakthrough in the Medenine–Métameur area. Irkens succeeded in entering the enemy's forward defensive lines but, in so doing, he lost 55 of his 80 employed tanks.

That afternoon, *General* Cramer, who had just returned to Africa from his convalescence and reassumed command of the *DAK*, recommended calling off the attack. With a heavy heart, Rommel agreed.

Three days later, Rommel transferred command of *Heeresgruppe Afrika* to *Generaloberst* von Arnim. He then flew to Rome, where he had an audience with Mussolini on 9 March.

On 13 March, Rommel met Hitler at the *Führer* Headquarters. A decision was made concerning the disposition of the forces. The non-mobile portions of the Italian 1st Army were to be pulled out of the line at Mareth and brought back to the Gabes position, which had yet to be established. The mobile forces remained in place. They also received permission to pull back in case the enemy threatened to break through or bypass them.

Orders were issued concerning logistics and the desperately needed reconstitution of the forces in the field. It was hoped that the bridgehead around Tunis could at least be held until the fall.

Rommel wanted more, though, and was not afraid to say it to Hitler's face. He asked that the front be pulled back 150 kilometers. That would free up 300 Italian artillery pieces that could then be incorporated into the main defensive lines. If that were to be done and the promised logistics and reconstitution efforts undertaken, Rommel believed the bridgehead could hold out for another year. That would obviously delay the Western Allies' efforts to land on the European continent for at least as long.

Rommel wanted to fly back to Africa, but he received orders to go on his cure in order to restore his health. Hitler's last words to Rommel concerning Africa: "Get better, so that you're back on top of things. I guarantee you that you will be leading operations from the Tunisian Bridgehead against Casablanca."

Rommel had left Africa for good. The battle for the Tunisian Bridgehead drew to a rapid close. One of the soldiers who had served under Rommel for two years said the following to the author concerning the last two months: "Rommel was no longer in Africa. All at once, it was as if someone had let the air out of the tires!"

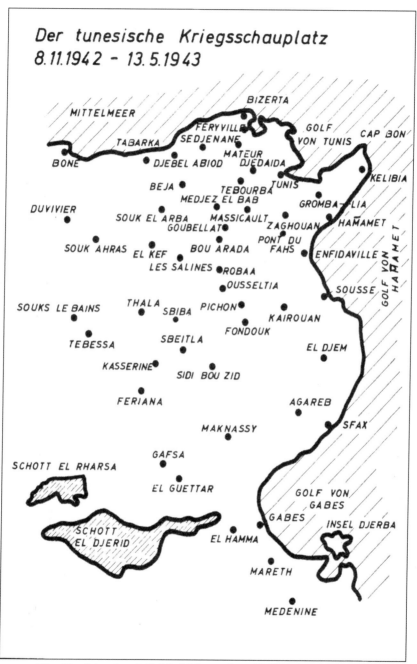

The Tunisian battlefield, 8 November 1942 to 13 May 1943.

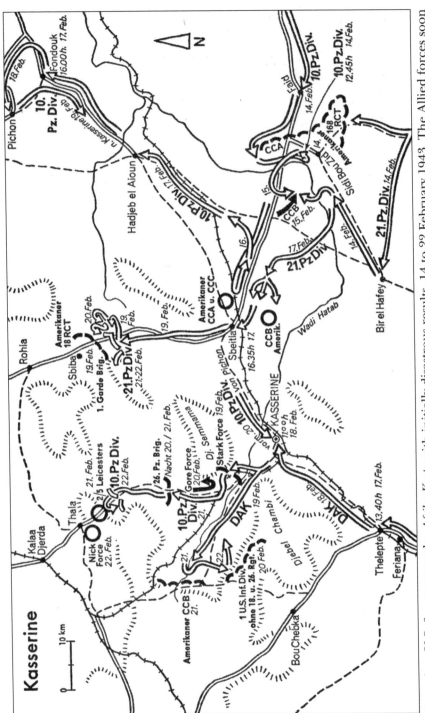

Kasserine: U.S. forces meet the *Afrika Korps* with initially disastrous results, 14 to 22 February 1943. The Allied forces soon held a firm defensive line and forced Rommel to stop the offensive. U.S. troops quickly learned the hard lessons of war and gave a good account of themselves.

Generalmajor Neumann-Silkow.

Werner Marcks, a battle group commander in Africa.

Battle group commander Geißler.

General der Panzertruppe Gustav von Vaerst.

General der Panzertruppe Crüwell

The command vehicle has broken down and Rommel takes an interest in the repairs.

Generalleutnant Seidemann, the last *Luftwaffe* commander in Tunisia.

Generalleutnant Friedrich Weber, commander of the *334. Infanterie-Division.*

Generalleutnant Borowietz, commander of the *15. Panzer-Division* in Tunisia.

Generaloberst von Arnim, at left, with *Generalmajor* Weber at Pont du Fahs.

Oberst Lang (middle) and *Oberst* von Barenthin (left) pinpoint positions during operation *Eilbote*.

Major Lueder, commander of *sPz.Abt. 501* (right), confers with his intelligence officer. The *501* was an independent *Tiger* unit.

The Tunisian winter was cold and wet. A *Tiger* negotiates a shallow stream.

Half-tracks and motorcycles of a reconnaissance unit follow the *Tiger*.

An armored spearhead, including *Panzer III* and *Tigers*, advances toward Kairouan.

The massive 56-ton *Tiger 1*, the most powerful tank in the theater. However, it was committed in numbers too small to make a difference to the final outcome.

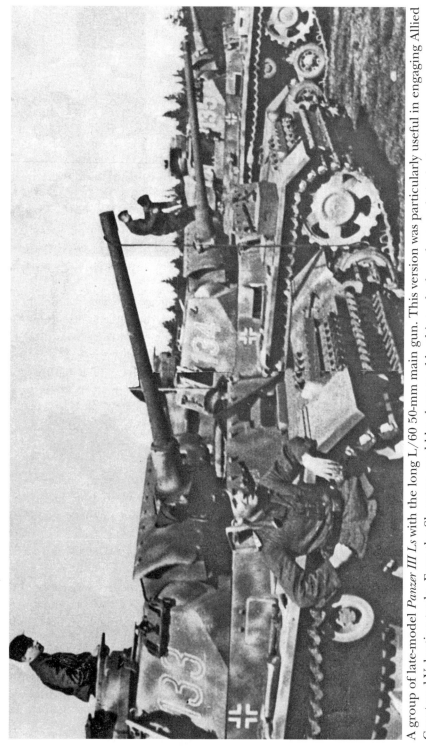

A group of late-model *Panzer III Ls* with the long L/60 50-mm main gun. This version was particularly useful in engaging Allied Grant and Valentine tanks. Even the Sherman could be destroyed by this tank, though at a relatively short range.

CHAPTER 13

The End in Africa

In the northern sector of the Tunisian Bridgehead, *Division* von *Manteuffel* was committed. It was an *ad hoc* formation consisting of a wide variety of elements, including a *Bersaglieri* regiment. It was employed north of the *Djebel Abiod*. The legendary armor commander Manteuffel was able to hold that position until 28 March. When the enemy launched an offensive on 30 March, the Axis lines began to waver. In the second attack that followed, they were forced back to an area 20 kilometers east of Cape Serrat–St. Jefna–Station de Nair.

While that fighting was going on, the 8th Army had started Operation "Pugilist" along the Mareth Line. In its first assault, the 50th and 51st Infantry Divisions entered the positions of the "Young Fascist" Division defending in the Zigzaghou *wadi.*

On his own initiative, *Generalmajor* Borowitz, the commander of the *15. Panzer-Division,* came to the aid of his Italian comrades with his division on 21 March. *Panzer-Regiment 8* and *Oberst* Irkens helped turn the tide against the enemy forces that had broken through, knocking out six tanks and scattering the enemy's infantry with high-explosive rounds. Montgomery called off the attack.

In the vicinity of the *Djebel Tebaga,* Mannerini's battle group was pressed back. *Generaloberst* von Arnim, who arrived on the battlefield on 23 March, gave Colonel General Messe permission to move the non-mobile elements of his 1st Army back to the Akarit position.

At first light on 26 March, the New Zealand 2nd Infantry Division attacked. It was joined in the attack by the British 1st Armoured Division. By evening, a deep penetration had been achieved. If the attack succeeded in reaching the sea, the entire Italian 1st Army would have been cut off.

The *15. Panzer-Division* was alerted and rolled into the southern flank of the enemy's attack forces and held them up. That allowed the *21. Panzer-Division* and the *164. leichte Afrika-Division* to pull back to El Hamma, where they established a blocking position. The 8th Army's attacks on 27 and 28 March could not break through there, and the 1st Army was able to withdraw to the Akarit position. The *Centauro* Armored Division fought bravely at Guettar against a two-fold superiority.

228

The U.S. II Corps, which had been directed to support the 8th Army's attack, was unable to make much progress. Its two divisions were pushed back. The U.S. 9th Armored Division, which had been directed to break through to the coastal plain near Sened, was stopped and defeated by two small German battle groups: *Kampfgruppe Medicus* and *Kampfgruppe Lang*.

Even though the Axis forces defended successfully, the logistics issue was a problem that would not go away. No more ships made it through to Tunis after 23 March. The enemy's air superiority was oppressive.

The few German fighters were no longer in a position to hold their own against the Western Allies' air superiority. They flew escort for the few *Stuka* formations that remained on African soil. The efforts of the *Luftwaffe* had been relegated into insignificance, especially since there was hardly any fuel available to launch aircraft.

On the evening of 4 April, the III Corps of the 8th Army assaulted the first three hill positions of the Italians' XX Army Corps. The *90. leichte-Afrika-Division*, which was in support of the Italians, was able to turn back the British in its sector. Nevertheless, when it looked as though the 8th Army would force a breakthrough, *Oberst* Irkens and his few remaining tanks launched a counterattack along with the mechanized infantry of *Hauptmann* Pätzold. In the early-morning hours, the attacking forces ran into a British supply column, which was either destroyed or captured. The Germans reached the area that had been penetrated, sealing it off and clearing it. When the 50 enemy tanks attempted to roll back through to their own lines, they were engaged by the tankers of the *15. Panzer-Division* and the *Flak* that had been attached to them. A number of British tanks were destroyed.

In addition to driving back the enemy, 20 tanks from *Panzer-Regiment 5* that had been stranded in the area of the penetration due to a lack of fuel were refueled and saved from certain capture or destruction.

Panzer-Regiment 8 was ordered to screen the withdrawal of the *90. leichte-Afrika-Division*, which was scheduled for the coming night. *Generaloberst* von Arnim had ordered the withdrawal. In order for the wounded to be evacuated and also allow the severely tested infantry to cover the 300 kilometers, the *Luftwaffe* had to give up its supplies of fuel. That allowed the trucks to be fueled, and the *Luftwaffe* was actually instrumental in saving the infantry forces.

During the evening of 8 April, the lead elements of the 8th Army reached the Gabes–Gafsa line and the road there. The rearguards of the *DAK* repeatedly turned around to try to slow the advance of the 8th Army. On 10 April, Montgomery reached Sfax; three days later, his lead elements were just outside the tank ditch at the Enfidaville position.

THE ALLIED ADVANCE IN THE NORTH

At the same time, the Allied forces in the north had reached Cape Serrat and taken it by 1 April. At Heidous, the Free French and Moroccan forces, coupled with elements of the U.S. 1st Armored Division, achieved a penetration in the sector of Manteuffel's *ad hoc* division. Hasso von Manteuffel personally led his reserves in a successful effort to seal off the penetration.

On 7 April, the 78th Infantry Division attempted to take "Longstop Hill," which was being held by the mountain troops of the *334. Infanterie-Division.* The Germans were forced to pull back, step-by-step, but they were able to continue controlling the hill.

The fighting in the Tunisian Bridgehead approached the end. From 14 to 16 April, the newly arrived British 4th Infantry Division attacked *Kampfgruppe Lang* of the *334. Infanterie-Division,* which was holding at Sidi Nsir.

During the night of 19/20 April, the 8th Army opened its offensive against the Enfidaville position. The city fell, and Montgomery shifted his attack's main area to the coastal area, since he estimated that the German-held positions from Enfidaville to Zaghouan would cost too many casualties.

On 24 April, "Longstop Hill" finally fell to the 78th Infantry Division. That opened the gates to Tunis.

The final round of fighting started. Divisions from the Allied forces stormed from all sides. Nineteen large formations, including four armored divisions, were advancing on Tunis. The German formations, increasingly burned out, pulled back to Tunis and the Cape Bon Peninsula. Individual pockets of resistance held out until the beginning of May.

Oberst Irkens, in his role as *Panzerführer Afrika,* threw 70 tanks from all of the armored formations against the enemy. More than 1,000 tanks were rolling forward to break through to Tunis. When he finally disengaged from the enemy, he had 20 tanks left. His men had accounted for 90 of the Allies' seemingly inexhaustible supply of armor.

During the night of 6/7 May, the remaining tanks of *Heeresgruppe Afrika* rolled back to the El Aila airfield, west of Tunis. There was a series of smaller engagements, until the last of the ammunition had been fired off and the fuel consumed. The remaining seven operational tanks were driven into a *wadi.*

The Allies continued their attacks on the morning of 7 May, with the artillery hammering into the ever-shrinking bridgehead. Allied airpower smashed pockets of resistance. They were able to do that without any aerial opposition, since the last *Luftwaffe* formations had left the continent.

At 1740 hours on that day, the first Allied formations entered Tunis, splitting the forces of *Heeresgruppe Afrika* into two. By the next morning, all of the city was in the hands of the English.

It was not until 9 May, however, that the Allies were able to break through east of Bizerta Lake and take Fort Farina. The last order of the *5. Panzer-Armee* was issued at 1524 hours: "Destroy documents and equipment—Good-bye —Long live Germany!" The next day, the British 6th Armoured Division broke through at Hammanlif. It was followed by the Indian 4th Infantry Division, which then turned in the direction of Cape Bon. By the evening of 12 May, it had completely occupied that northernmost peninsula of Tunisia.

The divisions of the Germans' "Middle Group" sent their last radio transmissions during the morning of 12 May to *Heeresgruppe Afrika*. The field-army group's last command post was at Ste. Marie du Zit. *General der Panzertruppe* Cramer had been able to get there before the capitulation with the last two armored vehicles of the *DAK*. Around 1100 hours on that day, von Arnim sent a message to Rome indicating that his command post was surrounded on two sides. Immediately thereafter, he made a surrender offer to the Allies. It was *General der Panzertruppe* Cramer who sent the final message, however:

To: German Armed Forces High Command
Ammunition expended. Weapons and materiel destroyed. The *Deutsches Afrika-Korps* has fought to the point where it is no longer capable of fighting."

Early on the morning of 13 May, General Alexander sent a message to the Prime Minister in London:

Sir, it is my duty to inform you that the Tunisian Campaign is over. All enemy resistance has ceased. All of Africa is ours!

✠

The end in Africa was just as catastrophic as that in Stalingrad. In addition to 130,000 German personnel, some 180,000 Italian personnel were taken captive. What was even more serious: the fighting morale of the Italians had been broken. They had lost the fight for their colonial possessions and were then in fear for their homeland, since the writing was on the wall that the Allies would soon kick open the door to "Fortress Europe."

In all, one hundred thousand soldiers of all nations lost their lives in the fighting for North Africa.

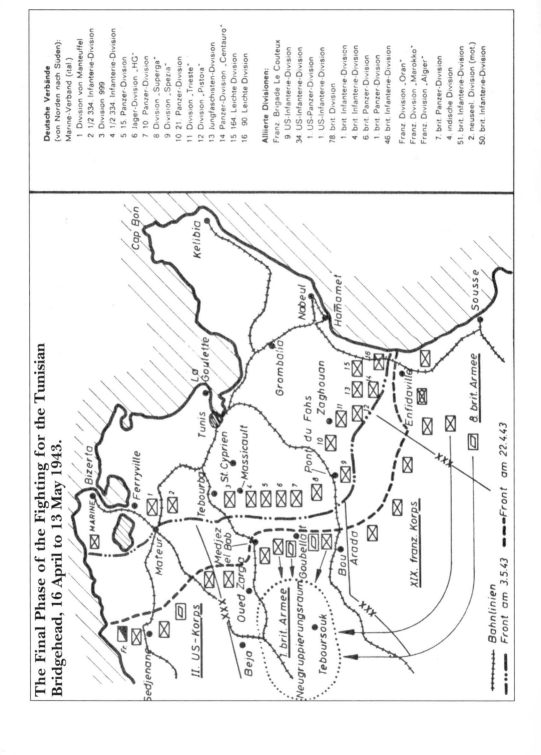

The Final Phase of the Fighting for the Tunisian Bridgehead, 16 April to 13 May 1943.

Deutsche Verbände
(von Norden nach Süden):

Marine-Verband (ital.)

1 Division von Manteuffel
2 1/2 334. Infanterie-Division
3 Division 999
4 1/2 334. Infanterie-Division
5 15. Panzer-Division
6 Jager-Division „HG"
7 10. Panzer-Division
8 Division „Superga"
9 Division „Spezia"
10 21. Panzer-Division
11 Division „Trieste"
12 Division „Pistoia"
13 Jungfaschisten-Division
14 Panzer-Division „Centauro"
15 164. Leichte Division
16 90 Leichte Division

Alliierte Divisionen:

Franz. Brigade Le Couteux
9 US-Infanterie-Division
34 US-Infanterie-Division
1 US-Panzer-Division
1 US-Infanterie-Division
78. brit. Division
1. brit. Infanterie-Division
4. brit. Infanterie-Division
6. brit. Panzer-Division
1. brit. Panzer-Division
46. brit. Infanterie-Division

Franz. Division „Oran"
Franz. Division „Marokko"
Franz. Division „Alger"
7. brit. Panzer-Division
4. indische Division
51. brit. Infanterie-Division
2. neuseel. Division (mot.)
50. brit. Infanterie-Division

Bizerta
MARINE
Ferryville
Sedjenang
Fr.
II. US-Korps
Beja
Mateur
Oued Zarga
Medjez
el Bab
Goubellat
Neugruppierungsraum
1. brit. Armee
Teboursouk
Tebourba
Tunis
St. Cyprien
Massicault
Pont du Fahs
La Goulette
Grombalia
Zaghouan
Bou Arada
XIX. franz. Korps
Cap Bon
Kelibia
Nabeul
Hammamet
Enfidaville
Sousse
8. brit. Armee

Bahnlinien
Front am 3.5.43
Front am 22.4.43

APPENDIX A

Rank Comparisons

U.S. ARMY	BRITISH ARMY	GERMAN ARMY
Enlisted Men		
Private	Private	*Schütze*
Private First Class	Private 1st Class	*Oberschütze*
Corporal	Lance Corporal	*Gefreiter*
Senior Corporal	Corporal	*Obergefreiter*
Staff Corporal		*Stabsgefreiter*
Noncommissioned Officers		
Sergeant	Sergeant	*Unteroffizier*
	Staff Sergeant	*Unterfeldwebel*
Staff Sergeant	Technical Sergeant	*Feldwebel*
Sergeant First Class	Master Sergeant	*Oberfeldwebel*
Master Sergeant	Sergeant Major	*Hauptfeldwebel*
Sergeant Major		*Stabsfeldwebel*
Officers		
Second Lieutenant	Second Lieutenant	*Leutnant*
First Lieutenant	First Lieutenant	*Oberleutnant*
Captain	Captain	*Hauptman*
Major	Major	*Major*
Lieutenant Colonel	Lieutenant Colonel	*Oberst Leutnant*
Colonel	Colonel	*Oberst*
Brigadier General	Brigadier General	*Generalmajor*
Major General	Major General	*Generalleutnant*
Lieutenant General	Lieutenant General	*General der Fallschirmjäger, etc.*
General	General	*Generaloberst*
General of the Army	Field Marshal	*Feldmarschall*

APPENDIX B

The *Afrika Korps* Order of Battle in North Africa

5. leichte Division

Arrived in Tripoli 14 February 1941. Reinforced, reorganized, and renamed as the *21. Panzer-Division* on 1 October 1941.

Commanders:

Generalmajor Johannes Streich, 20 February 1941–22 July, 1941.

Generalmajor Johann von Ravenstein, 23 July 1941–1 October, 1941.

Main Combat Formations:

Panzer-Regiment 5

1./Panzerjäger-Abteilung (mot)¹ 33

Panzerjäger-Abteilung (mot)² 39

Machinengewehr-Bataillon (mot) 2

Machinengewehr-Bataillon (mot) 8

I./Artillerie-Regiment (mot) 75

Flak-Abteilung (mot) 605

Flak-Abteilung (mot) 606

Aufklärungs-Abteilung³ (mot) 3

1./Pionier-Bataillon⁴ (mot) 39

10. Panzer-Division

Transferred to Tunisia in November 1942. Destroyed in the final fighting for Tunis and never reconstituted.

Commanders:

Generalleutnant Wolfgang Fisher, 2 August 1941–1 February 1943.

Generalmajor Fritz Freiherr von Broich, 1 February 1943–12 May 1943.

Main Combat Formations:

Panzer-Regiment 7

Panzerjäger-Abteilung (mot) 90

Infanterie-Regiment (mot) 69

---

1. *(mot)* = motorized.

2. *Panzerjäger* = antitank.

3. *Aufklärungs* = reconnaissance.

4. *Pionier* = engineer.

Infanterie-Regiment (mot) 86
Sturmregiment "Hermann Göring" (mot) (Luftwaffe)
Infanterie-Bataillon (mot) A4
Artillerie-Regiment (mot) 90
Flak-Gruppe Böhmer (Luftwaffe)
Kradschützen-Bataillon⁵ (mot) 10
Pionier-Bataillon (mot) 90

15. Panzer-Division

Parts of the division arrived in Africa in late April of 1941. By the middle of June, the division had completed its transfer.

Commanders:

Initial commander: *Generalmajor* Heinrich von Prittwitz, 22 March 1941–10 April 1941.

Final commander: *Oberst* Willibald Boroweitz, 12 December 1943–13 May 1943.

Main Combat Formations:

Panzer-Regiment 8
Panzerjäger-Abteilung (mot) 33
Schützen-Brigade (mot) 15
       Infanterie-Regiment (mot) 115
       Infanterie-Regiment (mot) 200
       Maschinengewehr-Bataillon (mot) 8
       Kradschützen-Bataillon (mot) 15
Artillerie-Regiment (mot) 33
Aufklärungs-Abteilung (mot) 33
Pionier-Bataillon (mot) 33

21. Panzer-Division

Formed from the *5. leichte Division* on 1 October 1941 in a considerably strengthened state.

Commanders:

Initial commander: *Generalmajor* Johann von Ravenstein, 1 October 1941–29 November 1941.

Final commander: *Generalmajor* Heinrich-Hermann von Hülsen, 25 April 1943–13 May 1943.

Main Combat Formations:

Panzer-Regiment 5

---

5. *Kradschützen-Bataillon* = motorcycle batallion.

Panzerjäger-Abteilung (mot) 39
Infanterie-Regiment (mot) 104
Artillerie-Regiment (mot) 155
Aufklärungs-Abteilung (mot) 3
Pionier-Bataillon (mot) 200

90. leichte Afrika-Division

This division was initially designated as *Afrika-Division z.b.V.*[6] in August 1941. In March 1942, the division was reinforced and reorganized as *90. leichte Afrika-Division.*

Commanders:

Initial commander: *Generalmajor* Max Sümmermann, 17 July 1941–10 December 1941.

Final commander: *Generalleutnant* Theodor Graf von Sponek, 22 September 1942–12 May 1943.

Main Combat Formations:

Panzerjäger-Abteilung (mot) 190
Infanterie-Regiment (mot) 155
Infanterie-Regiment (mot) 200
Panzergrenadier-Regiment[7] (mot) Afrika
Kolbeck-Bataillon
Artillerie-Regiment (mot) 190
schwerste Infanteriegeschütze-Kompanie[8] 707
schwerste Infanteriegeschütze-Kompanie 708
Aufklärungs-Kompanie (mot) 580
Pionier-Bataillon (mot) 900

164. leichte Afrika-Division

Arrived in Africa in July 1942 from Crete.

Commanders:

Initial commander: *Oberst* Carl-Hans Lungerhausen, ? August 1942–31 August 1942.

Final commander: *Generalmajor* Kurt Freiherr von Liebenstein, 13 March 1943–13 May 1943.

Main Combat Formations:

Panzergrenadier-Regiment (mot) 125

---

6. *z.b.V.* = for special duties.

7. *Panzergrenadier* = armored infantry.

8. *schwerste Infanteriegeschütze-Kompanie* = heavy infantry gun (150mm) company.

Panzergrenadier-Regiment (mot) 382
Panzergrenadier-Regiment (mot) 433
Artillerie-Regiment (mot) 220
schwerste Infanteriegeschütze-Kompanie 707 [9]
schwerste Infanteriegeschütze-Kompanie 708
Flak-Abteilung (mot) 609
Aufklärungs-Abteilung (mot) 220
Pionier-Bataillon (mot) 220

334. Infanterie-Division
Arrived in Africa in December 1942 from the Grafenwöhr training area in Germany.
Commanders:
Initial commander: *Oberst* Freidrich Weber, 13 November 1942–15 April 1943.
Final commander: *Generalmajor* Fritz Krause, 15 April 1943–8 May 1943.
Main Combat Formations:
Infanterie-Regiment (mot) 754
Infanterie-Regiment (mot) 755
Gebirgs-Infanterie-Regiment[10] *(mot) 756*
Panzerjäger-Abteilung (mot) 334
Artillerie-Regiment (mot) 334
Pionier-Bataillon (mot) 334

999. leichte Afrika-Division
Formed in late 1942 initially as the *999. Afrika-Brigade* primarily from court-martialed soldiers. Redesignated *999. leichte Afrika-Division* in in March 1943 and two of its regiments transferred to Tunis.
Commanders:
Initial commander: *Generalleutnant* Kurt Thomas, 23 December 1942–1 April 1943.
Final commander: *Oberst* Ernst-Günther Baade, 2 April 1943–13 May 1943.
Main Combat Formations (actually served in Africa):
Afrika-Schützen-Regiment (mot) 961
Afrika-Schützen-Regiment (mot) 962
Artillerie-Regiment (mot) 999
Pionier-Bataillon (mot) 999

---

9. Companies 707 and 708 transferred from the *90. leichte Afrika-Division* in August 1942.

10. *Gebirgs-Infanterie-Regiment* = mountain troop regiment.

Division von Broich/Division von Manteuffel

Organized from miscellaneous German units in Tunisia. This unit was the first to meet U.S. forces in combat at Tebourba in November 1942. Redesignated as *Division* von *Manteuffel* on 7 February 1943.

Commanders:

Initial commander: *Oberst* Fritz Freiherr von Broich, 18 November 1942–5 February 1943.

Final commander: *Generalleutnant* Bülowius, 31 March 1943–9 May 1943.

Main Combat Formations (March 1943):

Fallschirmjäger-Regiment[11] (mot) "Barenthin" (Luftwaffe)

Panzergrenadier-Regiment (mot) 160

Bersaglieri-Regiment[12] (mot) 10 (Italian)

       Infanterie-Bataillon (mot) XVI

       Infanterie-Bataillon (mot) XXXIV

       Infanterie-Bataillon (mot) LXIII

IV./"Afrika"-Artillerie-Regiment (mot) 2

Flak-Kampftruppe (Luftwaffe)

Fallschirmjäger-Pioneer-Bataillon (mot) 11 (Luftwaffe)

Division "Hermann Göring"

A *Luftwaffe* formation that was heavily involved in the final battles in Tunisia. Two battalions of the *Jäger-Regiment* were sent to Tunisia in November 1942 to assist in its defense. By March 1943, the majority of the division had been transported to Tunis. The division was largely destroyed in Africa but was reconstituted in southern France and Italy.

Commander:

Generalmajor Joseph Schmidt, March 1943–9 May 1943.

Main Combat Formations (April 1943):

I./Panzer-Regiment "Hermann Göring"

II. & III./Grenadier-Regiment "Hermann Göring"

I. & III./Jäger-Regiment "Hermann Göring"

1./Artillerie-Regiment 90

2./Artillerie-Regiment 190

I. & II./Flak-Regiment "Hermann Göring"

2./Werfer-Abteilung 1[13]

Aufklärungs-Abteilung "Hermann Göring"

---

11. *Fallschirmjäger* = parachute troops.

12. *Bersaglieri* = mountain troops.

13. *Werfer* = rocket launcher.

Fallschirm-Brigade Ramcke

The brigade completed its arrival in Africa by 17 August 1942 and was officially placed under the command of *Panzerarmee Afrika*. Positioned on the southern part of the Alamein front, the brigade was presumed destroyed when the front collapsed on 3 November 1942. However, the indefatigable Ramke and his tough parartoopers captured a complete British supply column for an armored division. The now fully-motorized *Brigade Ramcke* successfully completed a 200-mile trek through enemy territory, much to the astonishment of Rommel.

Commander:

Generalmajor Bernhard Ramke, 16 July 1942–November 1942.

Major von der Heydte, November 1942–12 May 1943.

Main Combat Formations:

On its arrival in Africa, the brigade consisted of three *Jäger-Bataillone*, one *Panzerjäger-Kompanie*, one *Artillerie-Abteilung*, and one *Pionier-Kompanie*. The brigade had no organic transport capability and initially used the transport capacity of *Flak-Regiment 135*.

APPENDIX C

Luftwaffe Fighter and Destroyer Units in North Africa

II./Jagdgeschwader 2 Tunisia, November 1942–March 1943.

6./Jagdgeschwader 3 Africa, November 1942–March 1943.

7./Jagdgeschwader 26 Africa, May–July 1941.

II./Jagdgeschwader 26 Tunisia, November 1942.

I./Jagdgeschwader 27 Africa, April 1941–November 1942.

II./Jagdgeschwader 27 Africa, September 1941–December 1942.

III./Jagdgeschwader 27 Africa, December 1941–November 1942.

II./Jagdgeschwader 51 Tunisia, November 1942–April 1943.

I./Jagdgeschwader 53 Tunisia, November 1942–March 1943.

II./Jagdgeschwader 53 Tunisia, November 1942–March 1943.

III./Jagdgeschwader 53 Africa/Tunisia, December 1941–March 1943.

III./Jagdgeschwader 53 Africa/Tunisia, December 1941–March 1943.

Lehrgeschwader 2 Africa/Tunisia, July 1942–March 1943.

II./Jagdgeschwader 77 Africa/Tunisia, December 1942–March 1943.

III./Jagdgeschwader 77 Africa/Tunisia, October 1942–May 1943.

III./Zerstörergeschwader 26 Africa/Tunisia, February 1941–May 1943.

Highest-Scoring *Luftwaffe* Aces in North Africa, April 1941– December 1942

Name	Unit	Aerial victories
Hans-Joachim Marseille	*I./Jagdgeschwader 27*	151
Werrner Schroer	*I. & III./Jagdgeschwader 27*	61
Hans-Arnold Stahlschmidt	*I./Jagdgeschwader 27*	59
Gustav Rödel	*II./Jagdgeschwader 27*	52
Gerhard Homuth	*I./Jagdgeschwader 27*	46
Otto Schulz	*II./Jagdgeschwader 27*	42
Gunther Steinhausen	*I./Jagdgeschwader 27*	40
Friedrich Körner	*I./Jagdgeschwader 27*	36
Karl-Heinz Bendert	*II./Jagdgeschwader 27*	36
Rudolf Sinner	*I. & II./Jagdgeschwader 27*	32
Karl-Wolfgang Redlich	*I./Jagdgeschwader 27*	26
Ferdinand Vögel	*II./Jagdgeschwader 27*	25
Ludwig Franzisket	*I./Jagdgeschwader 27*	24

All the pilots listed above flew the *Messerschmitt Bf 109 E, F,* and *G* variants.

The Highest-Scoring Common-wealth Aces in North Africa, April 1941–December 1942

Name	Unit(s)	Aerial victories
Clive Caldwell	112 & 250 Squadrons	20
A. E. Marshall	73 & 250 Squadrons	16
J. L. Waddy	4, 92, 250 & 260 Squadrons	15
E. M. Mason	80 & 274 Squadrons	15
L. C. Wade	33 Squadron	15
J. Dodds	274 Squadron	14
B. Drake	112 Squadron	14
P. G. Wykeham-Barnes	80, 274 & 73 Squadrons	13
A. W. Barr	3 Squadron (R.A.A.F.)	12
V. C. Woodward	33 Squadron	12
J. H. Lapsley	80 & 274 Squadrons	11
A. C. Bosman	2 & 4 Squadrons (S.A.A.F.)	10
R. H. Gibbes	3 Squadron (R.A.A.F)	10

The fighter aircraft used were the following: Hawker Hurricane Marks 1 and 2, Curtis Tomahawk/Kittyhawk, and Supermarine Spitfire Mark 5.

The R.A.A.F. designation denotes the Royal Australian Air Force.

The S.A.A.F. designation denotes the South African Air Force.

APPENDIX F

The Highest-Scoring U.S. Army Air Force Aces in Tunisia, November 1942–May 1943

Name	Unit	Aerial Victories
Levi R. Chase	33rd Fighter Group	10
Sylvan Feld	52nd Fighter Group	8
Claude Kinsey Jr.	82nd Fighter Group	7
Arnold Vinson	52nd Fighter Group	7
Norman MacDonald	52nd Fighter Group	6
William Momyer	33rd Fighter Group	6
Meldrum Sears	1st Fighter Group	6
Virgil Smith	14th Fighter Group	6
Thomas White	82nd Fighter Group	6
Roy Whittaker	57th Fighter Group	6
John Wolford	1st Fighter Group	6
John Bradley	33rd Fighter Group	6
Robert Byrne	57th Fighter Group	6

The main types of fighter aircraft flown by the U.S.A.A.F. were the Curtis P-40F Warhawk, the Bell P-39D Airacobra, the P-38 F&G Lightning, and the Supermarine Spitfire Mark 5.

APPENDIX G

The *Regia Aeronautica*

The Italian Air Force is usually overlooked in most accounts of the fighting in Africa, although it was engaged in combat for longer than its *Luftwaffe* ally and many units fought to the end in Tunisia.

The *Regia Aeronautica* was hampered by both outdated, underpowered aircraft[1] and woefully inadequate logistic support.

Italian pilots were generally considered more skillful than their German counterparts but were somewhat less aggressive and determined. Also, the Italians were more likely to engage in dog-fighting, the Germans preferring hit-and-run tactics.

However, the courage, aggressiveness, and determination of Italian torpedo-bomber pilots was exceptional.

It is very difficult to compile a list of Italian aces in North Africa as no official list of aerial victories currently exists. Additionally, many victories were scored by Italian pilots in East Africa, over Malta, and in the defense of Sicily.

---

1. The situation changed somewhat with the introduction, in late 1941, of the excellent *Macchi MC 202* powered by the German DB 601 engine.

APPENDIX H

German and British Tank Tactics in North Africa

The Germans employed their tried and tested *Blitzkrieg* tactics in the desert with the expected successful results. Actually, combined-arms tactics is a more accurate way to describe the German tactics. Armored, infantry, artillery, combat engineers, and air support were all carefully integrated into the attack plan. The Germans placed great emphasis on maintaining the momentum of the attack by maximizing the effectiveness and mutual support of all the units involved. Effective and timely command and control was also considered essential. Rommel was an absolute master at quickly summing up a situation and reacting accordingly. By contrast, the British command structure was much more rigid and inflexible.

In the interwar period it was recognized that tanks operating independently were vulnerable to artillery and antitank fire. Also, tanks could take ground but only hold it with difficulty; infantry and artillery support was essential. The British came to the same conclusion but seemingly ignored the concept in the early fighting.

The Germans tended to avoid large-scale tank-versus-tank engagements where possible. They preferred to lure the British tank regiments within range of concealed antitank guns and hull-down[1] tanks by feigning a retreat by their armored units. Bravely, but recklessly, the British tank units usually attacked the German positions head-on. The usual outcome of this mechanized cavalry charge was the destruction of British armor. The employment of the 88-mm *Flak* gun was most effective in these instances and it developed an almost mythical reputation as a long-range tank killer. The British also had an equivalent weapon, the 3.7-inch antiaircraft gun, but it was almost never used in the antitank role as it lacked suitable ammunition and the artillery regiments were reluctant to use it in the front lines.

The British tanks could not effectively engage the German dug-in guns with high-explosive rounds as the standard 2-pounder tankgun was only supplied with armor-piercing solid shot. In contrast German tank were supplied with a mixture of high-explosive and armor-piercing shells. The early models

---

1. The hull-down position is where a tank is dug-in or behind a ridge with only its turret visible.

of the *Panzer IV* were armed with a low-velocity 75-mm cannon and used primarily as an infantry support weapon. Antitank guns could be engaged using high-explosive well beyond their effective armor-piercing range.

The first effective blunting of a *Blitzkrieg*-style attack was by the Australians at Tobruk in April 1941. A series of mutually supporting defensive positions with machine-guns, antitank guns, and artillery was constructed. These positions were surrounded by dense mine fields consisting of a mixture of antitank and antipersonnel mines. The German tanks were allowed to come within close range of the concealed antitank guns before firing from all available guns was commenced. The machineguns and artillery separated the supporting infantry from the tanks and kept the tanks closed-up. The infantry allowed the tanks to overrun their positions before engaging the supporting infantry and forward artillery. Tanks were used for immediate surprise counterattacks.

This form of defense, which calls for both coolness under fire and a high degree of discipline, brought the German attack to an ignominious halt. German prisoners later admitted that nothing like that had happened to them before.

Although the British forces soon relearned the lessons of combined arms, most of their subsequent offensives from El Alamein onwards were relatively ponderous set-piece battles. These offensive operations relied on overwhelming numerical superiority in armor and infantry and the use of massed air and artillery support.

Select Bibliography

Primary Sources

Barnikol, Dr. H. A. *Kriegserlebnisse in Tunesien.* Unpublished manuscript: ?

Hambuch, Rudolf. *Einsätze des FJR 5 in Tunesien.* Unpublished manuscript: ?

Heilmann, Ludwig. *Fallschirmjäger auf Sizilien.* Unpublished manuscript: ?

Kesselring, Albert. *Kesselring's Views of the African War.* Unpublished manuscript: ?

Nehm, Heinz. *Zwei Einsätze in Tunesien.* Unpublished manuscript: ?

Nehring, Walther K. *The Development of the Situation in North Africa.* Unpublished manuscript: ?

———. *Die erste Phase der Kämpfe in Tunesien.* Unpublished manuscript: ?

———. *North African Campaign Volume II (1942).* Unpublished manuscript: ?

Ramcke, Bernhard Hermann. Personal information provided to the author. Unpublished manuscript: ?

Sauer, Paul. *Combat Reports of Kompanie Sauer in Tunisia.* Date unknown.

———. *Kampfgruppe Sauer im Einsatz..* Unpublished manuscript: ?

Student, Kurt. *Memoirs.* Unpublished manuscript: ?

Secondary Sources

Agar-Hamilton, J., and L. Turner. *Crisis in the Desert.* Capetown, 1952.

———. *The Sidi Rezeg Battles 1941.* Capetown, 1957.

Alman, Carl. *Balkenkreuz Über Wüstenland.* Oldenburg, 1943.

———. *Ritterkreuzträger Des Afrikakorps.* Rastatt, 1968.

Barnett, Corelli. *The Desert Generals.* New york, 1961.

Barré, Georges. *Tunisie, 1942–1943.* Paris: ?, 1950.

Bender, Roger, and Richard Law. *Uniforms, Organization and History of the Afrikakorps.* San Jose, 1973.

Bernig, Heinrich. *Hölle Alamein.* Balve (Germany): ?, 1960.

Carell, Paul. *The Foxes of the Desert.* New York, 1961.

Carver, Michael. *El Alamein.* New York, 1962.

———. *Tobruk.* Philadelphia, 1964.

Ciano, Count Galeazzo. *The Ciano Diaries 1939–1943.* New York, 1946.

Chalfont, Alun. *Montgomery of Alamein.* London, 1976.

Churchill, Winston, S. *The Second World War, Volume IV.* London, 1951.

Divine, A. *Road to Tunis.* ?: ?, 1944.

von Esebeck, Hanns. *Helden Der Wüste.* Berlin, 1942.

Haupt, Werner, and J. Bingham. *Der Afrika-Feldzug 1941–1943.* Dorheim, 1968.

Irving, David. *The Trail of the Fox.* London, 1977.

Jacobsen, H., and J. Rohwer. *Decisive battles of World War II: The German View.*
    New York, 1965.

Kesselring, Albert. *Kesselring: A Soldiers Record.* New York, 1954.

Liddell Hart, Basil. *The German Generals Talk.* New York, 1948.

————. *The Rommel Papers.* New York, 1968.

Macksey, M. C. *Afrikakorps.* New York, 1968.

Massimello, Giovanni, and Giorgio Apostolo. *Italian Aces of World War 2.*
    Oxford, 2000.

von Mellenthin, F. W. *Panzer Battles.* Harman, 1958.

Montgomery, Field Marshal Bernard Law. *Memoirs.* London: ?, 1966.

Moorehead, Alan. *The Desert War.* London, 1965.

Nehring, Walter K. *Die Geschichte der Deutschen Panzerwaffe 1916–1945.* Berlin,
    1969.

Pitt, Barrie. *The Crucible of War: Western Desert 1941.* London, 1980.

————. *The Crucible of War 2: Auchinleck's Command.* London, 1982.

————. *The Crucible of War 3: Montgomery and Alamein.* London, 1986.

Playfair, Ian. *The Mediterranean and the Middle East.*

————. *Volume 1: Early Successes against Italy.* London, 1954.

————. *Volume 2: The Germans Come to the Aid of Their Ally.* London, 1956.

————. *Volume 3: British Fortunes Reach Their Lowest Ebb.* London, 1960.

————. *Volume 4: The Destruction of Axis Forces in North Africa.* London, 1966.

Ramcke, Bernhard Hermann. *Fallschirmjäger damals und danach.* Frankfurt
    am Main: ?, 1951.

————. *Vom Schiffsjungen zum Fallschirmjägergeneral.* Berlin: ?, 1943.

Scheibert, Hans. *Deutscher Panzergrenadier 1939–1945.* Dorheim, 1966.

Scheibert, Hans, and C. Wagener. *Die Deutsche Panzertruppe 1939–1945.* Bad
    Nauheim, 1966.

Schmitt, Heinz. *With Rommel in the Desert.* London, 1951.

Seemen, Gerhard von. *Die Ritterkreuzträger 1939–1945.* Friedberg: Podzun-
    Pallas-Verlag, 1976.

Shores, Christopher. *Luftwaffe Fighter Units Mediterranean 1941-1944.* London,
    1978.

Shores, Christopher, and Ring, Hans. *Fighters over the Desert.* New York, 1969.

Shores, Christopher, et al. *Fighters over Tunisia.* ?, 1974.

Trevor-Roper, Hugh, ed. *Blitzkreig to Defeat.* New York, 1965.

Warlimont, Walter. *Inside Hitler's Headquarters 1939–1945.* New York, 1964.

Weal, John. *Junkers Ju 87 Stukageschwader of North Africa and the Mediterranean.*
    London, 1998.

Wilmot, Chester. *Tobruk.* Sydney, 1944.

Young, Desmond. *Rommel–The Desert Fox.* New York, 1950.

Index